Recasting the

the

Imperial
Far East

Based on extensive research in British Foreign Service records and in U.S. State Department documents, this study sheds new light on the Anglo-American rivalry in China in the period between the defeat of Japan and the triumph of the Chinese Communists. Disputing the dominant historiographical perspectives of both Anglo-American and East Asian studies, the author rejects the Cold War approach of Soviet-American rivalry as the focus of analysis and concentrates instead on the relatively neglected dimension of Anglo-American relations, detailing the significant tensions between a rising imperial power (the United States) and a declining imperial power (the United Kingdom) over China policy issues.

What emerges from this study is a rich picture of conflict, rivalry, and disagreement between American officials who acted as if they were natural heirs to Britain's dominant prewar position in China (among Western powers) and British officials who viewed the United States with only partly disguised contempt and were loathe to concede the field to the upstart Americans. Congruent with the revelations that result is a new and timely perception of the behavior of American power in the Far East, and fresh insights on the roots of wars to come in Korea and Vietnam.

Recasting the

the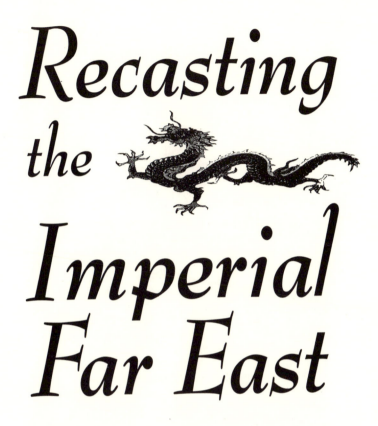

Imperial
Far East

Britain and America
in China, 1945-1950

LANXIN XIANG

An East Gate Book

M.E. Sharpe
Armonk, New York
London, England

An East Gate Book

Library of Congress Cataloging-in-Publication Data

Xiang, Lanxin, 1956–
Recasting the imperial Far East: Britain and America in China,
1945–1950 / Lanxin Xiang.
p. cm
Includes bibliographical references and index.
ISBN 1-56324-459-4.—ISBN 1-56324-460-8 (pbk.)
1. Great Britain—Foreign relations—China. 2. China—
Foreign relations—Great Britain. 3. United States—
Foreign relations—China. 4. China—Foreign relations—
United States. 5. Great Britain—Foreign relations—1945–
6. United States—Foreign relations—1945–1954.
7. China—Foreign relations—1912–1949.
8. China—Foreign relations—1949–
I. Title.
DA47.9.C6X53 1994
327.51017521—dc20   94-30256
CIP

Printed in the United States of America

The paper used in this publication meets the minimum
requirements of American National Standard for Information Sciences—
Permanence of Paper for Printed Library Materials, ANSI Z 39.48-1984.

∞

BM (c) 10   9   8   7   6   5   4   3   2   1
BM (p) 10   9   8   7   6   5   4   3   2   1

Contents

Preface

In late October 1950, as the tension in Korea was mounting, Sir Maberly Esler Dening arrived at Hongkong. Whitehall had announced that, as the British Foreign Office's top man on the Far East, Dening would make a routine tour of several Asian countries. Communist China was not on the list, not only because there were not yet diplomatic relations between the two nations, but also because Dening, widely known at the time as ambassador-designate to China, was not the appropriate person to enter China as a special envoy at that time. However, Dening's main mission was to go to Peking; not even his private secretary was aware of it.

Dening was an expert on Japan and a key architect of British Far Eastern policy during and after the war. After ending a successful tour as Lord Louis Mountbatten's political adviser at the Southeast Asian Command, Dening returned to London after the war and soon became assistant undersecretary for Far East affairs. Later, he also served as chairman of the Foreign Office's Far Eastern Committee. Dening's assignment to Peking at this juncture was a desperate move. The Labour government was on the brink of a breakthrough in negotiations with the Chinese Communists when the Korean conflict erupted. Washington's strategy of forcing the allies to support its China policy by linking the Korean conflict immediately to Peking was leading the United States precipitously toward an armed showdown with Communist China. One of Dening's major tasks was to give the Chinese a chance to vent their spleen against the Americans and to reassure them that the U.S. policy did not necessarily enjoy support from the Allies.

As Dening anxiously awaited an entry visa that was being delayed by the Chinese, news came that General Douglas MacArthur had ordered the crossing of the Thirty-eighth Parallel—where the Chinese had drawn the line. Thus, the frustrated British envoy went to Japan, where he became convinced that MacArthur's "saber-rattling" had definitely goaded the Chinese into the conflict. As the Chinese engaged MacArthur shortly thereafter, all hopes for political settlement with China—Britain's preferred policy option—were smashed. By the mere presence of their troops in Korea, the British found themselves at war with China.

Dening never made it to Peking as the British ambassador; he ended up in Tokyo instead. He knew that the postwar British problems in the Far East, particularly in China, largely hinged on one factor: the Anglo-American relationship. He was convinced that an erroneous U.S. policy in China would eventually drag Britain through the mud.

Ever since the publication of Christopher Thorne's studies on Far Eastern diplomatic history from multilateral perspectives, the Anglo-American relationship in various parts of the world has attracted scholarly attention.[1] Thorne's multiarchival approach is both rewarding and demanding. It requires historians to understand the multiple cultural settings that affect international events and to transcend often biased single-country perspectives.

Anglo-American relations in China is not a new subject. Thorne had done extensive work on the Manchurian Incident and the wartime Anglo-American conflict over China. From the American side, the Sino-U.S. relationship has long been a field of study by itself. Thus, it seems risky to choose a subject that has presumably been "overstudied." My topic appears to fall into the sphere of either a big historical category such as U.S.-East Asian relations—a major preoccupation of American diplomatic historians—or Anglo-American relations—a subject of great importance to the British historical profession. But having looked at postwar historical writings, I find my topic to have been, in fact, grossly "understudied." In most cases, historians of Anglo-American relations have ignored those relations in the Far East, not least perhaps because Anglo-American relations there jar the prevailing notion of a "special relationship." Often preoccupied with strategic studies, scholars of postwar history inevitably focus their attention on the U.S.-USSR confrontation, a perspective that tends to minimize conflicts within the "special relationship."

For scholars of U.S.-East Asian relations, the Anglo-American dimension seems insignificant. Perhaps it makes American scholars uncomfortable to consider U.S. policy in the same context as the British because this basically suggests the replacement of one imperial power by another—a view that may seem unjust to many American historians who believe in still another "special relationship": between the United States and China.

This study focuses on the question: Was there an Anglo-American special relationship in the Far East after World War II? And if not, why? The irony of Sino-American relations in the 1940s is that they both reached their peak and fell to the bottom quickly. Great Britain was the best witness to this puzzling and entangled diplomatic tale. Although scholars tend to focus on wartime Anglo-American relations in China, few have paid much attention to the British policy toward China after the war; there has been a tendency to dismiss the British as helpless onlookers rather than to regard them as active players in China from 1945 to 1950. This may be due to the habit of reading back into history the incurable weakness of the British Empire at the end of the war, a notion that often runs counter to how the British perceived themselves and the way they were perceived by other countries at the time. After all, it was President Franklin D. Roosevelt who proposed that Britain become one of the "Four Policemen" to guarantee world peace. More importantly, it is hard to ignore the fact that Britain had played a pivotal role in the beginning of the Cold War.

From the Opium War of 1840 to the end of the war against Japan in 1945, Britain experienced a century-long reign as the leading power in a vast country that was culturally hostile to Western civilization. However, compelled by a weak economic position after World War II, the British exercised typical pragmatism by accepting a secondary role in China, although this did not imply that they blindly followed the American lead. In reality, London (especially the Foreign Office under Ernest Bevin) had made every effort to influence the American China policy, even if often unsuccessfully. Presumably, Great Britain was the country that best understood the mentality of her former colony, the United States; therefore, British perceptions and observations of the problems in postwar American China policy are undoubtedly valuable in assessing the behavior of the United States in the Far East.

This study tries to move away from both the dominant framework of American East Asian scholarship and the traditional Cold War approach. Its focus is relatively modest: Anglo-American behavior in the Far East, rather than East Asian diplomatic history in general. This focus allows me to set aside the dominant Cold War dimension, since the Soviet Union had contributed surprisingly little to this Anglo-American dispute over China.

From another angle, this dispute must be put into a broader Anglo-American context. For both sides, there seemed to be an organic link between their policies in the Far East and those in Europe. Thus, this study also attempts to trace insiders' thinking in both Washington and London on the subject of China. The emphasis given here to the roles of the British Foreign Office and the U.S. State Department is prompted not so much by a penchant for "traditional diplomatic history" as by reality. During the period under study, foreign policy professionals on both sides of the Atlantic temporarily had gained great power in policy making—largely as a result of weak policy direction from the top. Policy-making processes were left to the Foreign Office and the State Department, where strong leadership usually prevailed. Both the White House and Number Ten Downing Street seemed to have minimized involvement in foreign affairs. Compared with the high wartime dramas of summit conferences and personal diplomacy between Franklin Roosevelt and Winston Churchill, the postwar Anglo-American diplomatic relations were marked by the absence of summit meetings. It was not until the end of 1950 that President Harry S. Truman and Prime Minister Clement R. Attlee faced each other over conference tables again. The last time they had met was in 1945.

Finally, this study does not strictly fall under "China Studies." Although Chinese-language materials were frequently consulted, they were used sparingly because of their nonarchival and inconsistent nature. At this stage, it is too early to say whether or not recent Chinese materials made available will radically change our perspectives. For the moment, we have to wait for one promising new source of reliable information: archives of the former Soviet Union concerning the full story of the Yenan-Moscow ties.

Note

1. See Christopher G. Thorne, *The Limits of Foreign Policy* and *Allies of a Kind*.

Acknowledgments

A work of this nature cannot be done without encouragement from others. I am especially grateful to Professor David Calleo, who has taught me all the subtleties about transatlantic relations and constantly encouraged me to finish this work. I would also like to thank Tom Row, who as a great friend and fellow student has seen this work through all stages. I must also express thanks to Kendall Myers, John Harper, Patrick McCarthy, Adrian Lyttleton, Doak Barnett, and David Kelly for their kind help at different stages. Errors in judgment are of course mine only.

Part of chapter six appeared in *Journal of Contemporary History*, volume 27, no. 2, April 1992, pp. 319–44. I must thank the editors of this journal for allowing me to use it in this book. The Harry S. Truman Library Institute was most kind to provide me with a grant.

Finally, I must thank my wife, Ying Chu, and I would like to dedicate this book to her and to our son, Jeffrey, whose grandparents happened to be on the opposite sides of the Chinese Civil War.

Recasting the Imperial Far East

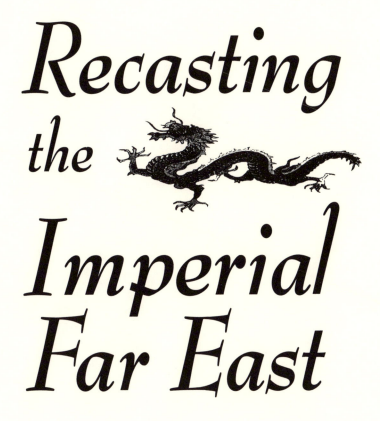

1

The "Strong China" Controversy

One of the most salient disputes between Britain and the United States throughout World War II was over the issue of a "strong China." Ostensibly the issue was more polemic than substantive, but behind the rhetoric lay a deep-rooted conflict of interest over what the Far East would be like after the war. Although less frustrating than the Cold War, the Anglo-American disputes reflected a painful process of adjustment—a process of "succeeding John Bull" by the United States, as D. C. Watt calls it.[1]

The controversy appeared in many forms. In the military sphere, it was the dispute over the Burma Campaign that brought the controversy sharply into focus: Should Allied military priority be given to China or to European colonial possessions? In the politico-diplomatic sphere, it was the favorite American notion of a "strong China" that fueled the dispute. The British had grave doubts about the notion, which was promoted personally by President Roosevelt. The "strong China" controversy was often obscured by Allied preoccupation with Europe, but as the war in Europe drew to an end in early 1945, the question of China's future began to loom large.

Under the circumstances, any expression of doubt about the "strong China" concept could have triggered a politico-diplomatic storm. The controversy touched on all aspects of Anglo-American dispute throughout the war: the question of colonial empires and the lend-lease aid connected with them; China's future role in Asia; economic competition in China; and the issue of Hongkong, which stood out as a case so explosive that Winston Churchill was provoked to declare, "Hongkong will be eliminated from the British Empire only over my dead body!"[2]

The controversy was also evident for people handling China policy. From an institutional viewpoint, the Anglo-American conflict over China involved a wide spectrum of policymakers from the highest levels down to the lower echelons. There were two striking parallels between London and Washington from 1945 to 1950. First, there was a legacy of wartime during which China policy was the prerogative of those at the top. Both sides indulged in personal diplomacy while the government bureaucracy was largely ignored. Second, after the war, there was a kind of laissez-faire at the top, and professional diplomats for a time regained considerable power in making policy regarding China. Thus, from late 1945 onward, the Department of State and the Foreign Office both exerted decisive influence, as their files later reflected.

Near the end of the war against Japan, President Roosevelt's personal representative, Major General Patrick J. Hurley, found his counterpart in Lieutenant General Sir Adrian Carton de Wiart, the British prime minister's personal representative in China.[3] Hurley was sent to China with a two-fold purpose: to bring about the unification of China under Chiang Kai-shek and to "keep an eye on European imperialism."[4] Carton de Wiart's mission was less ambitious: ostensibly for military purposes, he was to serve as a liaison between Lord Mountbatten and Generalissimo Chiang. In practice, however, he assumed wide political responsibilities to counterpoise not only Hurley but also General Albert Wedemeyer. Besides, Carton de Wiart was running, in Hurley's words, "most of the widespread British intelligence system in China."[5]

At the departmental level, many officials had remained in office since 1941. In London, the Foreign Office relied heavily upon men long involved in Asia such as Sir Humphrey Prideau-Brune, principal adviser on Chinese affairs; Maberly Esler Dening, foreign office representative; Sir Horace Seymour, ambassador to China; and John Cecil Sterndale-Bennett, former ambassador to Turkey, now head of the Far

Eastern Department. In Washington, the formulation of Far Eastern policy remained in the hands of the group led by Joseph Grew, often dubbed the "pro-Japs" team. Although Stanley Hornbeck, longtime director of the Far Eastern Division, was given an embassy post in the Netherlands in 1943, the Grew team seemed well protected after Cordell Hull was succeeded by Edward Stettinius, who wrote his predecessor in January 1945 that he was "taking good care of [Joseph] Ballantine, Joe Grew and other people."[6]

In sharp contrast to the British officials, who cooperated well with political appointees, there was constant conflict between career officers at the State Department and Ambassador Hurley. The nagging issues between them also often centered around the concept of a "strong China," yet their differences were more tactical than fundamental. The department officials favored a policy of flexibility, which they deemed practical to bring about a "strong China," while Hurley was pursuing a policy of overt support for Chiang Kai-shek exclusively. It was reported by Drew Pearson that Hurley would wave his fists whenever criticisms of his policy were heard in Chungking.[7] The Chiang government was, however, very satisfied with his work. As Chinese Foreign Minister T. V. Soong wrote in a personal letter to Stettinius dated in March, "Pat Hurley has been going great guns since the day he arrived. He has helped us tide over many ticklish situations."[8]

Another important source of friction came from President Roosevelt's elusive character and management style. Hurley was always handicapped by Roosevelt's unwillingness to issue "written instructions"; instead, the president had a penchant for intimate oral briefings. During these private sessions, Roosevelt was able to cover many sensitive and controversial topics with Hurley, such as Indochina, Burma, Thailand, Hongkong, and so on. Hurley interpreted these concerns as having policy implications, and so he would pursue these issues with great personal zeal, often antagonizing the State Department, which was kept in the dark as to these briefings.

Roosevelt, moreover, granted few favors to his foreign policy experts as well as to historians in this regard. His inner thoughts were carefully concealed. He died in office with no memoirs, leaving a legacy of wartime diplomacy that seemed decisive for the postwar world but subject to many different interpretations. It is difficult to ascertain the impact of the Delano family's long association with the China trade upon his "strong China" policy, which above all was reflected in his "Four Policemen" (United States, Britain, Soviet Union, and China) scheme for the postwar world order. It is no less frustrating for historians to determine how his personal views of Chiang Kai-shek had affected his policy. He met Chiang four times during the Cairo Conference, yet there is no record of his personal impression of the man who was to become essential in his grand design for Asia.[9]

On the whole, there were more continuities than breaks in the China policies on both sides of the Atlantic. The continued Anglo-American dispute over China was clearly reflected in the rivalries between officials in the field. The fierce conflict between MacArthur and Mountbatten was well known. There was also intense rivalry between Carton de Wiart and Wedemeyer, between Wedemeyer and Mountbatten, and between Hurley and almost everyone else. It was in this complicated setting that the "strong China" controversy evolved.

The "strong China" controversy pointed to a much wider context than the narrow parochial conflict of interest in China proper. It must be seen in the context of overall Anglo-American relations at the end of 1944, when perhaps the worst crisis in the Anglo-American association since Pearl Harbor occurred. The new year was to open with a chilly windstorm blown from London across the Atlantic. The 30 December issue of the *Economist* published a leading editorial entitled "Noble Negatives." The author, believed to be Owen Fleming, vented his spleen on the American attitude toward Britain, saying, "The British have been having a bad time in the U.S. of recent weeks. The outburst of criticism [triggered by the Sforza affair] has been one of the most violent and sustained of the war years." Moreover, he stated that "Britain is stealing a march on the poor repressed American exporter, Britain has no intention of fighting the Japanese, [and] Britain is not really fighting in Europe. . . . Britain is imperialist, reactionary, selfish, exclusive, restrictive." The editorial went on to charge that, "All is painfully familiar, the only novelty in the recent epidemic is the evidence that [the] American government itself—or at least part of it—is more anxious to provide ammunition for the miscontents than to correct their wild misstatements." The author asked

> Just how much British safety can be gambled on American good will? In the political sphere, is it right to refrain, in the hope of obtaining American support for a general and universal system of security, from making special arrangements to assure British safety? In the economic

sphere, is it right to surrender the means of safeguarding British inter-ests, as Bretton Woods and the American commercial proposals would have us do, in the hope that American policy will be stable and sound? What is the conclusion of British policy toward America?

The author further declared, "Let an end be put to the policy of ap-peasement which, at Mr. Churchill's personal bidding, has been fol-lowed with all the humiliations and abasements." He concluded that, "Hypocrisy is a common Anglo-Saxon failing—indeed, a failing of the rich and comfortable, all over the world" and "the British have many times made themselves cordially disliked by it. But that does not ex-empt them from feeling resentment when they are the objects of other people's hypocrisy."[10]

The *Economist*'s outburst produced a great media and political sen-sation. The headlines on both sides of the Atlantic read like: "British Frankness Has Good Effect in U.S." (*Daily Telegraph*); "So the British Have Dared to Hit Back" (*Daily Herald*); "Anglo-American Back Chat" (*New York Herald Tribune*); "Cross Talk" (*Daily Mail*); "U.S. Comment on British Touchiness" (*Manchester Guardian*), and so forth. The London Foreign Office generally agreed with the editorial, but officials there were more concerned with future developments. A top-secret report by William Stephenson, who headed the British Secu-rity Coordination, an espionage agency based in New York, warned that "the worst [is] yet to come." He summarized a "composite view of American friends," saying

> the present crisis indicated [that] (1) the coalition of American political factions, which has supported pro-British wartime deals and measures, is crumbling through defection of middle liberals who see their democratic principles forsaken for power politics; (2) the hardening toward Britain is spreading quickly in official circles; [and] (3) the foregoing has produced a protest wave to date of isolationism and economic nationalism (the America Firsters are coming out of their cracks on the walls).

The report went on to say that unless diverted, the developing situation will produce the following results:

(1)   Opposition to mutual aid measures.
(2)   American liberals would not oppose the stopping of aid to Britain because fear of continuing European power politics makes Amer-

ican imperialism seem a comparatively minor evil. Meanwhile, conservatives would rejoice because stoppage of the capital goods' flow to the U.K. will handicap Britain in postwar trade, giving American business a larger share of world markets than otherwise obtainable.

(3)   The above circumstances and business aspirations will stimulate latent nationalism.

(4)   This nationalism will result in ruthless American postwar exploitation of every economic advantage, untempered by liberal internationalism.[11]

Meanwhile, in Washington, President Roosevelt and Secretary of State Stettinius were besieged by the press for reactions to the irritating article. As Stettinius recorded, "Unfortunately, other British papers had followed the *Economist*'s lead. Even the London *Times* demanded that America 'put its cards on the table.' " Stettinius then wrote a memo for the president, stating that this article's appearance reflected the fact that "the British were undergoing a strain in adjusting to a secondary role after having always accepted a leading one."[12]

While Mediterranean policy triggered the *Economist* crisis, the issue of China was no less explosive. As J. C. Donnelly, head of the North American Department in the Foreign Office, recalled a few months later, "there is no doubt at all that American misconceptions of our attitude towards China and the Far East generally . . . are another pocket of equally explosive gas. It would be a bold man who would say that no matches will fall." Donnelly advised his colleagues to be well prepared because, "We shall not find ourselves seriously incommoded by waves of unanimous criticism such as bedeviled us in December and January in relation to the Sforza Incident and the crisis in Greece."[13]

Indeed, China at the beginning of 1945 was a hot topic in Washington. Patrick Hurley blamed his failure in 1944 to bring the Kuomintang (KMT) and the Chinese Communist Party (CCP) together on European imperialism. As the ambassador wrote to Washington on 24 December 1944:

Foreign influence, composed of a group of imperialist nations now fighting for reconquest and re-establishment of their colonies in Southeast Asia, presents the greatest opposition to the unification of China.

This group is trying to convince the Chinese that everything the United States does to unite and strengthen China interferes [in] her internal affairs.[14]

Hurley's charge was, however, not supported by concrete evidence showing that Britain or the other colonial powers had a definite plan to divide and weaken China. Representative Mike Mansfield (D., Montana), who had just completed an official trip to China, presented a more balanced view. In his conversation with John Carter Vincent, chief of the Division of Chinese Affairs, the congressman remarked, "Britain . . . would not be averse, because of the Empire considerations, to a perpetuation of a weak China." But the British, "as [a] matter of policy, were not working to prevent a united China . . . [although] they are not working for such a China."[15]

The Anglo-American controversy over the idea of a "strong China" had endured throughout the war, but the allied military preoccupation had prevented it from exploding before the Japanese could be defeated. When the end of the war seemed imminent, the China issue became politicized and began to dominate the politico-diplomatic aspect of U.S.-British relations with regard to China. In reality, the concept of a "strong China" posed three questions that were not clearly distinguishable from one another at the time. First, was China a strong power in 1945? Second, would China become a strong power after the war? And third, could a "strong China" be brought about mainly with foreign help? Both London and Washington had advocates and opponents of these ideas. Few policymakers seemed to believe the first notion, but to say so openly was to be politically insensitive. While it is difficult to fathom President Roosevelt's thoughts about the first two questions, he apparently believed that China could become "strong" with the help of American power. Prime Minister Churchill, on the other hand, was the most outspoken opponent of all three notions. With his acute sense of power politics, Churchill perceived Roosevelt's "strong China" scheme as creating a "faggot vote for the United States."[16] In a talk with Hurley in April, Churchill claimed that the whole idea of a strong China was "a great American illusion."[17]

The Foreign Office, however, had a more subtle view: only with Anglo-American collaboration could a strong China be brought into being; it felt handicapped by the undiplomatic outspokenness of the prime minister on China. On 12 January, London received a telegram from Sir Horace Seymour, ambassador to China, reporting that, "Political gossip is again rife in Chungking. A topic much discussed is the alleged unwillingness of HMG to see the emergence of a strong and prosperous China."[18] Seymour undoubtedly believed that a certain number of Americans and Chinese, holding similar views, confirm each other's opinions.

John C. Sterndale-Bennett, head of the Far Eastern Department, suggested to Foreign Secretary Anthony Eden a few days later: "It is, I think, desirable to do what we can to kill the idea that we do not want to see a strong and prosperous China." He went on to suggest that the foreign secretary take the opportunity during the coming parliamentary debate to announce that a weak and disunited China would be a constant source of trouble. The suggestion was, however, turned down because of "unsuitable timing."[19] Not until 25 January did the Foreign Office succeed in inserting such a declaration into Lord Gascoyne-Cecil Cranborne's speech in the House of Lords, but the effect was rather limited.

What was most frustrating to London was its inability to discern the inner thoughts of American policymakers on China. Four main issues made Anglo-American cooperation in Asia problematic: (1) the use of lend-lease aid to regain colonies, (2) the policy toward the KMT-Communist dispute, (3) postwar economic plans in China, and (4) the policy toward the Soviet Union in East Asia. As for the lend-lease aid, despite U.S. qualms, London believed that Americans would find it difficult to separate Britain's war efforts against Japan from its efforts to restore the colonial empire. A war cabinet memo sent to the Far Eastern department pointed out that "presumably, the fact that the Japanese happen to be in Burma or Malaya or Sumatra should not lay us open to suspicion that our operations were entirely directed at regaining our lost colonies."[20]

The biggest puzzle was, of course, China's internal dispute and Russia's intentions. Britain was not at all enthusiastic about getting involved in what its own long experience in China suggested was yet another of China's interminable domestic disputes. After Joseph Grew made a statement in January that the American government was using its good office to bring about a compromise between the KMT and the Communists, John Keswick, a former Shanghai tycoon now serving as British counselor at the Chungking embassy, asked John Carter Vincent why the U.S. government even "recognized" the communists, as

Keswick believed the Americans were only strengthening Yenan's hand and that "they are likely to be less willing to compromise than before."[21]

From Britain's point of view, the Russian factor did not loom large in China in early 1945. London believed that Stalin was momentarily satisfied by the secret "Big Three" agreement signed at Yalta. Known as the Livadia Agreement, the covert deal provided Stalin with a strong incentive to enter the war against Japan (i.e, restoring many Czarist privileges in Manchuria before 1905). These privileges did not undermine Britain's strategic or economic interests in southern China.

The American suspicion of British intentions in China remained strong. However, in the United States, China was regarded as one of the most trusted partners in the postwar world. As Secretary Stettinius informed the Chungking embassy in January: "a Princeton opinion poll reveals that, in early December [1944] . . . China ranked second among countries, following Canada, in response to the question [of] 'whether or not you think (each) can be trusted to cooperate with other countries after the war.' "[22] Although the State Department was skeptical about Hurley's exaggerated charges against Britain, it was too afraid of being duped by Britain's cunning diplomacy. This fear was enhanced in January when the American ambassador to Kabul, Afghanistan, obtained a top-secret circular from the Foreign Office to various British missions abroad, which advised its diplomats not to plead with the Americans for help as if asking for "personal favors" but to let them see their real interests were also at stake in cooperating with London.[23] In a memo written by John Paton Davies, second secretary at the Chungking embassy, it was predicted that "the British may well get what they want—a disunited China with the southern half of the country a British, and if we so desire, American sphere of influence."[24]

The Anglo-American crisis also triggered a public "strong China" debate, which was brought into sharp focus by an article written by Nathaniel Peffer, professor of international relations at Columbia University. Published in the January 1945 issue of *Transatlantic*, the essay raised the sensitive question, "Is China a great power?" and attempted to argue why Anglo-American attitudes differed in a fundamental way. He believed that Americans took for granted that China was a great power, while the British did not consider nor want it so. Peffer sharply criticized the popular American thesis, illustrated by

Walter Lippmann's book *U.S. War Aims*, that America's enthusiasm about China was prompted by her "incontinent passion for self-sacrifice in the cause of liberty and idealism. Thus China has been the victim of injustice . . . and, America cannot bear injustice." Peffer went on to say, "Speaking scientifically . . . I believe this to be erroneous. If I were speaking informally, I should call it nonsense . . . a more profitable approach is to start with the question, is China a great power?" In Peffer's view, on the basis of facts, China was not. But as the United States worked toward that goal for its own self-interest, Britain, also for self-interest, did not seem to want a strong China at all.[25]

Peffer's efforts to point out several scenarios contained in the notion of a "strong China" received great attention in both London and Washington. A. L. Scott at the Foreign Office's China desk commented on 23 January: "This article is, I suppose, typical of American opinion that we don't want a strong, united China . . . but I believe that our more realistic and factual approach will earn (and confer) greater benefits in the long run."[26] Moreover, Thyne Henderson, in charge of the China desk, commented a few days later: "In any case one has to treat with facts, not dreams. We hope our colonies will some day govern themselves but we do not at present treat them as Dominions (though the U.S.A. here again, would approve of such action). . . . If we did, it would not be the best way to bring about such an end." "Similarly," Henderson continued, "if the Americans insist on treating China now as a Great Power, instead of a potential one, they and China will suffer from such a policy."[27]

On 3 February, the Peffer article was again the topic of argument between Sterndale-Bennett and John Allison, a Far Eastern expert and second secretary at the American embassy in London. According to Sterndale-Bennett, Allison thought Peffer summed up rather well the differences in the American and British viewpoints on the "strong China" notion. Sterndale-Bennett disagreed, saying the essay was based on the mistaken assumption that there was a difference of views between Britain and the United States and that the British were going about saying that China was not a strong power and never could be. He added, "I took the opportunity to draw his attention to the statement in Lord Cranborne's speech in the House of Lords on January 25th."[28]

Within the British government there was widespread anxiety over America's true intention in China. A widely circulated secret paper prepared at the Indian office by Humphrey Trevelyan pointed out in

March that, "The foreign policy of the United States is not always notable for clarity, definition or consistency, but if there is one country about which she has made up her somewhat unpredictable mind, that country is China." Trevelyan interpreted the essential American attitude toward China as "a general conviction that the U.S. cannot be secure with an aggressive power facing her in the Pacific, and that a friendly and strong China is the best guarantee of American security in the Far East of the future." More importantly, "Many anticipate that China is to be the El Dorado of the American exporter, and some hope that, now that the mantle of Britannia is giving way, at least in the Pacific, to the business-suit of Uncle Sam, the Open Door will remain open only for the citizens of the United States." Trevelyan concluded that, "Though critical of interference by the chancelleries of Europe and freely attributing them to the motive of "Power Politics," the United States does not hesitate to interfere in domestic politics of another country."[29] J. C. Donnelly believed that Trevelyan's paper "covers the ground extremely well."[30]

Britain's suspicion of America's double-talk was well founded, since behind all the lofty talk of FDR's postwar grand designs, such as the "Four Policemen" scheme, there was a hard-nosed realpolitik player too. At the Yalta Conference, Roosevelt seemed quite comfortable to make a secret deal with Stalin by exchanging China's territorial rights for Russia's entry into the war against Japan. Yet this naked power politics did not dampen the attack on British imperialism. Once satisfied, Stalin was expected to stay out of the Chinese internal dispute and, in fact, he kept most of his promises throughout the civil war. From the American perspective, the Livadia Agreement stabilized the Soviet factor in China—which was considered a wild card at the time—and staved off a big-power confrontation in Asia and the Pacific.

Both London and Washington foresaw potential troubles for the future, but they viewed the result of the Livadia Agreement from different perspectives. Washington feared that Stalin's new foothold in Manchuria might prompt him to interfere with Chinese politics. Strategically, the Soviet naval bases in Dairen and Port Arthur could be a potential nightmare in the face of American preeminence in China after the war. Politically, the Livadia Agreement could well become an explosive issue at home, for it had blatantly underwritten an imperialistic policy.

London, however, foresaw no direct threat to British interests in

China as a result of the agreement. When preparing the Livadia Agreement in October 1944, the war cabinet accepted the Foreign Office's argument that "British vital interests in the Far East were mainly in the region south of latitude 32° N while those of Russia are in the region north of that parallel." Therefore, "if we are prepared to meet Russian wishes as far as we can in respect of this northern region, there would seem to be no necessity for a clash between our respective interests."[31] The Foreign Office memo was more concerned with the possibility of a Soviet-American clash of strategic interests in the Pacific.

In January, the war cabinet's joint planning staff concluded that "provided that Great Britain are prepared to accept Russia's predominance in these areas (i.e., areas adjacent to the Soviet Far East region) and collaborate in preventing a revival of German and Japanese military power, Russia is unlikely to follow an aggressive policy."[32]

Facing all the uncertainties in China, Britain was anxious to get the Americans to put their cards on the table. This was the game Washington refused to play. On 22 January, Neville Butler, acting superintending undersecretary for Far East affairs of the Foreign Office, suggested to American Ambassador John Winant a British-American conference on Far Eastern questions to be held at the departmental level. Winant was instructed to turn it down.[33] Washington, in fact, viewed such proposals with a wary eye. Throughout January, there were widespread rumors that the British and the French had reached an understanding regarding colonial policies after the war. The Americans feared that the British, by colluding with the French, intended a hegemony in Western Europe as well. Ambassador Jefferson Caffery in Paris concurred with Winant in London that "the British were maneuvering themselves into a position where they would be considered the leaders and advocates for the French in Washington." Caffery noted that the recent trip by Richard Law to Washington was accompanied by Jean Monnet.[34]

The Anglo-American mutual suspicion further percolated through every level of the bureaucracy. Back in Chungking, British and American officials were often at loggerheads concerning the issue of a strong China. The Foreign Office instructed its Chungking embassy in January to reassert British influence in China. A telegraph for war cabinet circulation stated:

[The reasons why an effort on our part [to help China] seems desirable are (a) it is a general Allied interest to avoid a collapse in China; . . .

(b) to continue in the role of passive spectator cannot fail to have an adverse effect on our prestige and future standing, not only in China but elsewhere in Asia; [and] (c) if America continues until the end of the war to exercise a virtual monopoly in China, the effect will be not only to *weaken* our own future position but also to detract from the UN conception which has caught the imagination of the Chinese. Moreover, China in any case prefers not to place herself in the hands of a single power.[35]

The British personnel in the field, however, found things easier said than done. Many of their American colleagues adopted a cool, if not hostile, attitude toward any active participation of the British in Chinese affairs. Ambassador Hurley was particularly reluctant to see British involvement in the KMT-CCP dispute. He reported that Britain's imperial maneuvers were unduly facilitated by the lend-lease and that Carton de Wiart even had a personal American lend-lease airplane to engage in these activities.[36] Carton de Wiart angrily reported to the prime minister in February, "The Americans are playing up to the Chinese 100%, and you will find them solidly together at San Francisco [UN Conference]. On the other hand I think the Chinese think the Americans are becoming too proprietary here."[37]

American suspicion of the British intention in China also permeated through less overtly political activities. Humphrey Trevelyan reported bitterly in March that, "when recruitment of Englishmen for the Far Eastern Office of the UNRRA [United Nations Relief and Rehabilitation Administration] was being considered, a high [American] UNRRA official informed the British representative that they would be glad to have British officials, provided that they were not imperialists."[38]

The negative American attitude toward Anglo-American collaboration in China put heavy pressure on the Foreign Office. In March, during interdepartmental reevaluation of British China policy, Sterndale-Bennett wrote a long paper calling for concrete measures to be taken to restore British influence and to dispel the myth of the "weak China" policy said to be adopted by the British government. Sterndale-Bennett believed that in 1942 Britain had made a mistake in not insisting on China as a special entity beyond the American strategic sphere of influence. As a result, "the Americans are today virtually monopolizing China." In view of mutual suspicions engendered by the "strong China" controversy, what were the alternatives for Britain?

Sterndale-Bennett believed that the greatest problem at the time was political—to overcome the deadlock between the government of China and the Communists. He noted that "direct intervention or too close association with American efforts in this direction may be unwise. Our best course may be simply to keep a constant watch for opportunities of exerting a discreet influence either with the Chinese or the Americans."[39] Meanwhile, he suggested using financial and diplomatic means to regain influence in China.

The British Treasury Department regarded this call for spending on China as unrealistic. The Chancellor of the Exchequer doubted that Britain would be in a solvent position at the end of the war.[40] The Foreign Office sought other means to beef up British efforts in China. On 21 March, Anthony Eden wrote A. V. Alexander, First Lord of Admiralty, raising the question of responding to the Chinese military attaché's earlier suggestion of Anglo-Chinese naval cooperation. "So far as I am concerned," wrote Eden, "I am only too glad to find some field in which we are able at this difficult time to strengthen relations with China." After Churchill's approval on 30 March, the project was launched involving one cruiser, two "V"-class submarines, eight coastal craft, and one Hunt-class destroyer. The British also offered to train one thousand naval officers for China.[41] In view of the virtually nonexistent Chinese navy at the time, the project was thought to be an important source for British influence in postwar China.

Meanwhile, the Foreign Office was seeking any opportunities for Anglo-American consultation on China. On 2 March, Sterndale-Bennett raised the issue with Ambassador Winant, saying that there was "a lack of collaboration and . . . it was difficult to obtain a true picture of what is going on in China."[42] Because of this, he expressed strong hope that General Hurley would be able to accept the Foreign Secretary's invitation to visit London.

Hurley was back at Washington to confer with Roosevelt and Stettinius in March. The president, despite his failing health, remained an acute observer of Chinese affairs. By no means convinced of Britain's support for his "strong China" policy, as illustrated by such weak presentations as Lord Cranborne's speech in January, FDR decided to send Hurley to both London and Moscow in his dual capacity as the president's personal representative and ambassador to China. Hurley was instructed to obtain cooperation from the British and Soviet governments for the American policy to support the Nationalist government of China and unite the Chinese military forces to bring the war with Japan to a speedy end. Hurley was also briefed by the president to raise colonial issues with Churchill, particularly the issue of Hongkong.[43]

The Hurley Mission was perhaps FDR's last effort to induce Big-Three cooperation and approval for his version of a "strong China." But the results of the trip did not reach him before his sudden death on 12 April. According to Hurley's record, the trip to Moscow was successful. Stalin promised not to support the so-called Communists in China, though William Averell Harriman and George Kennan remained skeptical of this pledge.[44] The trip to London, however, was "hell-raising." After considerable anxiety and careful preparation, the Foreign Office was dismayed to learn that Hurley's trip had turned out dreadfully. As a top-secret brief prepared for Eden pointed out, the trip's principal objective was to clarify American policy toward the KMT-CCP dispute, but this was clearly unobtainable, given Hurley's attitude.[45] The real drama developed between a vehement British prime minister and the American special envoy with an Irish temper. According to Hurley, "In the discussion with Churchill and Eden, questions pertaining to the reconquest of colonial and imperial territory with American men and lend-lease supplies and the question pertaining to Hongkong and other problems were interjected by the British." Churchill branded the American long-range policy regarding China as the "great American illusion." Hurley further recounted, "The President briefed me regarding Hongkong and authorized me to discuss it if the question were introduced. Churchill flatly stated that he would fight for Hongkong to a finish. In fact he used the expression 'Hongkong will be eliminated from the British Empire only over my dead body!' . . . I then pointed out that if the British decline to observe the principles of the Atlantic Charter and continue to hold Hongkong, then Russia would possibly make demands in regard to areas in North China."[46] At this point, Churchill stated that Britain was not bound by the Atlantic Charter at all.

After the Churchill-Hurley talk, the prime minister was still in a fighting mood. He sent a handwritten note to the Foreign Office, stating, "I took him up with violence about Hongkong and said that never would we yield an inch of the territory that was under the British flag."[47] Hurley's meeting with the Chiefs of Staff committee also bored his hosts. A. L. Scott reported that the meeting consisted almost entirely of a monologue by Hurley; no discussion took place about specific issues.[48]

Monologue, however, was not just Hurley's personal style. There was no evidence that the Americans were prepared to discuss any significant or special issues. After the Churchill-Hurley talk, the Foreign Office promptly held a much-desired conference with Hurley's entourage in the hope of getting something concrete. The meeting proceeded cordially but yielded few results. According to a State Department record, Sterndale-Bennett felt that "the British were not being kept close enough in touch with American plans and policy in China, either in military or in the politico-economic field." He, then, asked his American colleagues whether or not there was any prospect of success in bringing the Communist Party and the Nationalist government together. Robert Smyth, the American counselor at the Chungking embassy, suggested that Sterndale-Bennett ask Hurley directly. The Americans apparently did not want to answer any substantial questions. A frustrated Sterndale-Bennett concluded that, "The situation in China, where the U.S. was in a position to be of immediate aid and the British could only be of secondary assistance, was almost the reverse of the situation which existed in Turkey." In Turkey, the British government was in a position roughly comparable to that of the United States in China. However, as he reminded his guests, the United States had real interests in Turkey, economic or otherwise. It was his hope that "similar collaboration could take place in Chungking so that British and American policy and actions in China could be as closely aligned as possible."[49]

The death of President Roosevelt did not change the prospects for improved Anglo-American collaboration in the Far East. President Truman continued to carry on Roosevelt's "strong China" legacy. In May, Truman sent Harry Hopkins to Moscow on a mission similar to Hurley's—to obtain further assurance from Stalin regarding China and other policies. To London's chagrin, there was no prior consultation with the British government. Truman was facing a rapidly changing situation from that faced by Roosevelt. In FDR's time, a "strong China" was more a fiction than a reality. When the war ended in Europe in April, it became urgent for the American government to bring the fiction into reality. Under the circumstances, Truman relied heavily upon career diplomats, because he was not yet in a position to pursue personal diplomacy. The State Department, which had lost much of the policy initiative during the period of the Roosevelt-Hurley duo, strove to regain control. The dormant feud between the department and Hurley quickly came to a head.

The State Department had long favored a strategy of flexibility in dealing with China, though there was hardly any serious dispute at the higher levels about which horse the U.S. government would back. The department was particularly concerned about Hurley's inflexible policy, which would damage the "long-term objective" in China as defined by a joint paper endorsed in January by the State, War, and Navy Coordination Committee (SWNCC), an earlier form of the National Security Council (NSC). According to the paper, the U.S. short-term goal in China was to induce military victory over Japan, while its long-term aim was to bring about the unification of China. For the former aim, Chiang Kai-shek was the only candidate who could lead China, but for the latter aim, Chiang was not necessarily the only one.[50] Hurley's policy placed both short- and long-term American interests into Chiang's basket and was, therefore, considered ineffective in inducing the generalissimo to adopt political reforms—a condition the department regarded as essential for long-term stability in China. On 7 May, the department informed Hurley that a new policy memo prepared for the secretary of state to use in the San Francisco conference contained the following position:

> We continue to support Chungking, ... but, in pursuance of our long-term objective and against the possible disintegration of the existing government we have to maintain a degree of flexibility to permit cooperation with any other leadership which may give greater promise of achieving unity and contributing to peace and security in East Asia.[51]

In appearance, Hurley had no choice but to accept such a position. In practice, the flamboyant general was busy firing his associates at the embassy. One after another, foreign service officers were, in Chungking's parlance, "Hurleyed" out of China. Anyone who disagreed with him encountered difficulties. Most officers who were kicked out of Chungking were in the China service, although Hurley never confined his targets to that office alone. In May, the military attaché's office prepared a memo that appeared to disagree with Hurley's unbridled criticism of the British China policy. The memo argued that (1) many Chinese actually preferred to let Britain retain Hongkong as a Crown Colony; (2) Sino-British relations had improved from the low point of 1942; and (3) the British were realistic in their cautiousness toward the KMT-Communist dispute, and they deliberately let the

Americans take the lead to set precedents in dealing with a postwar new China. In short, the memo seemed to believe that British policy was more sensible than that of the United States. Hurley was outraged. He wrote to Stettinius, charging that the memo "sets forth British imperialist propaganda—and while the supporters of this propaganda may be entitled to their own views in the premises, I know of no reason why American officers serving in China should undertake to sponsor such propaganda or to disseminate it within the American Government."[52]

American bureaucratic infighting, which became more evident after the death of President Roosevelt, was encouraging news to London. British ambassador to Washington Lord Halifax watched the development with acute interest. As he reported to Eden on 21 May, "The State Department has one bucking-bronco ambassador in its hands and it does not quite know what to do with him. He is ebullient, energetic Patrick J. Hurley." Halifax emphasized that, "Hurley holds the No. 2 job in the world. No. 1 is Moscow. Both China and Russia these days are more important than London, where relations are happy and serene."[53]

London was anxious to benefit from this internal dispute. Early in 1945, General Carton de Wiart obtained information through an intelligence network about the rivalry between Hurley and Wedemeyer, reporting that, "Hurley was rather sour that he had not been given an English decoration" particularly since Wedemeyer had received one. London decided to take action in April to ascertain the possibility of awarding a military decoration to Hurley. The effort was abandoned when the State Department objected to it on the grounds that Hurley, now a civilian, was ineligible for such an honor.[54]

The imminent Potsdam Conference put heavy pressure upon the Foreign Office, which had been kept in the dark about any changes in American China policy. London tried again to use the opportunity of the conference to revive the idea of departmental consultation with the Americans. At first, the British embassy had "pitched into Ballantine pretty strongly" that John Carter Vincent and Eugene Dooman, the Far Eastern experts attending the conference, should visit London on their way home. But Washington was not interested in the idea. Then Sir Alexander Cadogan, the permanent undersecretary, took it up with James Byrnes, the new American secretary of state, at Potsdam. Byrnes simply thought it inadvisable.[55] The frustrated Sterndale-Bennett wrote to L. H. Foulds, the Far Eastern Department's representative at Potsdam: "I do not know why the Americans are so shy about meeting us." He went on further, "We have not anything formal or elaborate in mind but merely think that even if Carter Vincent and Dooman were able to spend a day here on their way back it might be useful to make their acquaintance and exchange ideas with them."[56]

Throughout the summer, the issue of Hongkong became urgent in both London and Washington. Hurley firmly believed that Hongkong and Indochina were "two major controversies affecting the present military situation and the future of democracy and imperialism in Asia that are still unsettled." He advised President Truman in May to demand possession of all used and unused lend-lease equipment and say that no credit or additional gift at the expense of the American taxpayer would be given to Britain until it shows a more understanding attitude toward the American policy on Hongkong and toward democracy all over the world. He added, "I think you would find Britain amenable to reason."[57]

In practice, economic sanctions against a major ally were not feasible. The State Department also thought the option to use American forces to retake Hongkong "politically undesirable."[58] There seemed nothing the Americans could do to affect British repossession of Hongkong. President Roosevelt told Hurley in March that, "if Churchill refused this [the return of Hongkong to China], he would go over Churchill's head in an appeal to the King and the parliament."[59] It is doubtful that Truman was in a position to do the same.

The war cabinet in London was very much preoccupied elsewhere when the alarm about Hongkong was heard. In a gloomy mood concerning Europe, General "Pug" Ismay, the imperial chief of staff, wrote to his close friend Carton de Wiart in May:

> Life is very difficult these days. When the eagles are silent, the parrots start to chatter. When the war of the giants is over, the squabbles of the pygmies begin. Quite apart from all the complexities tidying up Europe in general, and Germany in particular, Tito must need choose this particular moment for being tiresome, and de Gaulle for being—de Gaulle![60]

A few weeks later, Carton de Wiart reported to Ismay that, "Hongkong is certainly a very sore point with the Americans here." The imperial chief of staff was greatly alarmed and wrote back promptly: "I do not quite understand what do you mean when you say 'Hongkong is certainly a very sore point with the Americans here.' Do they object to our having it again, because of our imperialistic tendencies. Or do they want it for themselves? Whom do you include in the 'Americans here'?" Carton de Wiart replied that both American objections were possible and that by the "Americans here," he meant Wedemeyer, whom he presumed represented American opinion.[61]

In London, consensus had long been reached on the issue of British forces retaking Hongkong. Despite the general election in July and August, the Labour Party also supported Churchill's position on Hongkong. In fact, in November 1944 Clement Attlee affirmed, on behalf of Churchill, that "no part of the British Empire is excluded from the declaration" (referring to Churchill's statement that he was not the king's first minister to preside over the liquidation of the British Empire), when asked by a Conservative M.P. whether Hongkong was included in it. The questioner then expressed satisfaction that such an assurance came from a Labour leader.[62] Fate decreed that the task of retaking Hongkong fell on the shoulders of the Labour Party eight months later.

Anglo-American conflict over a "strong China" went on well into the postwar period. As we have seen so far, no consensus or agreed policies were reached by August 1945, when the Japanese surrendered. The political and diplomatic aspects of this controversy were noisy and often in the open; the economic rivalry, however, was conducted behind the scenes, yet more intensely.

Anglo-American economic rivalry over China at the last stage of the war was largely a reversal of the picture in the nineteenth century. Given Britain's predominant position in China at that time, the Americans were striving for equal opportunities, which were often at the mercy of the British policy. In 1945 it was Britain's turn to ask for the "most favored nation" treatment. There was constant fear in London that the long-established British interests in China might be squeezed out in the face of the U.S. predominant position there as the result of the war. The Americans appeared to be able to defy any competition.

Wartime penetration of the United States into China was of a depth and thoroughness unimaginable for any foreign power in the last century. With their "Big Trio" (Hurley, Wedemeyer, and Nelson[63]) missions in China, the Americans were predominant in all fields—

political, economic, and military. Hurley assumed the task of political unification, Wedemeyer was the chief of staff of the Chinese military force, and Nelson created and ran the Chinese War Production Board as well as the Board of Transport. There were experts and advisers everywhere, from Chiang Kai-shek's private adviser, the missionary Dr. Frank Price, down to the men of SACO's naval intelligence program, who trained China's first modern secret police troops.[64]

The Americans, however, suffered from one handicap: they had had few established economic interests in China before the war compared to the British, who had penetrated deeply into the Chinese domestic economy. There were two kinds of trade in prewar China: trade *in* China and trade *with* China. The postwar American advantage in trade *with* China was without question, but it needed to build trade bases *in* China.

Britain's disadvantage in postwar China was obvious. Its trade with China predictably met strong competition from the United States, but worst of all, British trade suffered severely from a "strong China" policy that encouraged nationalism. Since the second half of the nineteenth century, the British had acquired expertise in doing successful business in a weak or divided China, and they were not prepared to deal with a strong one, especially one promoted by the United States. During the war, foreign extraterritorial rights, which had been the most effective protection for Britain's business activity in China, were abolished as the result of the U.S. "strong China" policy. The British were left in a particularly weak position vis-à-vis the assertiveness of Chinese economic nationalism. They felt vulnerable to Chiang's ambitious postwar program for industrialization, which was followed by a series of laws and regulations to control foreign economic activities. The British had long established themselves in shipping, banking, real estate, railway, mining, textile, and other fields. Having been wiped out by the Japanese during the war, the British found themselves in a position of having to restore their previous status under Chinese law.

With the abolition of extraterritorial rights, American businessmen would presumably suffer too. But this disadvantage was more than compensated for by the United States' dominant position and all the privileges attached to it. The prospects for long-term net gains whetted American business appetites. Under the circumstances, the U.S. "strong China" policy was perceived in London as a strategy for capturing the China market. Although the idea of an insatiable China market had proven in the past to be more fiction than reality, the dream had never died. The clichés were very much alive, and Anglo-American business communities were still under such illusions as "every Chinaman adds one inch to his shirt" or "each Chinaman smokes one pack of cigarettes a day." There was serious doubt in London that Americans would care about British interests, which were the largest foreign interests in China: direct investments alone came to about £200 million.[65] Such anxiety was well expressed by Sir George Sansom, British minister in Washington, as he reported to London on 29 December 1944: "There is plenty of information which shows in a general way what was on *a priori* grounds to be expected," namely, that American financial and commercial interests "look to China as a field of investment and enterprise which they will dominate and from which they hope, by sheer weight of financial and industrial strength, to EXPEL [sic] British and other competition." Sir George was greatly disturbed that "many American naval and military officers talk as if something like a monopoly of Far Eastern trade is a reward due to their contribution to the Pacific War. Some of them justify this sentiment by arguing that they are not fighting to restore an effete British imperialism in Asia." Moreover, "The Administration's program which involves a promise of '60 million jobs after the war' no doubt stimulates government agencies concerned with the future of American trade and industry to look upon the Far East as potential market of the highest importance."[66]

Despite widespread pessimism, the British government still believed there were conditions that would eventually work in favor of its position. The first was that the Chinese traditionally would not place all their eggs in one basket. The second was that the prewar position of the British business establishment had been a strong one. But most importantly, the American position was based on a strong and unified China, which remained very much a fiction. Nevertheless, London was deeply concerned with the possibility that Britain might be cut out of China's postwar industrialization program, for such a program, if implemented, was bound to involve a large amount of American credit and provide many business opportunities.

In a telegram to Sir Horace Seymour in Chungking in late 1944, Anthony Eden said that the present American dominance in China was possibly just a passing phenomenon that would disappear gradually with the special circumstances of the present time. Eden suggested that the position could also alter when trade was resumed and the flow of goods was again more on a commercial than a governmental basis. Eden emphasized that, "I am naturally anxious to see British influence and British trade restored in China, but . . . so far as Americans are concerned there seem to be influences working for and against such [Anglo-American] cooperation."[67]

Sir Humphrey Prideau-Brune, principal adviser on Chinese affairs, wrote a memo that was included in Eden's telegram to Seymour. He pointed out that "Perhaps the greatest obstacle to Sino-American-British cooperation is the latent suspicion in China and in the States of the imperialism which is believed still to colour British policy in the Far East." Thus, "once satisfied on this point China and America would both become more receptive and we should be on a good footing for offering help in solving the problem of the day." Sir Humphrey made a fateful prophecy: "the Communist problem, for instance, is the sort of thing which is apt only to become aggravated as a result of direct pressure by a single foreign power."[68]

The Americans were, however, not convinced of the benefits of Anglo-American cooperation in China—either politically or economically. The declared governmental policy was to promote a strong, independent, and prosperous China. Behind the rhetoric, the administration was also concerned with the question of how to utilize the newly obtained position in China to promote American business interests. Political unification was undoubtedly the top priority, for a civil war in China would surely blast the China market into pieces. The Americans had a unique stake in Chiang Kai-shek, as an OSS report pointed out clearly: "For Kuomintang, China's economic orientation towards the US is a matter of life and death. A Communist China can survive without America [sic] aid but seeks such assistance." Moreover, "the China Market is vital for the full utilization of America's expanded production facilities."[69]

The administration took concrete steps in early 1945 to bring about a "strong China" that would be economically dependent upon the United States. The first step was to prepare a modern commercial treaty with China. As John Carter Vincent explained in a memo in early 1945: "Our opinion is that such a treaty should be negotiated at an early date—prior to the conclusion of the war." The reason was that "it would be better to enter peace period with a basic treaty regarding commercial intercourse already in force rather than enter the peace without such a treaty; better for concerned American commercial interests and beneficial to our immediate post-war relations with China." It seemed to Vincent that the British did not want to negotiate such a treaty now because they were reluctant to deal with a fictitious "strong China"; thus, they "prefer the deferment of such treaty until after the war."[70]

The second step was to strengthen the already strong U.S. representation in Chungking. On 18 January, President Roosevelt approved a recommendation made by Donald Nelson that a man of outstanding qualifications be appointed to head the Foreign Economic Administration at Chungking and that he be given the rank of minister to work under the ambassador's general direction. Believing this recommendation did not go far enough, Hurley suggested that "a qualified officer, who is both politically and economically minded, be assigned to Chungking as over-all coordinator and supervisor of the various agencies dealing with civil matters."[71]

The third step involved putting pressure on Chiang's government to influence the making of laws concerned with foreign interests in post-war China. Judge Milton J. Helmick, a legal expert from New York, was sent to China to help the Chinese draw up such legislation as company law, banking law, and so on. The American business community, for its part, influenced these laws through channels like the National Foreign Trade Council and the China-America Council of Commerce and Industry. In February the State Department's *Daily Secret Summary* recorded that all the important points in the National Foreign Trade Council's memo, suggesting the establishment by the Chinese government of a simplified procedure for the registration of foreign firms, seemed to have been covered by Judge Helmick in recommendations he had drawn up and that these had been approved in principle by the generalissimo.[72]

The British, however, had much less leverage in China. Their major concern was whether or not the Americans would take British interests into consideration. As far as trade *with* China was concerned, the American competition could not be resisted, as a Foreign Office report admitted: "In general, British business presumably has to recognise that it will start off at a disadvantage with America in many aspects in China's post-war trade" since "America's ability to manufacture and ship capital goods and heavy machinery with rapidity . . . should enable her . . . to steal a march on British manufacturers." Furthermore, "the supply of wartime equipment is by no means unconnected with the supplying of peacetime requirements." The report predicted that if American factories, with the help of Donald Nelson and the lend-lease, were going to fill orders for the supply of Chinese wartime rail requirements, then those U.S. manufacturers would be in an obviously advantageous position for peacetime replacements. Thus, "HMG, if it meant to help British manufacturers, would therefore be well advised to scrutinize carefully the categories of 'war goods' supplied to China by US."[73]

The British government tried to set up an Anglo-American screening committee, but the suggestion was promptly turned down by the Americans. As Vincent reported, "We do not believe that such a screening committee would serve a useful purpose . . . moreover, with regard to the proposed conversations with the British on aviation . . . we favor their [Chinese] participation."[74] On 11 January, Vincent informed Ballantine and Grew that there were elements among the British who desired a weak and possibly disunited China in the postwar period. He believed that "our policy towards China is not based on sentiment. It is based on an enlightened national self-interest."[75]

The British were greatly worried about the American attitude. The War Cabinet Far Eastern Economic Subcommittee stated in January: "If the problem of our future commercial relation with China is to be on [the] basis of cash or commercial credit, we shall certainly not be able to compete with the Americans." But the report also asserted that, "Most important of all perhaps is the political necessity that we should recover as much as possible of our previous influence in China. The part we play in China conditions our whole position in the Far East." The subcommittee further called attention to the rapid pace at which the Americans were working toward a commercial treaty with China— although the time for Britain on this issue might not be ripe, London should closely watch this development.[76]

As for trade *in* China, the British were annoyed by numerous reports that America was embarking on a comprehensive plan for postwar economic development in China. The *Washington Post*, for example, reported in January that "a five-year guide for China's post-war industrialization by sprinkling 600 industrial plants is ready on paper at the FEA."[77] The *Shipping Digest* likewise reported on the close collaboration among Donald Nelson, the FEA, and the China-America Council

of Commerce and Industry in matters pertaining to the future development of China.[78]

Nevertheless, Britain's predominant position before the war in trade
in China enabled the Foreign Office to seek room for maneuver. G. A.
Wallinger, the commercial counselor and chargé at the Chungking
embassy, reported to Eden in February that the United States had undoubtedly established a sort of monopolistic control over the external
economy of China. While "there is a historical reason to believe that
the Chinese wish to distribute their eggs into different baskets, we
must, I think, add to the suspicion of British 'imperialism' the existing
doubts whether Britain either can or wishes to, help China to develop
herself." Wallinger believed that in the immediate postwar period, the
United States would surely take the lead in China's rehabilitation, but
he added,

> Is it not possible the existence of considerable vested interests in the old
> treaty ports may give us certain advantages at that stage over America,
> among such are export services, business management, shipping, bank-
> ing, insurance and the provision of many types of manufactured goods
> and if we include Empire products of such primary commodities as
> wool, wheat and rice. . . . It would therefore seem that there is a possi-
> ble line of approach to the U.S. authorities concerned with a view to
> *rationalisation* of Anglo-American cooperation in the post-war devel-
> opment of China.[79]

General Carton de Wiart also expressed the same thought when he
reported to the prime minister in April: "As to the Generalissimo, his
position is very difficult, he is virtually in the pay of the Americans
and no one else is in a position to help him at the present, he therefore
has to dance to the tune they play. His sympathy, I think, is more with
us than with them."[80]

In the meantime, London was busy preparing for the return of British business interests to China, especially in the fields of banking and
shipping. In February, Edmund Hall-Patch, the Treasury representative
to the Foreign Office, told Vincent in Washington, "It seems to me
desirable that the American and British banks should know what is in
each other's mind and ascertain how far it would be possible for them
to pursue a common policy on return to China."[81]

On 21 March, the Treasury sent a memo to the Foreign Office
affirming that the Bank of England considered it in the national interest
that Hongkong Bank be adequately staffed in Chungking. Moreover,

as prospects had appeared of a possible resumption of British trade with China in the near future, the Treasury wanted to inform the passport department that it was in favor of the bank's application.[82]

At the same time, a memo prepared by George Hall, chairman of the War Cabinet Armistice and Postwar Committee, concluded that (a) "it is of great political importance that we should recover as much as possible of our previous position of influence in China" and (b) "the preparation of a draft commercial treaty with China and of its supplement, the Consular and Establishment Convention, should be expedited."[83]

In the field of shipping, the British government carefully watched the postwar Chinese orientation; before the war it had always been veered toward Britain. When a Sino-American shipping negotiation was reportedly under way in New York, Sir George Sansom at the Washington embassy commented that joint companies between the Chinese and the British would be more profitable to the Chinese than a similar association with American interests because "British-built vessels could be supplied more cheaply, and thus in greater tonnage for the proportionate issue of stock, apart from the British advantage in operating experience, ability to recruit satisfactory crews, etc., in the Far East." Sir George advised the British shipping industry that if Holt's (Butterfield and Swire), Jardine's, and other British shipowners felt sufficiently confident of their ability to weather Chinese postwar nationalism, then the best thing to do was "clearly to expedite their preparations as quietly as possible with a minimum of disclosure of the sort that might drive Chinese into closer relations with American shipping interests than has been achieved to date."[84]

With the war's end in Europe, Anglo-American preparation for a return to business in China intensified. The economic activities that had hitherto been behind the scenes became increasingly more open and aggressive. The British were soon to discover that America's monopolistic tendencies were not a "passing phenomenon," as Anthony Eden had hoped, nor were such drives for monopoly concerned with rationalization of Anglo-American cooperation, as Wallinger had predicted.

British business representatives in China were even more astounded by the ruthless drive of American businessmen aided by their official missions. In the spring of 1945 a "G–5" section, which was created by Wedemeyer's headquarters, assumed wide responsibilities in steering the Chinese domestic economy. J. C. Powell, of Shell Company China, reported to London: "What does disturb us about G–5 is its unthinking treatment of very delicate parts of the Chinese political body. . . . We are astounded that G–5 publicly claims responsibility and credit for the control of inflation, for the Gold Policy, for China's reconstruction and post-war economic policies, etc."[85]

The aggressiveness of the Americans also shocked G. E. Price, Chungking representative of Swire and Sons, one of the leading British companies in China. As Price described:

> The aggressive American industrial salesmen in and out of uniform are having things very much their own way. They can talk about firm finance and early large-scale delivery. They seem to have an unlimited supply of technicians and planners unengrossed by the war to put at Chinese disposal. The Chinese have been made to realise that they are in a hurry and they turn first to the eager continent with an intact economy, not to Britain with a smashed one to repair.[86]

Even so, American business interests were hardly satisfied with the U.S. administration's efforts to facilitate their business activities in China. One sore point was over bureaucratic procedures. American business circles had a traditional lack of confidence in their diplomatic service abroad. A report in May on Anglo-American relations prepared by Mrs. Ehle, president of the Philadelphia organization *Leadership Panel*, cited a common American cliché that British diplomatic officials could always outsmart their American colleagues. The report pointed out further that "Business men feel this keenly in relation to consular services in the Far East. None of the business men questioned suggested that the activity of British officials on behalf of British traders was anything more than shrewd, experienced self-interest. . . . Executives who were asked why the British were, instead of us, in this field usually replied that 'the British have been at it longer,' or 'look at the men we have!' "[87]

Better cooperation between the British government and the business community in China disturbed many American businessmen. John Carter Vincent told Stettinius in July: "We have been plagued for some time and with some justification, by complaints of American businessmen with regard to this government's attitude toward the return of American businessmen to China. . . . some of them are directed against the severity of our policy in comparison with the British. It is a fact that British business people seem to find it easier to get into the country and are there in greater number than our own."[88]

The war in the Far East, thus, ended with intense economic rivalry between the two erstwhile allies over the future of their respective positions in China. Just as in the political field, economic cooperation was not achieved when the war ended in August. Furthermore, the "strong China" controversy was not confined to China proper; it also involved Anglo-American conflicting strategic visions for Southeast Asia.

By 1945, the United States was undoubtedly the dominant power not only in China, but also in all of the Far East. Among the Big Three, however, it was the only power that had no foothold in McKinder's "heartland"—the Eurasian landmass. The Anglo-American difference in strategic visions was characterized by the U.S. quest for hegemony versus Britain's desire to restore the balance of power. For the Americans, it would have been politically unwise to take over Britain's colonial possessions; such an action would have resembled the centuries-old European imperialism. Thus, throughout the war, the Americans, who were foreign to the Eurasian heartland, adopted a strategy to challenge the legitimacy of the British position in Asia, as was clearly demonstrated by the Anglo-American quarrel over the Atlantic Charter of 1941. But such a strategy would have been ineffective without native support; therefore, a strong China, perceived to be a natural ally of the United States in the battle against colonialism, was an ace up Uncle Sam's sleeve.

From the British viewpoint, the American anti-Empire campaign was "foreign" interference in Britain's "domestic" affairs. Because the United States in the past had not been averse to balance-of-power politics in the region, the British were convinced that the Americans were determined to replace Britain in the Far East.

Another British concern resulting from America's "strong China" policy was the possible revival of the ancient Chinese empire, which had a traditional interest in playing a leading role in the region. In a paper entitled "Modern China's Asiatic Empire," prepared by the Indian Office, Chinese "imperialism," as well as irredentist claims and policies were pointed out as endangering British Asiatic interests. The trouble spots in the postwar period were likely to be Burma, Siam, French Indochina, and other Southeast Asian countries. Economically, the paper envisaged an emergence of a "Nanking-Washington Axis," which would encourage Chinese expansion in Southeast Asia. The paper called for a united front within the British Commonwealth for the purpose of resisting "all Chinese and American schemes which would have the appearance of 'altruism' and 'internationalism.' " [89]

In early 1945, President Roosevelt was convinced by Hurley and Wedemeyer that the imperialist countries were using American lend-lease materials toward their colonial ends. The administration was alarmed by the report that the British, Dutch, and French governments had reached an understanding regarding the future political, economic, and security aspects of Southeast Asia.[90] Hurley told the Dutch ambassador in China, "If Britain and Holland thought that the U.S. was going to clear up the imperial mess for their imperialism in the Far East, they had better think again."[91]

Meanwhile, high tension existed between British and Americans over the Burma Campaign. Churchill's unwillingness to see a large group of Sino-American troops in Burma caused friction with the Americans, who wanted to open the Burma road to China as soon as possible.

Another nagging issue was French Indochina. In early 1945 the British attempted to sponsor French reentry into Indochina. President Roosevelt, however, insisted on dealing with any Indochina issues after the war, as he wrote to Stettinius in January: "I still do not want to get mixed up in any way with French Indo-China decision. It is a matter for post war."[92] General Carton de Wiart reported to the war cabinet in February: "In this part of the world what worries me is Indo-China. Wedemeyer considers it to be in the U.S. strategic sphere of interest and, therefore, will not allow Mountbatten to operate in any way unless he obtains Wedemeyer's consent."[93] Two weeks later, Carton de Wiart wrote to his friend General "Pug" Ismay, imperial chief of staff, that "The feeling between Mountbatten and Wedemeyer is strong about Indo-China, and the latter wrote a letter to Mountbatten . . . saying 'our views are 180 degrees apart on the question of Indo-China.' "[94]

At the same time, the issue of Siam or Thailand came to a head. According to Stettinius, "Thailand is a country with which Britain was at war. The British would treat the country as a *conquered enemy* while to us it would be a *liberated area*." Since Siam had collaborated with the Japanese during the war and was awarded with ceded territories from British Malaya, the Americans were convinced that the British were bound to pursue a "weak Thailand" policy. Hurley went so far as to suggest setting up a provisional free Thai government in Chungking," thus forcing the British to deal with Siam's postwar status quo through this government. Hurley warned that, "if our Government does not move forward in this matter the British will outmaneuver us and the Chinese and will obtain some degree of control over Thailand."[95] The British felt that American suspicion of its evil design on postwar Thailand was mixed "possibly with a desire to replace Britain in [its] former position of supremacy."[96]

The Anglo-American "strong China" controversy was symptomatic of a fundamental recast of Far Eastern international relations after the war. On the one hand, the British were painfully aware of their deteriorating position in the balance of power in the Far East. Since unilateral British predominance in the region had ended in the last decade of the nineteenth century, London had pursued a consistent policy of preventing any rival from attaining an ascendant position through Anglo-Japanese and Anglo-American alliances. The days of such a game seemed to be over in 1945. The British found themselves in a defensive position.

Notes

1. D. Cameron Watt, *Succeeding John Bull: America in Britain's Place, 1900–1975.*

2. Hurley to Stettinius, top secret, 14 April 1945, in U.S. Department of State, *Foreign Relations of the United States,* 1945, 7:331 (hereafter cited as *FRUS*).

3. Lieutenant General Sir Adrian Carton de Wiart had been assigned to Chungking since 1943. See A. Carton de Wiart, *Happy Odyssey: the Memoirs of Lieutenant-General Sir Adrian Carton de Wiart.*

4. Hurley to Truman, top secret, 29 May 1945, enclosed in Admiral Leahy's memo to the secretary of state, in which Hurley complained about the late president's reluctance to issue "written instructions." See National Archives of the United States (hereafter cited as *NAUS*), Decimal Files, RG 59, microfilm LM69, 893.00/5–2945.

5. Hurley to Stettinius, 31 January 1945, *FRUS*, 1945 7:40.

6. NAUS, Stettinius Records, RG 59, part 1, Section 3.

7. Drew Pearson's syndicated column, *New York Times,* 15 June 1945.

8. NAUS, Stettinius Records, RG 59, part 4, section 7, p. 51.

9. For an interesting discussion, see T. G. Fraser, "Roosevelt and the Making of America's East Asian Policy, 1941–1945," pp. 92–109.

10. "Noble Negatives," *Economist,* 30 December 1944.

11. U.K. Public Record Office (hereafter cited as U.K. PRO), Stephenson to

Michael Wright of British Washington Embassy, 5 January 1945, FO371 44559/AN/70/23/45.

12. NAUS, Stettinius Records, RG 59, part 3, section 5.

13. U.K. PRO, Minute by Donnelly, 26 June 1945, FO371 46171/F3917/36/10.

14. Hurley to Secretary of State, 24 December 1944, *FRUS,* 1944, 6:748.

15. NAUS, Decimal Files, RG 59, Memo of Conversation, microfilm, 893.00/1–645.

16. Quoted from Diana Shaver Clemens, *Yalta*, p. 48.

17. Hurley to Secretary of State, 14 April 1945, *FRUS,* 1945, 7:331.

18. U.K. PRO, Seymour to FO, 12 January 1945, FO371 46232/F409.

19. U.K. PRO, FO371 46232/F4097.

20. U.K. PRO, General Hollis (War Cabinet Office) to Sterndale-Bennett, FO-371 46324/F2152/91/G61.

21. U.K. PRO, Memo by Gore-Booth, 25 January 1945, FO371 46165/F873/135/10.

22. NAUS, Decimal Files, LM69/roll 1/893.00/1–1345.

23. NAUS, Decimal Files, RG 59, C. Van H. Engert to Secretary of State, 19 January 1945, 711/41/1–2945, box 3395.

24. NAUS, Decimal Files, Memo by Davies, 4 January 1945, microfilm 893.00/1–445.

25. Nathaniel Peffer, *Transatlantic*, January 1945.

26. U.K. PRO, Handwritten Minute by A. L. Scott, FO371 46170–72/F45/36/10.

27. Ibid., Typed Minute by Henderson.

28. U.K. PRO, Memo by Sterndale-Bennett, 2 February 1945, FO371 46232/F792.

29. U.K. PRO, Paper by Humphrey Trevelyan, May 1945, FO371 46170–72/F3917/36/10.

30. Ibid., Donnelly's Minute, 26 May 1945.

31. U.K. PRO, FO371 54073/F9836/8854/G61.

32. U.K. PRO, Top Secret, FO371 46336/F669/185/G61.

33. NAUS, Records of the Office of the Executive Secretariat, *Daily Secret Summary*, 22 January 1945, lot file 110/box 1.

34. NAUS, Records of the Office of the Executive Secretariat, RG 59, *Daily Secret Summary*, "British Efforts at Hegemony in Western Europe," 31 January 1945, box 4.

35. U.K. PRO, 11 January 1945, FO371 46232/F136.

36. Hurley to Secretary of State, 31 January 1945, *FRUS*, 1945, 7:40.

37. U.K. PRO, Carton de Wiart to Ismay, 28 February 1945, CAB 127 (Private Collections)/28(General Carton de Wiart Correspondence).

38. U.K. PRO, FO371 46170–72/3063/36/10, May 1945.

39. U.K. PRO, Paper by Sterndale-Bennett, "British Policy Toward China," 2 March 1945, FO371 46232/F133.

40. Ibid., Discussion Minutes by Hall-Patch and Cavendish-Bentik.

41. U.K. PRO, Eden to Alexander, 21 March 1945, FO371 46173/F1440/55/10.

42. NAUS, Decimal Files, Winant to Stettinius, 2 March 1945, microfilm 893.00/3–245.

43. Hurley to Stettinius, 14 April 1945, *FRUS*, 1945, 7:329–32.

44. Hurley to Stettinius, 17 April 1945, *FRUS*, 1945, 7:339.

45. U.K. PRO, FO371 46325/F2011/127/G61.

46. Ibid., see note 43.

47. U.K. PRO, Churchill's Handwritten Note to FO, FO371 46325/F2263/127/G61.

48. U.K. PRO, FO Minute by A. L. Scott, FO371 46325/F2218/1127/G61.

49. NAUS, Decimal Files, Memo of Conversation, microfilm 893.00/14–445.

50. *FRUS*, 1945, 7:34.

51. NAUS, Decimal Files, Stettinius to Hurley, 7 May 1945, box 3479, 711.93/5–745.

52. NAUS, Decimal Files, RG 59, microfilm 893.00/5–1845, roll 2.

53. U.K. PRO, Halifax to Eden, 21 May 1945, FO371 46170–72/F3163/36/10.

54. U.K. PRO, General Carton de Wiart Correspondence, April to May, CAB 127/28.

55. U.K. PRO, FO Minute, 30 July 1945, FO371 46383/F4797/4664/61.

56. U.K. PRO, Sterndale-Bennett to Foulds, 28 July 1945, FO371 46383/F4797/4664/61.

57. NAUS, Decimal Files, Hurley to Truman, top secret, 29 May 1945, microfilm 893.00/5–2945.

58. NAUS, Decimal Files, box 3497, 711.93/1–1245.

59. Hurley to Truman, ibid., see note 57.

60. U.K. PRO, General Carton de Wiart Correspondence, Ismay to Carton de Wiart, May 1945, CAB 127/28.

61. Ibid., 15 June 1945.

62. NAUS, Records of the Division of Chinese Affairs, RG 59, lot file 110, box 7: Hong Kong 1945.

63. Donald Nelson, formerly chairman of the U.S. War Production Board, was sent to China by FDR in the summer of 1944 as personal representative for economic affairs.

64. The Sino-American Cooperation Organization (SACO) was a program between the U.S. Navy Intelligence Group in China under Rear Admiral Milton Miles and the Chinese Military Intelligence under the notorious General Tai Li. The program trained special counterintelligence forces against the Communists.

65. U.K. PRO, FO Paper, December 1945, CAB 134/87.

66. U.K. PRO, Sansom to Eden, 27 December 1944, FO371 46179/F5571/16/60.

67. U.K. PRO, Eden to Seymour, 27 December 1944, FO371 46179/F5571/16/60.

68. Ibid., enclosure.

69. Office of Strategic Services Records, R & A Report, 13 June 1945, microfilm no.3316.

70. NAUS, Records of the Office of the Executive Secretariat, J. C. Vincent Files, Memorandum (no date, possibly January 1945), RG 59, lot files, Division of Chinese Affairs, box 1.

71. NAUS, Records of the Office of the Executive Secretariat, Daily Secret Summary, 18 January 1945, box 1.

72. Ibid., 16 February 1945.

73. U.K. PRO, Sansom to FO, 2 January 1945, FO371 46178/F293.

74. NAUS, J. C. Vincent Files, January 1945, lot files box 1.

75. Ibid., 11 January 1945.

76. U.K. PRO, Cabinet Memo, 17 January 1945, FO371 46179.

77. *Washington Post*, 7 January 1945.

78. *Shipping Digest*, 8 January 1945.

79. U.K. PRO, Wallinger to Eden, 14 February 1945, FO371 46178/F962/57/10.

80. U.K. PRO, Carton de Wiart Correspondence, 22 April 1945, CAB 127/28.

81. U.K. PRO, Memo by Hall-Patch, 15 February 1945, FO371 46178/F1379/57/10.

82. U.K. PRO, FO371 46178/F1835/57/10.

83. U.K. PRO, Memo of Cabinet, 24 March 1945, CAB/A.P.W. (45)/43.

84. U.K. PRO, Sansom to FO, 2 January 1945, FO371 46178/F293.

85. U.K. PRO, Powell to FO, 11 July 1945, FO371 46184/F4900/57/10.

86. U.K. PRO, Price to FO, 4 May 1945, FO371 46187/F3280/57/10.

87. U.K. PRO, quoted from a copy of the report in FO371 44555/AN1259/22/45.

88. NAUS, Vincent to Stettinius, 3 July 1945, J. C. Vincent Files, lot files, box 1.

89. U.K. PRO, Paper by O. M. Cleary, Indian Office, FO371 46282/F4220/4220/10.

90. NAUS, Daily Secret Summary, 1 January 1945, box 1.

91. U.K. PRO, Memo of Conversation, 12 January 1945, FO371 46170–72/F482/36/10.

92. NAUS, Stettinius Records, part 2, section 5.

93. U.K. PRO, Carton de Wiart Correspondence, 13 February 1945, CAB 127/28.

94. Ibid., 28 February 1945.

95. NAUS, Daily Secret Summary, 3 February 1945, box 1.

96. U.K. PRO, FO Paper, "British Policy in the Far East," December 1945, CAB 134/280 (1945).

2

The Japanese Surrender

The Japanese surrender in August 1945 was obviously a major turning point in world history. World War II was finally over and the "post-war" era had begun. Old dreams and plans were put in front of new reality. During the months after August, the Anglo-American controversy over China entered a new phase. The American concept of a "strong China" was tested, adapted, and eventually carried out in the form of mediation between the Kuomintang and the Communists in China. Did America's obsession with mediation indicate any fundamental changes in U.S. China policy? Or was it a policy of continuity and convenience? To answer these questions one has to look at the motivation behind the mediation efforts and at the political and military realities in China after August 1945 to determine whether the United States had other alternatives. American interests in China were incompatible with the idea of a "red star over China." Washington was more than anxious to see China enter America's new liberal world order.

The British had very different concerns. First, London had grave doubts about the prospect of mediation, which was viewed as a useless attempt. Second, the British strongly resented the American tendency to monopolize Chinese affairs, as shown by U.S. policies immediately after the war. Britain always considered such a single-handed approach to be detrimental to its interests.

It should be noted that both sides had new governments at war's end: the Truman administration was four months old, and the Labour government, only two weeks in office. But the change of guards did not make Anglo-American cooperation in the Far East any easier. The two new regimes preferred continuity to changes in their China policies.

While Truman's foreign-policy team was not entirely new at the beginning of the administration, British foreign policy depended on a man of great stature and influence. The new foreign secretary was Ernest Bevin, a powerful Labour politician and union leader. As an OSS report pointed out at the time of Bevin's appointment, "If any man in the Labour Party is equipped by experience and personality to impose his will upon the permanent officials of the British Foreign Office, Bevin is the man."[1] According to Alan Bullock, Bevin's main biographer, one of the top priorities in his policy agenda was the British Commonwealth and Empire, a priority that would attract a great deal of his attention to the Far East and the Pacific, because

> It fell to Bevin (and this was one of the reasons why Attlee had put him at the Foreign Office) to make clear to those who presumed too far that while Britain might no longer be as powerful as she had been, she was still the nation to be reckoned with and had no intention of being pushed around or left out of account.[2]

It is not surprising that another OSS report noted in October that "the Labour Government is as empire-minded as was its Conservative predecessor under Churchill."[3]

As far as general Anglo-American relations were concerned, the Labour cabinet was faced with a somewhat hostile American public. The Labour landslide seemed to many Americans like a "July Pearl Harbor." John Balfour, the British chargé in Washington, reported on 28 July: "American opinion as a whole has expressed astonishment at the extent of the landslide in favour of the Labour Party ... [but] some satisfaction is derived from the belief that the new Government will lay less stress on what are usually described here as 'Imperialist trends.' "[4]

But the American hope to see less British imperialism soon faded away over the issue of Hongkong. Meanwhile, in Chungking, there were also sharply different reactions among the Chinese to the British election. The Kuomintang's reaction was cautious, but the Communists were "jubilant," celebrating that the reactionary "appeasers" were gone.[5]

Truman's most important decision, which reflected the American public's as well as the administration's sentiments, was to end the lend-lease immediately, knowing the insolvent financial position of Great Britain. This decision alone greatly reduced Bevin's circumstances. Upon assuming the position at the Foreign Office, Bevin immediately felt the impact of a "financial Dunkirk." On 9 August, the new foreign secretary received a comprehensive report from Balfour on Anglo-American relations, which stated: "During recent months the concept has steadily gained ground" in the United States that "Great Britain has come to occupy a position on the world stage which in terms of power and influence is inferior to that of the United States and the Union of Soviet Socialist Republics." Balfour described the anti-British feeling in the United States as "a keen sense of rivalry and with the apparently ineradicable idea that nature has endowed the British with a well-nigh inexhaustible store of superior cunning," of which "they are only too prone to make the fullest possible use in international negotiations with the object of 'outsmarting' the more simple-minded Americans." Balfour thought the problem was more emotional than substantive:

> Whatever they find reason to complain of our actions, Americans did not fail to apply to us a number of ugly catchwords . . . e.g., balance of power, sphere of influence, reactionary imperialist trends, colonial oppression, old-world guile, diplomatic double-talk, Uncle Sam the Santa Claus and the Sucker, and the like. Anti-British outbursts are, as a rule, the result of the propensity of Americans to oversimplify vexatious issues which are beyond their immediate ken. They need not, therefore, unduly disturb us.[6]

Bevin was not easily convinced of the relatively optimistic thesis expressed by Balfour. He saw deeper roots in Anglo-American rivalry. In a private letter to his colleague Sir Stafford Cripps, president of the Board of Trade, on 20 September, Bevin stated:

> There does seem to be an assumption that Britain is down and out because of what she has done in this war. When the P.M. made his statement in the House on Lend-Lease we were met with headlines in the U.S. in certain papers calling us "Cry-Babies." We ignored it, but all this percolates through to the British people and while you will appreciate as I do that there are no more combative people if they feel they are being treated unfairly.

Bevin assured Cripps:

> I cannot help feeling that Britain has got to stand up for herself. I do think the time has come when the world must realise that though we have paid such a terrific price in this war we are not down and out. . . . Finally, there is no doubt that the attempt to put tremendous pressure upon us to alter our way of life and economy—to meet the desires of the worst elements of American capitalism is being resisted by our working people.[7]

Thus, as part of the general policy to prove that Britain was not "down and out," Bevin adopted a strong position in the Far East, where the Americans were most anxious to see the end of the British role. The desire to restore British influence in Asia prompted Bevin to accept the chairmanship of the cabinet's Far Eastern Committee, along with the other two committees he intended to preside over. Bevin continued the Conservative party's China policy of a passive attitude toward the Chinese domestic dispute but active towards restoring Britain's prewar position. During a conversation in September with T. V. Soong, Chinese foreign minister, Bevin stressed the British interests in the former treaty ports after the abolition of extraterritorial rights.[8]

Bevin was particularly irritated by the American attempt to belittle Britain's contribution to the war against Japan. In September, for example, an American film about the Burmese liberation caused an outcry in Britain, for it showed that Burma was liberated by a force of American parachutists and glider-borne troops, two Gurkha guides, and a Chinese officer; the British Fourteenth Army was forgotten.[9] Bevin took his revenge on Byrnes during the Moscow conference of foreign ministers when the American secretary of state was angered by a Soviet film about Manchuria, showing that the Red Army was the only force responsible for liberating China. Bevin laughed at Byrnes as they were both walking out of the film show, "You know, Jimmy, it reminds me of your American film about the war in Burma: all the fighting was done by Errol Flynn . . . without an Englishman in sight."[10] Indeed, the Foreign Office under Bevin was very sensitive to British publicity in the Far East. At one point, Sir Archibald Clark Kerr, former ambassador to China, suggested that London should create an interdepartmental committee on American opinion and the British Empire "as a sort of general staff for the projection of the British Empire."[11]

In the United States, the changes in the administration were much less dramatic with the same Democratic regime. But postwar reality in China forced the Truman administration to reexamine the effectiveness of the Roosevelt-Hurley China policy. The "flexible" policy favored by the State Department began to gain the upper hand. After four months in the White House, President Truman felt confident enough to build up his own foreign policy team. The appointment of Dean Acheson as undersecretary of state in August and the resignation of the so-called soft-to-Japs team led by Joseph Grew appeared to be of tremendous importance. Isaiah Berlin reported from the Washington embassy on 20 August: "That the day of surprise last-minute appointment did not pass with the late President became apparent when, two days after he had announced his retirement from the State Department, Dean Acheson was reappointed and promoted to the post of Under Secretary of State." Berlin continued, "Since Grew and Acheson have been leaders of the opposing State Department factions on soft or hard peace for Japan, the latter's promotion would not seem to foreshadow the kind of policies which Grew would work on with favor." Berlin further commented that Acheson's appointment was generally a victory for the new Byrnes-Cohen-Truman team over that of the Stettinius-Grew-Dunn group and the old school, and that "Acheson's general outlook is that of a liberal conservative. . . . Yet his talent, like that of Brynes, is that of the smooth, sometimes excessively smooth, negotiator rather than that of the administrator or overall planner."[12]

Indeed, the State Department under Byrnes and Acheson was annoyed with Patrick Hurley's rigid policy and style and more so with the weakened position of its embassy in Chungking. The department's China service was generally opposed to Hurley's policy. Through 1945, most of the career diplomats there were reassigned somewhere else. The result, as a Far Eastern Office memo revealed in late August, was a lack of impartial, comprehensive political reporting from China, which left the department in the dark on important matters. The memo pointed out further that "the departure of Messrs. Atcheson, Service, Davies, Freeman, Ringwalt and Sprouse has made the Embassy dependent upon the Kuomintang sources of information. Moreover, the Embassy's informal contact with the communists has been crippled."[13]

The department tried to mitigate the effect of the Hurley purge in

Chungking by assigning those who were "Hurleyed out" of China to some important positions at the Far East Office or the China Division. Moreover, John Paton Davies, Hurley's archenemy, was made George Kennan's right-hand man in Moscow. Dean Acheson made another move in September to promote John Carter Vincent from the position of chief of the China Division to director of the Far Eastern Department.

Despite the bureaucratic infighting, the Truman administration was determined to carry out the "strong China" policy left by its predecessor. The first test Washington encountered was on the status of Hongkong. The Americans had no plans regarding the Crown Colony, but the administration was known to oppose the British reentry by force. The British embassy in Washington reported on 25 August that, "Hongkong has become a symbol to Americans of an outdated era in the Pacific."[14]

Short of direct military intervention, there seemed little the administration could do to prevent Britain from recapturing the Crown Colony. More importantly, the Truman administration was handicapped by the secret Livadia Agreement, which allowed Stalin to regain Russia's pre-1905 position in Manchuria. It would be unwise to single out the issue of Hongkong while defending the Livadia Agreement. On 12 August the *New York Times* published Nathaniel Peffer's article which suggested that Britain's possession of Hongkong was "as if Manhattan were in [the] possession of another power." Peffer went on to make the comparison with Manchuria, "the most valuable port of China . . . [yet] alienated to another power."[15]

The Foreign Office was outraged by Peffer's charge. A. L. Scott of the Far Eastern Department commented, "To use a vulgarism, it is 'pure rot' to talk of Hongkong being a Manhattan island in the possession of another power." His colleague George Kitson, however, thought the Manchuria comparison very useful: "As Russia now has a naval base in Port Arthur as well a commercial harbour in Dairen, we have a strong case for retaining Hongkong as a counterpoise to these two."[16]

In London, consensus had long been reached over the retaking of Hongkong by British troops. In June, Ambassador Seymour told Sterndale-Bennett that, "If it could only be the British forces which recapture Hongkong, at least some of our troubles would be largely solved. But if we are merely given it back, very reluctantly by our allies, it will be a long time before we hear the last of it."[17]

In July, General L. Hayes, general officer commanding the British mission in the China theater, reported to London: "I feel it my duty to bring to notice a situation which I believe is becoming steadily worse. To use an Americanism, we are in fact being 'pushed around.' " Hayes continued, "The uneven balance between the American effort in China, on the one hand, and ours, on the other, can only be substantially redressed in our favour, in my opinion, by the recapture of Hongkong by British troops." Without that, according to Hayes, "nothing that the existing British military organizations in this country can do will ... contribute in the slightest degree to the restoration of our former prestige here."[18]

The immediate controversy over Hongkong was triggered by General Douglas MacArthur's General Order Number One, which deliberately avoided specifying if Hongkong was "within China," and thereby within the territory where Japanese troops were required to surrender to Chiang Kai-shek. Encouraged by this obvious omission, Chiang claimed that the surrender of Hongkong was his responsibility. The Labour government at once rejected Chiang's interpretation. Attlee pressed Truman to prevent a Chinese Fiume. But Truman replied that he had no objection to the surrender of Hongkong being accepted by a British officer provided "full military coordination is effected beforehand by the British with the Generalissimo on operational matters."[19]

London decided to effect a *fait accompli* by sending a naval fleet to "recapture" the Colony, where the Japanese resistance had already disappeared. Under the circumstances, Truman advised Chiang to make concessions. The Chinese leader, thus, made a face-saving move indicating his willingness to delegate authority to a British commander to accept the surrender.[20] The reaction of the Labour government to Chiang's offer was illuminating. Both Ambassador Seymour and General Ismay thought that Chiang's solution was acceptable from a military point of view, but Bevin refused to budge an inch. The Foreign Office informed the Chinese that the British government was regrettably unable to accept the suggestion, because Hongkong was British territory.[21] Carton de Wiart laughed heartily at Chiang's move, as he told General Ismay that, "The Generalissimo's latest decision authorising us to go to Hongkong and take the surrender is a bit of a teaser."[22]

Ambassador Hurley regarded this British line as a "threat of force . . . ignoring all courtesies." He then recommended that Chiang put the case to the court of world public opinion.[23] The Hongkong dispute poisoned Anglo-Chinese relations immediately after the war, while the United States government, though it provided half-hearted support to Chiang, gained in prestige with the Chinese. Thinking of quitting his job, General Carton de Wiart painted a gloomy picture to Ismay on 31 August: "I do not think there is much point in my being left here now and you should send someone to take my place. It's sad, our shares had gone up a lot, now they will go right down, and the Americans will have a clear field. It's no use my saying more."[24]

While Washington was preoccupied with the task of carrying out the "strong China" policy in the face of new realities, two immediate factors entered the picture of policy considerations. Internationally, the implementation of the Livadia Agreement directly threatened China's territorial integrity; the Hongkong dispute also fueled the fire. Internally, a unified Chinese central government did not really exist at the end of the war, despite various efforts made by the Americans.

As the starting point of World War II, China's ordeal had been the longest. The war, which was initiated in Manchuria, ended up ironically with yet another Manchurian controversy. International power politics did not fade away with the disappearance of the Greater East Asian Co-Prosperity Sphere. Roosevelt was dead. Churchill was out of office. Stalin was left alone to bargain with his two new partners, whose signatures were not on the Livadia Agreement and who could disclaim or forfeit this deal. Thus, the Russian factor seemed to loom large in China's future.

But the Russian factor should not be exaggerated. There was ample evidence that Stalin was quite willing to confine his ambition to fulfilling his czarist aim of acquiring privileges in Manchuria and forgo political involvement in the rest of China. On the one hand, Stalin felt no urgent need to reentangle himself in an internal dispute, dating from the 1920s, in which he had found himself unable to influence either side. While Chiang's anticommunist sentiment was both real and deep-rooted, the Soviet-Chinese Communist relationship had, since Stalin's meddling in the twenties, been anything but good. Given CCP leaders', especially Mao's, penchant for ideological and political independence, it seems unlikely that Stalin bore them any personal good will. On more than one occasion, Stalin laughed at Mao in front of his American guests. When James Byrnes went to see Stalin in October, the Soviet leader laughed heartily at Mao's claim to 600,000 troops. "All Chinese are boasters," he remarked.[25] On the other hand, Stalin's obsession with the security of the Soviet Union after the war makes it hard to believe that the prospect of a unified and powerful China, Communist or not, was very appealing. To a certain extent, Stalin's objective in China was parallel to that of the British. As Michael Schaller pointed out, "A divided China, or one ruled by a tottering KMT regime dependent on Moscow favor, may well have seemed to Stalin as an ideal arrangement."[26]

Reporting from Washington in late August 1945, Isaiah Berlin pointed out that no matter how severe the domestic situation was in China, "the Soviet Union does not, after all, propose to adopt Yenan as a Far Eastern Lublin."[27] Despite its economic and strategic value, Manchuria was not, and had never been, the center of China's economic and political activities. Since the October Revolution, Russia had ceased to be a great power identified with the West and Japan in the old treaty ports where the heart of China's finance and politics lay. Moreover, Stalin's demand on Manchuria, no matter how imperialistic, was legal in view of the Livadia Agreement. On the contrary, as we have seen in chapter one, there was no agreement, legal or otherwise, that had been reached at the war's end to regulate Big Power relationships in these old treaty ports. Thus, a clash of interests among the powers, particularly the United States and Great Britain, was not only possible but also probable in these places.

With the Russians in Manchuria and the Chinese Communists in the North, the American idea of a unified government under Chiang Kai-shek seemed remote in August 1945. Nevertheless, the Truman administration took prompt action to help Chiang control as many territories as possible. Under the direction of General Wedemeyer, Chiang was able to quickly control Southern China and the Yangtze Valley. This was the internal situation in mid-August 1945.

Under the circumstances, the American government had to decide, within a short time, whether to continue active involvement or remain passive. A passive strategy was hardly a choice, but it had two meanings. On the one hand, it meant a passive attitude toward Chinese internal affairs altogether. This would imply that after heavy political and monetary investment in China during the war, the United States would allow other powers to have a clear field. On the other hand, it could mean that, though actively involved in Chinese internal politics, the American government might adopt a passive attitude toward both factions in China, that is, serve as an honest broker with a neutral stand. This was certainly not the Roosevelt-Hurley policy. As an OSS report dated in June frankly pointed out, Hurley's China policy may be characterized as (a) exclusive support of the Chungking regime, despite the country's actual division into areas of separate rule; (b) exclusive economic support of Chungking (no economic assistance was given to non-Chungking elements); (c) exclusive military support of Chungking; and (d) exclusive political support of Chungking.

Hurley's policy was not based solely on fantasy. Although the State Department disliked its inflexible position, it could find no alternative to Chiang as far as American interests were concerned. Hurley's mediation activities in China in 1944 and 1945 were unsuccessful because of their biased nature. Could the Truman administration adopt a truly neutral stand in China? The rationale must be based on the interest of the Americans, who had a heavy stake in Chiang. Thus, before the administration was confident enough that Chiang would be capable of handling or defeating his Communist opponents, a passive strategy in both a general and a specific sense was simply not a viable one.

Throughout the war against Japan, Washington's confidence in Chiang's ability had declined gradually. Chiang himself was, of course, confident that he would be able to wipe out his opponents. Various indications reached Washington that Chiang, if not constrained, would rather use force against the Communists at the earliest possible date. Edwin Locke, Truman's private representative in China, sent the president a memo in early September, which expressed the worry that a Chinese civil war could not be avoided. Locke stated, "My feeling is that Chiang would rather fight than make major concessions to the Communists. He understands the use of force, and his record shows that in the past he has inclined toward military methods of settling issues." Locke suggested that "unless powerful influences are brought to bear on him from outside China, I think it very likely that he will fight the Communists at the first possible opportunity."[28] One OSS report made the American concern even clearer:

> Continuation of the present antagonism between the Kuomintang and the Communists is likely to result in open civil war. The present balance of forces in China is such that if neither side receives outside aid, the Kuomintang cannot wipe out the Communists. On the other hand, the Communists, if neither force receives outside aid, will probably be

able to gain ascendancy over the Kuomintang. If the Communists receive outside aid and the Kuomintang does not, the victory of the former is assured. If the Kuomintang receives outside aid and the Communists do not, the result will be an indecisive civil war of unprecedented savagery and duration. If both sides receive outside aid, the result will be a civil war whose duration and outcome will be determined in large part by nature and extent of foreign intervention.[29]

It seemed, therefore, that the U.S. government had only one choice: active involvement in China's internal dispute. A policy of "letting the Chinese stew in their own juices" was possible only if Washington did not care about the taste of the stew resulting from a civil war. Returning to the time when the Big Powers actively competed with each other was a daunting prospect. Contemplating alternatives, the OSS report acknowledged that "Short of backing separate regimes, Great Britain may compete in China by adopting conflicting policies on specific issues." Thus, "Britain may desire to have China maintain an agricultural economy and the U.S. might seek to industrialize the country. Such rivalry would have the effect of retarding the political and economic development of China and of increasing the antagonisms among the Great Powers."[30] This was certainly not what the United States had in mind for its ambitious new liberal world order.

Under the circumstances, the U.S. government expected to continue monopolizing Chinese affairs as during the war, no matter what the other two Big Powers might have to say. Yet there was a problem of legitimacy, since there was no international agreement to legitimize America's role as an arbiter in China's domestic dispute. Moreover, the military reality in August 1945 would not easily allow the United States to become an effective mediator in China. John Carter Vincent was skeptical of the U.S. willingness to use military assistance to the extent necessary for "reasonable stability" to prevail in North China and Manchuria.[31] Without direct American military intervention, the only alternative for an active policy was to effect a "coalition government" under Chiang's leadership.

As Washington became obsessed with the idea of a "coalition government," Chiang accepted this policy with the greatest reluctance. As a former warlord, he understood the importance of timing. He would rather have started eliminating the Communists right after the war, but his American ally wanted him to put his own house in order first. The third party in the mediation game, the Communists, seemed to have a real stake in the idea of a coalition government. Although Mao did not believe that Chiang was sincerely interested in such an idea, he saw it as a good opportunity to enhance his party at a time when the international community refused to accord it legitimate status. Militarily, he needed time to consolidate his position. Abandoned by Stalin in the secret deal at Yalta and bereft of supporters among the Big Three, Mao's political position was very difficult. For a time immediately after the Japanese surrender, the United States appeared to be in a strong position to hold the balance in China's domestic struggle. But the deep American commitment to Chiang soon made this position as an effective mediator increasingly more precarious.

The British, meanwhile, were neither enthusiastic about the American mediation policy nor keen to see the prospect of "Stars and Stripes over China." Despite ideological hostility toward the Chinese Communists, London refused to put its bet on the Chiang regime either. The British policy was not to tie itself to the Kuomintang Party or the existing setup of the Chinese government.[32] As for the possibility of a civil war, General Carton de Wiart put it bluntly to London: "I am not really worried about civil war which is after all usual here."[33] A Foreign Office memo thus analyzed the nature of the conflict in April: "Both the Kuomintang and the Communists invoke concepts of democracy." But neither "can be called democratic; they are in fact rival forms of dictatorship, self-charged with the duty of creating democracy, but holding different views as to what is meant by democracy and how much is now practicable."[34]

Based on these judgments, London believed that the best policy was to leave the Chinese to solve their own problems. But, given the American commitment to China, it seemed likely that foreign intervention was inevitable. The British hoped to avoid the prospect of an American monopoly, which would make things even worse. Maberly Esler Dening, Lord Mountbatten's chief political adviser, put it this way in early 1945: "Everything at present points to the fact that the United States intend to take a leading part in settling the future of the Far East. If they were not so ham-fisted in their conduct of international affairs, this might be all to the good." Dening warned that,

> We do not want to be dragged by the United States into a collision with Russia. On the other hand we want to be in a position to trade freely

with China in the Far East as well as setting our own house in order and we shall be wise to avoid international entanglements while at the same time endeavouring to secure our Empire position within the framework of the international security system. . . . At present American imperialism is in the forefront in the conduct of affairs in the Far East, and not only is there a tendency to try to elbow us out but also . . . a smearing campaign . . . to belittle everything that we do.[35]

Britain's past imperial experience in China suggested that the only workable arrangements were either policing the country with joint foreign forces or ending up with the partition of the country. The Americans, in short, would have to abandon their unilateral mediation efforts and collaborate with other powers. G. F. Hudson, an Oxford China expert working in the Foreign Office Research Department, suspected that the American government would have to support Chiang under whatever circumstances, even merely for ideological reasons. As he commented in a Foreign Office minute in June: "What is the alternative for the U.S. government? If the Americans do not support Chungking, they risk losing all their influence in China, for it is extremely unlikely that a Communist China would be any more pro-American than Tito's Yugoslavia is pro-British." He added, "the Moderator of the Church of Scotland might have more influence over the Catholic clergy than the Pope, but probably not. It looks *as if* the Americans will have to go on supporting Chungking, whether they like it or not, because the international allegiance of Yenan has already been given." Nostalgic for the prewar days, Hudson went on further: "When the crisis comes, the least perilous course will be for the Big Two [United Staes and USSR] to act frankly as eminent counsel for their respective clients and do their best to settle out of court (perhaps by territorial partition) without pretending they are not taking sides."[36]

In effect, Hudson hoped to reenact something like the Western suppression of the Boxer Rebellion in 1900. Sterndale-Bennett was also thinking along the same line, as he expressed to the Americans "his feeling that the only possible sure way to prevent the civil war in China would be for the U.K. and the U.S. to inform the Nationalist Government and the Communists that they must negotiate or that force would be used to see that this is done."[37]

London had, however, few practical policy options. Britain's active involvement in China would be discouraged by the United States, while its disengagement would not assure the safety of British interests. Moreover, since the American intervention in China would be carried out as a mediation, which appeared morally justifiable, it would be very difficult, as Ambassador Seymour pointed out, "to refuse to give support to the Americans if they really wanted it." But Seymour did not "believe our participation would affect the result."[38]

In August, the Chinese government succeeded in signing a Sino-Soviet Treaty of Friendship in Moscow, as prompted by the Livadia Agreement, whose content was not disclosed to Chiang until June. Chiang told Hurley personally that he was satisfied the Soviets had promised to: (1) assist in bringing about unification of the armed forces of China; (2) support China's efforts to create a strong, united, and democratic government; and (3) support the national government of China. Hurley thought that his chance to solve China's internal dispute had come. He urged Chiang to send an invitation to Mao Tse-tung. In Hurley's opinion, "If Mao accepts the invitation, the armed conflict between the Communist Party of China and the National Government may be reduced to a political controversy." And, "Chiang Kai-shek will now have an opportunity to show realistic and generous leadership."[39]

Meanwhile, in Washington, Secretary of State Byrnes recommended to Truman efforts to enhance U.S. military commitment to Chiang. As he reported to the president on 3 September: "Chiang desires a military mission to be known as American Military Advisory Group to assist and advise the Chinese Government in the creation of modern military forces." He added, "I recommend that as far as possible we endeavor to meet Chiang's wishes because it is obviously to our advantage to have the Chinese look to us for military advice."[40]

Throughout the summer of 1945, numerous press reports pointed to the American anxiety about Russian intentions in China and Stalin's influence upon the Chinese Communists. Stalin apparently felt that the Americans had exaggerated his influence in China. John Paton Davies, now working at the Moscow embassy, reported to George Kennan on 18 August: "Adam Watson of the British Embassy told me yesterday evening that Pavlov, Molotov's secretary, had called on him on 8/16 and during the course of conversation had expressed his 'perplexity' as to why the United States appeared to be so interested in China." Davies reported further that, according to Watson, Pavlov said the American embassy had sent three notes to the Soviet government regarding

China that day, but that no communications had come from the British on that subject. Davies went on to relate Watson's account:

> Pavlov remarked that the American Ambassador [Harriman] appeared to be intensely interested in the China situation, "his eyes glittered when the subject of China was mentioned." Pavlov said that the Americans appeared to be particularly interested in the Chinese Communists. He thereupon quoted Stalin's definition of the Chinese Communists as "margarine communists."[41]

Back in Chungking, Hurley based his judgment also on his utter contempt for the Communist strength. As he told Sir Horace Seymour on 19 August, "the Communists would not risk a civil war—the American officers in the area estimate that they have enough small arms and ammunition for three days only."[42] On 27 August, after putting pressure on Chiang to accept his mediation, the flamboyant general embarked on a self-appointed mission of solving China's domestic dispute.

The British did not believe that Hurley could make any progress. General Carton de Wiart thought it would make things worse, and that civil war could not be avoided. In his report to London on 25 August he noted that, "Wedemeyer is very worried about the Communists, but I think a good deal of the worry is caused by the fear of the trouble there will be in the U.S.A. on the subject of lend-lease arms being used in a civil war." He commented further, "Hurley is going to fetch Mao Tse-tung" in Yenan, but "I am afraid if Hurley does this it will send the Communist shares up higher still," thus making his success even less likely.[43]

Hurley was undoubtedly overoptimistic. The Chiang-Mao talks, known as the Chungking Negotiations, failed to yield substantial results, especially in relation to the chief objective of both Washington and Chungking to unify China's armed forces under Chiang. They did not succeed in this key issue, despite other nominal achievements such as the agreement to convene a national Political Consultative Council.

The American failure was expected in London. During the Chiang-Mao talks, the British acted with extreme care. By distancing themselves from the American China policy, the British wished to convey the message of neutrality in China's domestic dispute. General Carton de Wiart attended a private dinner party with Mao, Chou En-lai, and, on the British side, Colonel Gordon Harmon, an intelligence officer who had known Mao and Chou personally from his trips to Yenan. During the dinner, Carton de Wiart had an interesting but cordial debate with the Communist leaders. Carton de Wiart tried to blame the Communist side for the domestic impasse in China, noting that Mao "did not much like my remarks." Nevertheless, Carton de Wiart quickly emphasized that Britain did not want to get involved, for "I consider the Kuomintang–Communist controversy as concerning China and no one else, and I have no instructions, right or desire to meddle in it." The subtle message behind his statement was a criticism of the American policy. Carton de Wiart reported that he found Mao "is quite a good type of man, but a fanatic," and "his chief of staff [Chou] is much easier to deal with." He concluded that, "I am afraid that my meeting with Mao does not give me any more confidence in a settlement than I had before."[44]

After the Chiang-Mao talks, the Foreign Office declared in November that "evidently North China is to be a Communist enclave. We seem to be getting very near a Communist North and a Kuomintang Centre and South China."[45] To London such a scenario was a natural result of the Chinese internal conflict, and there was nothing to be alarmed about; this de facto division of China, which could last a long time, would not necessarily harm British interests in the Far East. But Britain's hope that the Chinese would stew in their own juices without American intervention was soon to fade away.

Exasperated at his own failure to solve the Chinese domestic conflict, Hurley decided to tender his resignation. The ambassador had already asked for the president's permission to resign in August, because he felt that he was increasingly out of favor in the White House and, at the same time, had to fight with a hostile State Department. He confided to Seymour on 19 August that "he has asked the permission of the President to resign his post. His mission here was a war job and he would like to move to Nanking, if it can be done soon, and then leave China and 'forget all about [it].' "[46]

In his resignation letter on 26 November, Hurley expressed again his usual irritation at the career diplomats: "Throughout this period the chief opposition to the accomplishment of our mission came from the American career diplomats in the Embassy at Chungking and in the Chinese and the Far Eastern Divisions of the State Department." Hurley recalled bitterly, "I requested the relief of the career men who were opposing the American policy in the Chinese theater of war. These professional diplomats were returned to Washington and placed in the Chinese and the Far East Divisions . . . as my supervisors." He went on to charge that:

> We began the war with the principles of the Atlantic Charter and democracy as our goal. Our associates in the war at that time gave eloquent lip service to the principles of democracy. We finished the war in the Far East furnishing lend-lease supplies and using all our reputation to undermine democracy and bolster imperialism and communism.[47]

Ignored by the White House, Hurley chose to make his charges and resignation public. With the support of Republicans in Congress, this triggered a political storm. When word reached Truman about Hurley's charges, the furious president exclaimed, "See what the son-of-a-bitch did to me." But Truman accepted the suggestion made at the cabinet meeting on the same day that he move quickly to make a dramatic appointment in order to "steal the thunder away from Hurley."[48]

The appointment of General George C. Marshall was announced the day after Hurley's resignation. Marshall, a respected military man and chief architect of the allied war strategies, was to assume the title of the president's personal representative in China with the rank of ambassador.[49] Thus, the administration opened another round of the American mediation efforts in China.

In Britain, reactions to Hurley's public charges were strong. In a feature article entitled "Hurley-Burly," the *Manchester Guardian* commented that: "Americans must have rubbed their eyes in astonishment on Tuesday when they read the statement made by General Hurley on resigning his post as U.S. Ambassador to China." And "even if allowances are made for what seems to have been a fit of bad temper, it is hard to avoid the impression that a man who can write such nonsense is hardly qualified to serve his country in a high diplomatic office."[50]

The Foreign Office was equally enraged by Hurley's address, making similar charges against Britain, at the National Press Club in Washington on 28 November. As. A. L. Scott commented, "The gallant General seems to be talking through his hat at times, more especially when he tries to make out that 'American policy definitely did not have the support of the imperialist civil servants of Britain in Asia.' "[51] Edmund Hall-Patch, assistant undersecretary for economic affairs, reported to London about his recent meeting with Hurley in Washington, saying "he is determined to stir up as much as possible and he has many dubious friends among the politicians who will give him every encouragement to do so."[52]

However, some satisfaction was expressed in the Foreign Office that the Hurley incident might lead to better Anglo-American understanding on China and to new directions in the U.S. policy on China. A. L. Scott commented on 29 November: "Hurley's policy had consistently been to give all possible moral and material support to the Central Government under C. K. S." And, "This is one of the very few cases in which we did not follow the American lead."[53]

The Chinese government felt uneasy, for it was not clear whether or not the Marshall Mission indicated a major change in American China policy from a partial to an impartial stand in mediation. As the British embassy in Chungking reported, "Kuomintang is a little nervous that his [Marshall's] impartial approach to the problem may force them, in return for continued American economic aid, to yield more in any bargain than the pressure of military necessity would have dictated."[54] A KMT newspaper, the *Chungking Daily,* stated in an editorial, "If Marshall desires to learn in advance the true facts of the Chinese internal situation, he would find Hurley a most reliable adviser."[55]

In late November, Madame Chiang Kai-shek told General Carton de Wiart during a private conversation that the generalissimo intended to give "greater returns to Britain from the original British investment in China if the United Kingdom would take a larger share in supporting Chiang." From its experience in China, the British embassy felt "it would be [a] mistake to react too eagerly to Chiang's approach." Bevin agreed with this judgment and instructed the embassy on 6 December, "In view of [the] Hurley affair . . . it would be desirable to avoid . . . reference to cooperation, lest this should be interpreted as eagerness on our part to profit by the uncertainty of American policy."[56]

London was considerably worried about the future direction of American China policy, of which it had no reliable information. It seemed that the American mediation started by Hurley would go on, but the surprise appointment of General Marshall left the Labour government completely in the dark as to the inner thinking of the administration. This uncertainty caused numerous speculations regarding the nature of the Marshall Mission. Ambassador Lord Halifax sent a report to Bevin on 2 December, summarizing his estimate of the impact of the

Hurley affair and the Marshall Mission. According to the report, Hurley had so far played a negative role in China, "instead of employing his position as Ambassador to heal the rift between Chungking and the Yenan Communists, he had used it to promote policies designed to involve the United States as an active participant on the side of the former." Lord Halifax pointed out further:

> As a former Republican possessed of no little Irish political acumen, the swashbuckling old cavalryman has no doubt hoped in this way to capitalize his personal sense of grievance to further the interests of his party and perhaps his own political ambitions. In this respect he has however been largely check-mated by the prompt counter-move of the Administration in securing the acceptance of the vacant post by General Marshall, a nationally esteemed figure.

With considerable anxiety about the Marshall Mission, Lord Halifax ended the report by saying: "The general conclusion of thoughts on the subject of China is well illustrated by a cartoon in the *Times Herald* [which] represents a perplexed Columbia standing behind a blindfold Uncle Sam advancing towards the edge of a precipice and enquires of him: 'Well, Sam, where are you going in the Far East, what's your policy?' To which Sam replies: 'I don't know where I am going. I am just on the way.' "[57]

Indeed, even General Marshall himself was not clear about his task. Having seen the pitfalls of the China mission and the dilemma of his friend Patrick Hurley, whom he originally recommended for the job, Marshall was determined to press for clearly defined "written instructions"—the absence of which had haunted Hurley ever since he took the China job in 1944. After frequent consultation with the State and War Departments, Marshall helped produce written instructions signed by Truman. The part of the instructions that was made public was largely a reiteration of the familiar American policy toward China: to bring about a strong, democratic, and unified China. However, it was the part that was hidden from the public that was essential, for which Marshall had also managed to secure the president's approval. Apparently, as a "mediator," in its usual sense of the word, the United States had to prepare for its failure and decide whether or not to take sides after the failure. Marshall broached this question at a meeting with the president, on 11 December, attended by James Byrnes and Admiral

Leahy, White House chief of staff. During the conversation, Truman told Marshall that he would have the authority to deal with all the political, military, and economic issues in China; in particular, he would assume the task of helping Chiang move his troops into North China for the purpose of releasing the Japanese in that region and taking over control of the railroads. Marshall pressed the question of what exactly he should do in case of a breakdown in mediation. In his opinion, there could be two cases: first, if the Communists refused to compromise, then support for the Kuomintang would be assured; and second, if the breakdown was due to Chiang's unwillingness to make what in Marshall's view were "reasonable concessions," the general inquired "whether or not it was intended for him to . . . go ahead and assist the Generalissimo in the movement of troops into North China." This meant that the U.S. government would have to swallow its pride and much of its policy in doing so. Marshall wanted to make sure it was the president's intention to support Chiang no matter what resulted from the mediation. The president and Secretary Byrnes "concurred in this view of the matter." Thus, there is little doubt that Marshall was sent to China by a government already committed to one side. Realizing enormous difficulties ahead, General Marshall recorded the conversation carefully and signed his name on the memo. Understandably, he intended to keep it as his top-secret official instructions.[58]

President Truman announced on 15 December, a few days before Marshall's departure, that the United States military forces, which were scheduled to withdraw soon, would remain in China under the direction of General Marshall so as to give the general strong leverage in Chinese internal affairs. The president denied the charge that this was tantamount to direct interference in China's internal dispute.[59]

London was not at all convinced by Truman's interpretation regarding the troops in China. George Kitson of the Foreign Office dismissed as nonsense the American denial that "U.S. support will not extend to U.S. military intervention to influence the course of any Chinese internal strife." He added that "US support has already had such effect by depriving the Communists of the virtual certainty of taking control of North China. . . . I shall be surprised if the statement has much effect in promoting a genuine settlement." Kitson believed that the statement was "an ingenious apologia for the policy already pursued by the United States in China in supporting the Nationalist Government," as well as "a reaffirmation of that policy, coupled with a promise of a loan which is served as an inducement to national unity under an administration favoured by American business interests."[60] Shortly after General Marshall's arrival in China, G. A. Wallinger, British chargé in China, reported to Bevin that General Wedemeyer had instructed his troops to pay attention to the revision of American military policy in China.[61]

In the meantime, Bevin was in Moscow attending the foreign ministers conference of the Big Three. The British foreign secretary fought a courageous, if somewhat isolated, battle over the China issue. The controversy started over section 4 of the joint communiqué regarding China. The Americans proposed a joint statement that said, "The Foreign Ministers reaffirmed ... the need for a unified and democratic China under the National Government and for the broad participation *therein* of democratic elements." The emphasis was on "therein"—a word the Russians wanted removed from their version while leaving the rest intact. Although the British argued that both versions signified interference in China's internal affairs, the Russians could not have cared less about this dispute. Thus, a quick understanding was reached behind Bevin's back; a Soviet-American compromise was presented to Bevin, calling for "the broad participation of democratic elements in the National Government and its central and local branches." Bevin and his team reacted strongly. As Sterndale-Bennett recalled later, "Mr. R. Campbell [assistant undersecretary for Far Eastern affairs] and I said that we could not of course accept this text either. We felt that it was not right for the three Powers to give joint advice in this sense, since it was in effect interference in the internal affairs of China." After the three ministers were left alone to break the impasse, Bevin's argument prevailed. The final version reaffirmed their adherence to the policy of noninterference in China's internal affairs and showed agreement as to the need for the broad participation by democratic elements in all branches of the national government. Apparently, London's purpose was to prevent the "Moscow Declaration" from providing any legitimacy to the unilateral mediation efforts made by the American government.[62]

Nevertheless, the Foreign Office had to accept the fact that the American decision regarding their unilateral mediation in China, however distasteful to London, could not be changed. The British embassy in China predicted in its *Monthly Report* for December that the American administration would be in an awkward position of having to reconcile "the sentimentalism of Miss Pearl Buck and the various 'isms' of other American pressure groups with the handling of practical issues."[63]

In the economic sphere, London refused to play the role of a passive onlooker in China. But the British ambition to restore prewar economic status in China was soon met with severe financial reality. The abrupt ending of the lend-lease aid to Britain left Bevin few resources to back up his active economic policy in China. During his first meeting with T. V. Soong in September, Bevin told the Chinese foreign minister that, although "Great Britain had for the past six years applied the whole of the industry to war purposes," it was his belief that "in about four years from now, Britain might be in a position to take her place in China's market for capital goods."[64]

Constrained by financial difficulties, the British were initially preoccupied with the efforts to recover prewar British interests. It was soon clear to London that Washington was not at all enthusiastic about Britain's return to China. On 20 August Bevin promised the House of Commons that the Labour government would assure all British subjects who had been liberated in the Far East of its "watchful care for their interests, for their re-creation of their industries and restoration of their normal life."[65]

Another prominent Labour leader, Sir Stafford Cripps, spoke at the House of Commons a month later of specific measures to restore British trade in China, such as immediately opening general consulates there and returning representatives of British firms to their commercial bases. Although Sino-British trade only took up about 2 percent of Britain's total foreign trade, Cripps believed that a new era had begun, and that since Britain had suffered a commercial "blitz," the China trade might become increasingly more important.[66]

London soon found out that this was easier said than done. Britain's desire to reopen her consulates in China was blocked, and the United States showed little interest in doing anything to help. In contrast, backed by Wedemeyer's troops, the Americans moved quickly at the time of Japan's surrender to reestablish American diplomatic outposts throughout China. Urged by Hurley, the State Department decided on 25 August to send Richard Butrick, acting chief of the Foreign Service Administration, to Shanghai, along with fifteen foreign service officers, to set up diplomatic representation as soon as possible. Meanwhile, General Wedemeyer obtained Chiang's permission to let U.S.

foreign service officers in China accompany army units in entering Shanghai and other liberated cities, ostensibly for the purpose of assisting civilian internees.[67]

The British found it difficult to reenter China. Their request for U.S. military units to transport their consular officers was ignored. Hurley reported to Washington on 25 August that, "Army headquarters here is being importuned (by the British and French) hourly to provide transportation for them, at a time when facilities are so restricted that it is only with greatest difficulty that Army is handling the transportation of key military personnel." Hurley was, in fact, delighted when he learned from a vice minister at the Chinese Foreign Office that Chungking would not approve Britain's reopening of consulates in Chinese cities unless London allowed China to open consular offices in such places in the Far East where the British dominated before the war. One such place, reported Hurley, was Rangoon in Burma.[68]

Although Washington realized that London might protest the fact that American officers alone were able to enter Chinese cities where official jurisdiction had not been established, Secretary of State James Byrnes instructed Hurley to ignore British requests for transportation and go ahead with the American plans: "Dept [State Department] does not feel that delays of reopening of consular offices in China should affect our urgent desire to have foreign service officers enter liberated areas."[69]

British business executives, most notably the "Shanghailanders," also found themselves in an awkward position when they tried to reestablish their interests in China. Shanghai had been the hub of British interests before the war. The British government in 1945 estimated that 76 percent of British assets and investments were concentrated in metropolitan Shanghai.[70] Under the effective protection of extraterritorial rights, British Shanghailanders had been dominant in shipping, banking, public utilities, wharfs and docks, and others. The Shanghailanders had enjoyed an incomparable advantage in utilizing Chinese resources and cheap labor. Equipped with capital and technology, they formed the most powerful foreign group doing business and trade *in* China and *with* China.

At the end of the war, British Shanghailanders faced at least two severe problems: (1) to recover their prewar properties seized by the Japanese (the recovery was complicated by the Chinese government's tendency to set an arbitrary value on the seized assets) and (2) to begin operating their companies and businesses under the new Chinese law. The new law designated many foreign-owned companies as in the category of "China company," on the grounds that these companies were either born in China or had little business activities outside China. A "China company" would, hence, be required to register and operate under Chinese law, losing many privileges enjoyed by a foreign company in such matters as taxation or monetary arrangements. The Shanghailanders naturally chafed at the possible consequences if their companies were so registered. George Kitson of the British Foreign Office reported in a memo in late August:

> British interests in the International Settlement at Shanghai, in particular, exceeded in scope and value those of any other foreign nation and it is therefore perhaps our duty to take the initiative in trying to ensure that these former international areas pass to Chinese administrative control in such a manner that British rights and interests are adequately safeguarded.[71]

However, Britain alone could not solve any legal problems with China. The only hope lay in joint Anglo-American pressure upon the Chinese for the re-creation of business. But London had little to offer Washington. In the meantime, the Americans were preoccupied with their own efforts. On 27 August, executives from three big companies (American Express, Chase Bank, and National City Bank) joined hands to convince Joseph Ballantine, director of the State Department's Far Eastern Office, that "with the surrender of the Japanese, it is imperative for the restoration of law and order in such cities as Shanghai and Tientsin that the banks be reopened at the earliest possible moment." They continued by saying, "We feel sure that you will agree with our opinion that this is the most essential provision for the safeguarding of American interests in China."[72]

Despite the difficulties that British business people encountered, there was widespread grievance among the Americans against British efficiency, especially in view of the rapid return and reopening of businesses by the Shanghailanders. On 1 September, Dean Acheson, the new undersecretary of state, received representatives from the Texas Company (China), British-American Tobacco Company (China), and Stark, Park, and Freeman, Inc. The three companies vigorously complained against the British in a joint memo:

> May we point out that our British friends find themselves in a more favorable situation in China than do the Americans. Even throughout the war the British followed a realistic policy since many British key commercial personnel were engaged in Free China on official war work. They now can and undoubtedly will immediately resume their normal commercial activities. In addition to this the British Government is encouraging Britons to return to China and affords them prompt air passage thereto.

Acheson observed that there was no dissent from the memo.[73]

These complaints were not without grounds. During the war the British paid much attention to postwar restoration of their position in China. Even former Shanghai tycoons were invited to work as diplomats; thus, they obtained intimate knowledge about the conduct of war in the China theater of operations. John Kerswick, a director of the Jardine Matheson, was made counselor of the embassy in Chungking.

The Americans were also keenly aware that the British efficiency in resuming their business in China was facilitated by their retention of the Crown Colony of Hongkong. The Labour government's insistence on the retaking of Hongkong by British troops left a bad taste in the mouth of the American government and public opinion. An opinion poll sponsored by the National Opinion Research Center based in Denver showed in September that only 28 percent of those polled favored, while 51 percent opposed, the British retention of the colony.

The U.S. government was concerned with the economic implications of the British retention of Hongkong, especially in view of the Anglo-Chinese Agreement of 1943 that abolished extraterritorial rights in China as a gesture of goodwill. A confidential paper written by Carl H. Boehringer, assistant chief of the Far Eastern Unit in the Department of Commerce, pointed out in October: "Hongkong was obtained by the British in accordance with the best traditions of Empire building." However, "with the surrender by Britain of extraterritorial rights in China and the uncertain future of British investments and trade in that country, Hongkong seemingly assumes a new and increased importance for the Empire." Boehringer believed that the British used prestige as an excuse to retain the colony, "but prestige alone would seemingly not have justified the British possession of Hongkong. The Portuguese had had nearby Macao for centuries but have gained relatively little prestige therefrom." Thus, "in the case of the British, it may be said that a happy combination of prestige and profits impelled them to acquire the colony and to develop it into one of the greatest ports of the world."[74]

The British had never underestimated Hongkong's importance. In 1938 a report by the Royal Institute of International Affairs (RIIA) pointed out that both Hongkong and Gibraltar were practically free ports and, consequently, served as centers for massive trading. Hongkong, however, offered "something more. Its function as an entrepot for trade for Southern China and Western Pacific has hitherto been performed in such a manner as to make it not only a prominent outpost of British trade, but also a great asset in the movement of international commerce." Therefore, "this rocky and picturesque island is, and ought to be, more than a commercial clearing house for it represents the main outpost of British influence and the only centre of British culture in the Far East."[75] According to another RIIA report in 1939, "Commercially Hongkong gives to the British Empire a *pied-a-terre* from which to participate in the economic development of the Chinese hinterland."[76]

In December 1945, a British company transmitted a letter written by its China representative, D. C. H. Mellon, to the Foreign Office, which stated: "The rapidity with which Hongkong is being rehabilitated will, I feel, have a very beneficial effect on Shanghai's life and even more so on the resumption of trade through Canton ... [and] though the U.S.A. are continuing lease-lend on a considerable scale, it is certain that the Chinese Government do not desire to become tied to Gold Dollar commitments if they operate through a barter agreement with the United Kingdom."[77]

With no Hongkong to take advantage of, the American government was extremely interested in concluding a commercial treaty with China. As Willard L. Thorp, assistant secretary for economic affairs, reported to Dean Acheson on 13 September: "Developments in the Far East make the early consummation of the treaty of major importance to both the United States and China ... [because] American business organizations are anxious for a definite and satisfactory legal basis on which to pursue trade and investment interests."[78]

Over the issue of the proposed Chinese Company Law, the Anglo-American interests also considerably differed. The American business community was not so concerned with the definition of a "China company" (for not many such firms were U.S. owned); instead they were primarily interested in reducing restrictions imposed upon "foreign companies." From August to December 1945, the American government put constant pressure on the Chinese for concessions regarding firms to be registered as foreign companies. In August, for example, the State Department virtually rejected the revised version of the Chinese Company Law on the grounds that it was not "modern" and was based on "continental and other legal concepts and theories with which Americans engaged in international trade are not familiar."[79]

The British saw the legal issue in a different light. Having acquired long experience in doing successful business in a practically lawless China, the British business community did not relish the American penchant for legalistic arguments on China. Moreover, since the British held a strong position in businesses "established in China," stricter Chinese regulations concerning foreign companies (i.e., newcomers and competitors) would not necessarily jeopardize British interests in China. A typical view was expressed by a leading British business representative in China when he told his American friends in October that

> No great concern should be displayed or efforts made to assist the Chinese in the modernization of their laws, since, in any event, the amended or revised laws cannot in practice be enforced. . . . They can probably be enforced to a great extent with respect to foreign as compared with Chinese Companies. Let the law be as bad and unworkable as possible, and let us continue to do business by arrangements as we have always done.[80]

After the Hongkong dispute, the Labour government found its position in China deteriorating. Many events after the British retaking of Hongkong led London to believe that the Chinese government, with tacit approval of the U.S. administration, was conspiring to discriminate against Britain. In August, for example, the Chinese refused to allow a British naval fleet's port call at Shanghai, despite the existence of the Sino-British Naval Program. The British Admiralty was furious; thus, it decided to ask the Chinese to pay for the expenses of training their officers in Britain, although the Foreign Office objected strongly. George Kitson voiced the fear that "if the Chinese are asked to pay . . . they will go elsewhere, i.e., to the Americans, and all the goodwill we were hoping to secure from the offer of the ships would vanish like snow in midsummer."[81]

The British embassy in China painted a gloomy picture in its *Monthly Report* for November: "The British position in China inevitably continues to suffer by comparison: there has been a noticeable tendency on the part of the Chinese Government to ask for such shipping and other facilities as the British official or commercial organizations may be in a position to afford [and] at the same time to discriminate in favour of the Americans where privileges and other activities are concerned."[82]

Among the American business executives in late 1945, there was a strong sense of changing guards in China. On 24 October, a secret *China Regional Directive* issued by the United States Office of War Information revealed that American business enterprises were planning to return to China in growing numbers and hoped to extend their scope beyond the treaty ports. The report pointed out further that:

> Businessmen in America are paving the way for such a return through the encouragement of cooperative enterprises such as China-America Council of Commerce and Industry and through the inclusion of their personnel in American Government-sponsored projects such as FEA and the Chinese War Production Board. Prewar American business in China was on a much smaller scale than that of the British, but the wartime record of American assistance to China, together with a monopoly of present shipping facilities, will give Americans a post-war advantage.[83]

The British public was increasingly alarmed by the prospect of complete American monopoly in China. On 14 October, George Johnson, a seasoned journalist, wrote a feature article in the *Daily Mail* entitled "Stars and Stripes Over China"—a quip apparently inspired by Edgar Snow's bestseller, *Red Star Over China*. The article observed that China's quiet, firm, and effective blockade against British commercial interests worked well from the American viewpoint. And although usually a behind-the-scenes operation, the blockade reached the point where British military intelligence activities were "bluntly discouraged in China and adjacent territories because in the post-war period no one wanted to feel any obligation to Britain." Moreover, Johnson continued, "This anti-British psychology has not been discouraged by our American ally." He went on to explain that

> Interesting now, in the post-war picture, is an analysis of the operations of the U.S. civilian organizations in China. Operating under Washington's direction, they were the Foreign Economic Administration with the

satellite sub-organizations of the Chinese Defense Supplies and Lend-Lease Administration; the civilian section of the O.S.S. and the great U.S. Government propaganda organization, the Office of War Information. . . .

Johnson claimed that American propagandists were everywhere and that, during the past two years, it had been difficult to visit even the remotest parts of China without meeting uniformed representatives of the U.S. State Department. He added that U.S. propagandists "have been working from Lanchow, gateway to Tibet, to the Gobi Desert of Mongolia." Furthermore, "A great plan to dam the Yangtze, known as the 'Yangtze Valley Authority,' will be one of the greatest engineering contracts of modern times." He continued, "Their geologists have plodded the old caravan trails to the fringes of Tibet and the wild western tribal countries. Their transportation divisions have been largely comprised of men" who, before the Sino-Japanese war, "were special sales representatives in China of such great companies as General Motors, Ford, Chrysler and so on." Johnson concluded that "The Americans have shown aggression and virility, and all along have kept in mind the post-war business world upon which so much of America's power depends."[84]

Feeling squeezed out of China, the Labour government was pressured to redefine British policy in China and the Far East as a whole. Under Bevin's direction, the Far Eastern Committee worked out in December 1945 a top secret memo entitled "British Foreign Policy in the Far East." It was the most comprehensive reexamination of the British position and policy in that part of the world. More than one hundred and fifty pages long, the memo—consisting of five parts and six annexes—reflected Bevin's typical toughness and resilience. Perhaps it proved the point made by John Fischer in the August issue of *Harper's* magazine, complaining that no matter how difficult the situation was, "the British almost always have a policy."[85]

The central theme of the memo indicated the need for temporary retreat from the "North of the Tropic of Cancer" and the diversion of the limited British resources to Southeast Asia in order to counterpoise American positions in Northeast Asia. The memo concluded that after six years of war in Europe and four in the Pacific, the military and economic strength of the United Kingdom "does not permit us to resume' at once all our prewar power, influence and responsibilities throughout the Far East. Willy-nilly we have to consider where our limited resources can be applied to the greatest effect."

The memo predicted that in both China and Japan the United States would play the principal role in the next few years. Before the war, the onus at the first sign of trouble in the North Pacific usually fell on the United Kingdom. However, the memo continued, "if others have now become the leading influences in North Pacific affairs, it is only right that they should also undertake the responsibilities and any odium attached to them." The memo doubted that either of the two Big Powers in the North Pacific was capable of managing the regional balance of power and, therefore, Britain's restraining influence there would be stronger if its attitude were realistic. The memo showed deep concern about Anglo-American relations in the Far East. Annex 2, entitled "Relations Between the United Kingdom and the United States in the Far East," stated the following:

> U.S. policy appears to be dominated by two partly conflicting considerations. These are (a) A drive for exports which has acquired [a] certain force of desperation from the feeling, which may or may not be well founded, that a vast export trade alone can exorcise the demon of unemployment at home. This desire for exports is not, however, counterbalanced by any corresponding degree of willingness to accept imports abroad. (b) A strange neo-imperialism of a mystical irrational kind. This is an emotional reaction to the end of the war. There is strong desire to bring back U.S. forces from Japan and elsewhere. . . . Nevertheless, America is conscious of special responsibilities to the world and . . . the United States may be expected to be much more willing than she was . . . to take an active part in world affairs, but it will be on condition that wherever possible America is allowed to take the lead.

In China, the Annex warned, a possible battlefield existed between British and U.S. interests because the United States had already spent a very large amount of money there during the war. The United States would be able to obtain returns on fresh investments in China only if there were a friendly government in power. Thus, "The United Kingdom . . . will probably be forced to fight a 'delaying action' for a few years before she is finally in a position to make a determined effort to establish her position." There was little doubt in the early postwar years that U.S. interests would attempt to take advantage of Britain's temporary difficulties in order to consolidate their advantages and ease out established British enterprises to obtain an exclusive foothold in China. The Annex concluded: "Britain will be on [the] defensive for some years; it is likely that she will have to make concessions. But it is essential that these should be made only in return for solid advantages, and not to be interpreted as evidence of weakness."[86]

British officials in the field seemed to be more pessimistic than the authors of the memo. General Carton de Wiart reported to London in November that "The Americans have appropriated Shanghai pro-tem., a fact a great many of the Chinese are resenting." Moreover, he admitted, the attitude of the Americans had changed; whereas they had been ready to help the British over many things before, they were definitely not inclined to do so now.[87] The general was particularly worried about British prestige in China. On 18 December, he wrote a personal letter to "Pug" Ismay, imperial chief of staff, asking that his personal airplane, an American-made Dakota, be replaced by a British one. He explained: "I seem to be doing a good deal of 'showing the flag' at present but I must say that when the operation starts by my having to step out of an American plane, I do not feel very proud," and "if I were provided with a good, fast British plane, it would certainly impress the Chinese." After Ismay made an effort, however, the idea was blocked at the Ministry of Air Force.[88]

Reluctantly, as the cabinet memo indicated, London decided at the end of 1945 to accept the secondary place in China. The Foreign Office moved quickly to reassert British influence in Southeast Asia, but there too, the British discovered with chagrin, the American government showed little willingness to cooperate. In the middle of December, Bevin wrote a memo reminding Prime Minister Attlee that on 18 October Attlee had presided over a meeting of ministers, which agreed that the machinery for dealing with political matters in the Southeast Asia Command needed strengthening.[89] At the meeting, the cabinet approved a memo written by Sterndale-Bennett, which stated: "The difficulties which we are meeting in various parts of the SEAC . . . raise once more the question whether SEAC is at present adequately organized to deal with the various political and economic problems now that fighting against the Japanese has ceased." The memo suggested transforming the SEAC into a regional security organization.[90] In the meantime, the British Foreign Office found increased U.S. activity in Southeast Asia disconcerting and irritating.[91]

The American policies in Southeast Asia were closely connected with the China policy. In most cases, Washington was able to solicit the support of the Chinese government. Hardly had the Hongkong controversy subsided when the issue of Siam was set aboil again. The British government tried to impose harsh terms of peace on Siam through such measures as the rice levy, in order to obtain food to feed the other parts of the British colonial empire in Asia. The Anglo-Siamese negotiation reached an impasse in October when the British refused to recognize the Siamese government unless these terms were accepted. Charles Yost, American representative at Colombo, reported to Washington in December that "The British . . . attach great importance to the acceptance by Siam of heavy penalties as a public admission of war guilt." He suggested to Washington that "Our best course would be to resume diplomatic relations with Siam immediately," a step that "would be likely to give the British serious pause and which might be the most effective move we could take to bring about reconsideration of their policy by the British."[92] On 19 December, under heavy American pressure, the British government had to revise the terms imposed upon Siam, especially the "rice levy" clause.[93]

Indochina remained another sore spot. When the Chinese blocked the French reentry into Indochina at the end of the war, Jean Daridan, French chargé at the Chungking embassy, told K. C. Wu, acting foreign minister of China, that it would have "a very bad effect and might gravely prejudice Sino-French relations should the French troops not be permitted to proceed to Indo-China." General Wedemeyer, acting as Chiang Kai-shek's chief of staff, emphasized difficulties, in transporting troops. Ambassador Hurley knew of no provision in the Potsdam Declaration for the Japanese surrender in Indochina to be made to anyone other than the generalissimo as the supreme commander of the China theater.[94]

London attached great importance to Indochina not just for reasons of European colonial prestige. As the lengthy British cabinet memo, called "British Policy in the Far East," pointed out: "The security of French Indo-China is of particular importance to the defense of Southeast Asia as a whole."[95] At the end of the war, Lord Mountbatten proposed a joint Anglo-French operation in the surrender of Indochina, but Washington vehemently opposed it. Instead, the American government decided to have the Japanese in the north part of Indochina surrender to Chiang Kai-shek and those in the south, to Mountbatten.[96] London believed this decision to be disadvantageous. After the Japanese surrender, troubles continued to mount in Indochina. General Carton de Wiart reported to London in October: "I believe 75% of the trouble in Indo-China has been caused by the Americans who are violently anti-French in this part of the world, whatever they may be elsewhere."[97]

Another source of concern in London was the American quiet penetration into the "Jewel of the Crown"—India. According to the long cabinet memo of December, "There is a strong tendency among many sections of [American] public opinion, if not in the Administration itself, to regard any nationalist movements among the peoples of Southeast Asia as well as India, with sympathy." Coupled with this tendency was "the resentment of U.S. business at its restricted access to various colonial and other markets which have been sheltered by tariffs or exchange restrictions"—a resentment strengthened by "the urgent reconstruction needs of the countries concerned and the temporary inability of Britain and other European countries to supply their requirements."[98]

The London *Daily Mail*'s article by George Johnson also charged that: "Across India, American big business has been openly courting the major Indian industrialists who were—and are—one of the most powerful influences behind Congress." Moreover, "the great proportion of news in the Indian Press comes from the American-flavoured A.P. and the U.P. agencies, which are ousting the British-flavoured news of Reuter."[99] Consequently, when Hurley was making the rounds attacking the State Department and European imperialism, the American consul general at Bombay reported to Washington that Hurley's remarks were very popular in India.[100]

The year 1945 opened with a major Anglo-American crisis and ended with greater mutual suspicion. The Americans became more involved in China's internal dispute at the same time the British were being effectively squeezed out of China. The British had long entertained the cliché, "We have the brains, they have the money bags."[101] At the end of 1945, though London quietly decided to play second fiddle in China, the Americans did not seem to enjoy Britain's playing at all.

Notes

1. NAUS, OSS Report, R & A Report, 4 August 1945, microfilm no.3323s.
2. Alan Bullock, *The Life and Times of Ernest Bevin*, vol. III, p. 51.

3. NAUS, OSS Report, *R & A Report*, 15 October 1945, microfilm no. 3411.

4. U.K. PRO, Balfour to FO, 28 July 1945, FO371 44557/22/45.

5. U.K. PRO, Seymour to FO, 30 July 1945, FO371 46232/F4649.

6. U.K. PRO, Balfour to Bevin, 9 August 1945, FO371/AN2560.

7. U.K. PRO, Bevin to Cripps, 20 September 1945, FO800/US/45/25.

8. U.K. PRO, Memo of T. V. Soong's Conversation with Bevin, 17 September 1945, FO800/FE/45/49.

9. *News Chronicle* (London), 9 September 1945.

10. Bullock, *Life and Times of Ernest Bevin*, p. 211.

11. U.K. PRO, Clark Kerr Papers, August 1945, FO800/300/332–7.

12. Isaiah Berlin, *Washington Despatches*, p. 608.

13. NAUS, Memo by J, Friedman, *Policy Memoranda*, RG 59, lot files 110, box 9.

14. Berlin, *Washington Despatches*, p. 608.

15. Nathaniel Peffer, *New York Times*, 12 August 1945.

16. U.K. PRO, FO Minutes, FO371 46417/F6104/36/10.

17. U.K. PRO, Seymour to Sterndale-Bennett, 15 June 1945, FO371 46232/F3063.

18. U.K. PRO, Carton de Wiart Correspondence, 26 July 1945, CAB 127/28.

19. *FRUS*, 1945, 73:509.

20. Ibid., p. 511.

21. Ibid., p. 512.

22. U.K. PRO, Carton de Wiart Correspondence, 28 August 1945, CAB 127/28.

23. Aron Shai, *Britain and China, 1941–1947: Imperial Momentum*, p. 119.

24. U.K. PRO, Carton de Wiart Correspondence, 28 August 1945; CAB 127/28.

25. U.K. PRO, British Embassy in Moscow to FO, 1 November 1945, FO371/53561/F887.

26. Michael Schaller, *The US Crusade in China, 1938–1945*, p. 39.

27. Berlin, *Washington Despatches*, p. 607.

28. NAUS, Decimal Files, Edwin Locke, Memo for the President, microfilm 893.00/9–445.

29. NAUS, OSS Report, R & A Reports, 13 June 1945, microfilm no. 3166.

30. Ibid.

31. NAUS, Decimal Files, Vincent to Acheson, 15 November 1945, microfilm 893.00/11–1545.

32. U.K. PRO, FO Minute, 10 September 1945, FO371 43647/F13726/116/10.

33. U.K. PRO, Carton de Wiart Correspondence, 30 October 1945, CAB 127/28.

34. U.K. PRO, FO Memo, 24 April 1945, FO371 46167/F2464/35/10.

35. U.K. PRO, Dening to Sterndale-Bennett, top secret, 17 January 1945, FO371 46325/F411/124/61.

36. U.K. PRO, Memo by Hudson, 7 June 1945, FO37146170–72/F3065/36/10.

37. NAUS, Daily Secret Summary, 15 November 1945, box 2.

38. U.K. PRO, FO Memo, 24 April 1945, FO 371 46167/F2464/35/10.

39. *FRUS*, 1945, 7:446.

40. Memo for the President, 3 September 1945, Harry S. Truman Papers,

President's Secretary's Files, box 173: China 1945, Harry S. Truman Library, Independence, Missouri (hereafter cited as Truman Library).

41. NAUS, Decimal Files, Davies to Kennan, 18 August 1945, microfilm 893.00/8–1845.

42. U.K. PRO, Memo of Conversation by Seymour, 19 August 1945, FO371 46171/F6682/36/10.

43. U.K. PRO, Carton de Wiart Correspondence, Carton de Wiart to Ismay, 23 August 1945, CAB 127/28.

44. U.K. PRO, Carton de Wiart Correspondence, 6 September 1945, CAB 127/28.

45. U.K. PRO, FO Memo, FO371 46172/F11359/36/10.

46. U.K. PRO, Memo of Conversation by Seymour, 19 August 1945, FO371 46171/F6682/36/10.

47. *FRUS*, 1945, 7:722–23.

48. Gary May, *The China Scapegoat: The Diplomatic Ordeal of John Carter Vincent*, p. 139.

49. *FRUS*, 1945, 7:747.

50. *Manchester Guardian*, 29 November 1945.

51. U.K. PRO, FO Minute by Scott, 4 December 1945, FO371 46172/F11528/36/10.

52. U.K. PRO, Memo of Conversation by Hall-Patch, December 1945, FO371 46172/F11513/36/10.

53. U.K. PRO, FO Minute by Scott (handwritten), FO371 46172/F11513/36/10.

54. U.K. PRO, Seymour to FO, December 1945, FO371 53561/F1736.

55. *Chungking Ribao* (Chungking Daily), 4 December 1945.

56. U.K. PRO, FO371 46232/F10617.

57. U.K. PRO, Halifax to Bevin, 2 December 1945, FO371 46171/F11127/36/10.

58. *FRUS*, 1945, 7:767–69.

59. Ibid., p. 772.

60. U.K. PRO, FO Minute by Kitson, 21 December 1945, FO371 46172/F11861/36/10.

61. U.K. PRO, Wallinger to Bevin, 27 December 1945, FO371 53678/F518/515/10.

62. U.K. PRO, Sterndale-Bennett to FO from Moscow, 27 December 1945, FO371 53561/F53110.

63. U.K. PRO, *Monthly Report* by Chungking Embassy, December 1945, FO371 53561/F1236.

64. U.K. PRO, Chungking Embassy to FO, FO 371/53561/F2294.

65. *Parliamentary Debates*, Commons, vol. 413 (1945), col. 293.

66. Ibid., vol. 415, cols. 8–9.

67. *FRUS*, 1945, 7:1460.

68. Ibid., p. 1462.

69. Ibid., p. 1464.

70. U.K. PRO, Paper by Far Eastern Committee, 31 December 1945, CAB 134/280.

71. U.K. PRO, FO371 46238/F6134/60/10.

72. NAUS, 21 August 1945, RG 59, lot files 110, box 5.

73. Ibid., 1 September 1945.

74. NAUS, Confidential Memo by Boehringer, "Economic Importance of Hongkong," lot files 110, box 7.

75. Royal Institute of International Affairs, *The British Empire*, p. 106.

76. Royal Institute of International Affairs, *Political and Strategical Interests of Hongkong*, p. 21.

77. U.K. PRO, 13 December 1945, FO371 53642/F2369/116/10.

78. Thorp to Acheson, 13 September 1945, Name Files, Clayton-Thorp Papers, box 16, Truman Library.

79. *FRUS*, 1945, 7:1124.

80. Ibid., p. 1245.

81. U.K. PRO, Kitson to Young (Admiralty), 28 December 1945, FO371 46177/F12154/55/10.

82. U.K. PRO, FO Minute, 11 December 1945, FO371 53561/F67.

83. NAUS, Decimal Files, microfilm 893.00/10–2445.

84. George Johnson, "Stars and Stripes Over China," *Daily Mail*, 14 October 1945.

85. John Fischer, *Harper's*, August 1945.

86. U.K. PRO, "British Foreign Policy in the Far East," 31 December 1945, CAB 134/280.

87. U.K. PRO, Carton de Wiart Correspondence, 11 November 1945, CAB 127/28.

88. Ibid., 18 November 1945.

89. U.K. PRO, Bevin to Attlee, 13 December 1945, PREM8/189, FE General.

90. Ibid., see enclosure.

91. NAUS, Daily Secret Summary, October 1945, box 1.

92. Ibid., 14 December 1945.

93. Ibid., 19 December 1945.

94. *FRUS*, 1945, 7:462.

95. U.K. PRO, "British Foreign Policy in the Far East," 31 December 1945, CAB 134/280.

96. *FRUS*, 1945, 7:462.

97. U.K. PRO, Carton de Wiart Correspondence, 14 October 1945, CAB 127/28.

98. U.K. PRO, "British Foreign Policy in the Far East," 31 December 1945, CAB 134/280.

99. George Johnson, "Stars and Stripes Over China," *Daily Mail*, 14 October 1945.

100. NAUS, Decimal Files, Donovan to Byrnes, microfilm 711.93/12–1445.

101. Richard Gardner, *Sterling Dollar Diplomacy*, p. xvii.

3

The Marshall Mission

Nineteen forty-six was George C. Marshall's year. Despite some two years in the 1920s as commanding officer of the American garrison in Tientsin, Marshall did not acquire adequate knowledge about China, for Tientsin was an international city. Upon arrival at Shanghai on 20 December 1945, General Marshall knew his position was going to be very difficult and contradictory. It was the same contradiction that ruined Hurley's mission, notwithstanding the vast differences in temperament and ability that separated the two men.

The contradiction lay, first, in the fact that Marshall was expected to mediate as a neutral party between the Nationalists and the Communists, while at the same time the U.S. government recognized and supported only one side, the KMT regime, as the sole legal government of China. Such a position undoubtedly encouraged the Nationalists to believe that the United States would not, and could not, abandon them, no matter how much the Americans grumbled and criticized.

Second, the Kuomintang's belief that Washington would support its regime became all the more plausible at a time when problems between the United States and the Soviet Union were mounting in Europe. Chiang's belief was further strengthened three months after Marshall began his mission in China, when Winston Churchill inaugurated in his Fulton speech what was later called the "Cold War" period. Thus, just as Chiang started to lose interest in any negotiated settlement with Mao, the Communists increasingly suspected that the U.S. government was not really neutral.

Shortly before his departure for China, General Marshall asked again if his understanding of President Truman's intention was correct:

> I stated that my understanding of one phase of my directive was not in writing but I thought I had a clear understanding of his [Truman's] desire in the matter, which was that in the event that I was unable to secure the necessary action by the Generalissimo which I thought reasonable and desirable, it would still be necessary for the United States Government through me, to continue to back the National Government of the Republic of China—through the Generalissimo within the terms of announced policy of the U.S. Government.

According to Marshall's record, both President Truman and Undersecretary Acheson explicitly confirmed this understanding.[1]

But General Marshall was not simply the victim of this inherent contradiction in the U.S. China policy; in part he was its author. It was Marshall's decision in March to start aid projects to China—this meant to the Nationalists exclusively. These projects involved such matters as training military personnel and providing equipment for the KMT army, air force, and navy, as well as lend-lease supplies, surplus material sales, and sea- and airlifts for the KMT troops to Manchuria and North China.

With full backing of the president and freedom from bureaucratic infighting, Marshall appeared to be as confident as when he was the Allied military planner during the war. When his long-time friend, General Albert Wedemeyer, told him bluntly upon his arrival in Shanghai that his task might turn out to be an impossible one, Marshall flared up—an unusual occurrence for a man of his integrity.[2] Like many military men, Marshall had a distaste for career diplomats. But, unlike Hurley, Marshall was quick and willing to learn. As the mission grew increasingly difficult toward the end of 1946, Marshall's relationship with State Department officials became closer. This was, of course, also because Marshall was informed in May that he was secretary of state-designate. Moreover, through his arduous experience during the war, Marshall had become an excellent de facto diplomat himself. Persuasion, negotiation, and concession were nothing new to him.

Thus, despite his limited knowledge of China, Marshall never faced the problem of "how to deal with our erstwhile allies in that part of the world." He knew their intentions only too well. However, one moot point neither Marshall nor his Washington colleagues were clear about was the current status of the Moscow-Yenan connection. Throughout the war, there were various conflicting reports about that relationship. As Hurley's reports were considered unreliable, the most authoritative view was perhaps provided by the American embassy in Moscow. On 10 January, a month after Marshall's arrival in China, George Kennan sent him a long telegram, implying that "Yenan enjoyed what might seem to be a surprising degree of independence of Moscow."[3] The reasons he cited were:

(1) Chinese Communists had little reason to be grateful to the USSR. They had survived and grown not because of but despite relations with Moscow. Adherence to early Comintern directives resulted in near disaster for the CCP. And in the Sino-Japanese conflict, the USSR armed only the Chungking faction, which used some of those arms in blockading Yenan. Soviet stripping of Manchuria was like "plucking plums on which the CCP had long had their eye."

(2) The Chinese Communist Party was the most mature of all communist parties and had developed its own brand of Marxism and indigenous traditions.

(3) Chinese Communists were not a fugitive band of conspirators. For ten years they had had an established de facto regime, their own army, and civil administration. Consequently, they had developed substantial vested interests.

(4) Chinese Communists had taken on a nationalist coloration. From 1936 to the Japanese surrender, they were confronted with, and their propaganda concentrated against, an external foe. Rapid expansion of their armed forces and civilian following was largely on the basis of nationalism.

Although there is no evidence that General Marshall was influenced by this telegram, he did show a certain amount of personal respect for the Chinese Communists. More importantly, Marshall would often try to dispute the KMT view that the Chinese Communists always danced to the tune Stalin was playing.

As far as the British were concerned, General Marshall knew all along that London did not see eye to eye with Washington over its Far Eastern policy as a whole and over its China policy in particular, even though the Foreign Office took great pains to register official support for the Marshall Mission. London did not believe that the Big Three's Moscow Declaration on China in December 1945 had authorized any continued American involvement in China. However, the British had no choice but to endorse the Marshall Mission in public, which after all was a mediation effort.

London did not consider the mission workable; the Foreign Office was not convinced that China's internal dispute could be solved by foreign mediation. Ambassador Seymour, upon hearing the announcement of the mission, flatly told London: "It will hardly succeed."[4] But the British government found it impolitic to oppose the mission; the Foreign Office preferred to wait and see. The long memo in December 1945 pointed out that China's future as a unified modern state lay in the balance. The British did not want to appear to back one faction against another, lest any schism in China threaten to become permanent. However, the British realized "It will require nice judgment to decide where one consideration begins to override the other, and this will throw special responsibilities on the men on the spot." The memo further indicated that "There is a very real underlying unity in China arising from her long cultural and racial consciousness, which seems certain to take national form in due course, but it will be difficult if meanwhile we have to come to terms with it in an amorphous state."[5]

After a few months in the Foreign Office, Bevin became very critical of the whole U.S. policy in the Far East. In December 1945, the foreign secretary invited comments on a memo he had prepared for the cabinet from Ambassadors Halifax and Seymour. Halifax found that the secretary of state's criticism of U.S. policy in the Far East and Latin America was too severe, while Seymour agreed with Bevin, adding that Americans believed they enjoyed what Wendell Wilkie called "a reservoir of good will" by not having been engaged in wars with China and other states in East Asia. Moreover, Seymour believed that a majority of the East Asian states welcomed U.S. help and intervention, which was therefore "not power politics but good policemanship."[6]

The significance of the Anglo-American disagreement over China policies lay far beyond the mediation issue. It was America's hegemonic approach to international affairs in general—reflected in her efforts to monopolize Chinese affairs—that worried London in early 1946. Such an approach rejected the idea of Anglo-American collaboration or "ganging up," which had after all been the cornerstone of

American foreign policy since the Monroe Doctrine. The reality that the United States had outgrown the Anglo-American framework in diplomacy became even harder for London to swallow, for at the end of the war British policymakers were torn between the pride of being a world-class empire and the humiliation of having to beg for American money to make ends meet. The most irksome of all was the negative attitude the Americans adopted over the loan to be extended to Britain. Washington made it clear that a loan would be forthcoming only if the British gave up part of their imperial pretensions.

From a global perspective, the Americans seemed convinced that they could obtain a safe world by being a "peacemaker" and "mediator"—a viewpoint London had loathed for decades. From this vantage, Washington did not need Britain's collaboration lest it be duped by the British supercunning, as had happened many times in the past. There was a bipartisan realization in London that the U.S. obsession with mediation was not only unrealistic but also detrimental to British interests all over the world. Though keen on annulling the U.S. role as the world's supermediator, the Foreign Office found no practical strategy to pursue. It, thus, fell upon Winston Churchill, the wartime hero most familiar with American affairs and His Majesty's loyal opposition leader, to break the Anglo-American impasse over the loan negotiations and other issues.

In early February, a top secret memo written by Isaiah Berlin from Washington reflected the typical British anxiety at the failure to influence American thinking: The Russians had thus far found themselves in a position where they could freely maneuver, as between the divergent attitudes of Britain and the United States. Such maneuvers, the memo said, "can only be arrested by a concerted prior agreement between the Americans and ourselves on various issues." Berlin admitted that in the absence of such an agreement, the British government found itself in the disadvantageous position of being thrown back on its own resources and caught in a squeeze play. Thus, the memo concluded, "there seems to be no harm in discreetly exercising our powers of persuasion along these lines on policy—shaping Americans at all levels."[7]

Isaiah Berlin's call was soon answered by Winston Churchill. Ever since his failed election campaign, Churchill had been active in influencing Western policies toward the Soviet Union. His solution was to foster, by whatever means, an Anglo-American alliance in order to utilize the U.S. power to serve Britain's interest when the actual British power could no longer meet the requirements of her global commitments. The Labour government had been well informed of Churchill's activities and intentions since October 1945, when the ex-prime minister took a "vacation" in the United States. In fact, the idea of Churchill's delivering a speech at Fulton, Missouri, was reported to Attlee by Lord Halifax in October, before it was announced by the White House on 19 December 1945.[8]

In November 1945, Washington demanded the possession of a group of Pacific islands that belonged to the British, but had been occupied by General MacArthur during the war. Bevin was uncertain and unfamiliar with the wartime arrangements concerning this issue. He wrote a personal letter to Churchill, who was asked to "burn the letter" after reading it. The former prime minister jumped at the opportunity to elaborate on his thinking about Anglo-American relations, most of which would reappear in his famous Fulton speech a few months later. In Churchill's view, it was to the long-term advantage of Britain and the Commonwealth to have their external and strategic interests so interwoven with those of the United States. From this viewpoint, the more strategic areas they held in joint occupation the better. But he advised Bevin that, although the United States was far more powerful than the British Commonwealth, Britain must insist upon coming in on equal terms.

To achieve this objective, Churchill believed it was essential to preserve indefinitely the organization of the Combined Chiefs of Staff Committee, from which would arise the continued interchange of military and scientific information and intelligence, as well as the similarity and interchangeability of weapons, common manuals of instruction for the armed forces, interrelated plans for the war mobilization of civil industry, and interchange of officers at schools and universities. Churchill ended his letter to Bevin by saying, "You are indeed fortunate that this sublime opportunity has fallen to you and I trust the seizing of it will ever be associated with your name."[9]

In reply, Bevin cautiously agreed with Churchill about joint bases, but as far as an Anglo-American alliance was concerned, he said, "I must keep the UN in mind."[10] Nevertheless, Bevin was not surprised when Churchill made his thesis public at Fulton, Missouri, a few months later.

Some prominent Americans shared the British concern about America's role as mediator. Walter Lippmann was one of the most outspoken ones. In an article published in *Collier's Magazine* on 26 January, Lippmann criticized the fact that the United States was called upon to "discharge the role of mediator" in many fields of international affairs.[11] This statement drew much attention in London. Most of the British press praised Lippmann's insights. The *Economist* stated in a leading article: "American diplomacy, in recent months, has concentrated on getting agreement—sometimes, it has seemed, regardless of the merits." It went on further, "The new doctrine of 'mediation' holds that America should never be a principal but always neutral. . . . Similarly, it was lack of imagination on the American side which, in so many British eyes, made the conditions attaching to the loan so painful."[12]

Michael Wright, first political counselor at the British embassy in Washington, saw Lippmann's article in a different light. As he wrote to the Foreign Office: "There is an obvious lack of clarity on at least one essential point. There are two distinct types of mediation. In one case the mediator is not a partner to a dispute and has no direct interest in its solution. In the other case he stands to gain or lose." Wright pointed out further that, "Lippmann's thesis by no means carries with it the assumption frequently made by others that Britain (or the Commonwealth) is a junior partner to the United States." Thus, the real problem for the mediator lay in self-image, as Wright warned that

> The role of mediation, whether interested or disinterested, leads to self-righteousness and criticism from the sidelines. The concept of the junior partner at least connotes the idea of consulting your partner on matters of common interest. . . . The concept of mediation, on the other hand, carries with it the idea of pressing your own solution upon both sides, and there is always the temptation for the mediator to take advantage of the weaker party.[13]

Sitting in Washington, Wright could not have summarized better the Anglo-American friction over China in 1946. He apparently resented the treatment Britain received from her former ally, the United States, which was worse than a junior partner. Under the circumstances, the Foreign Office greeted Churchill's Fulton speech with extraordinary zeal and relief.

In early 1946, Bevin was having a hard time with the Americans. The Anglo-American loan negotiation seemed to be getting nowhere.

American public opinion on the whole opposed such a loan without strings attached. The American press fed this public sentiment with numerous attacks on Britain's bargaining attitude, typically reflected in her intransigence over imperial trading and payment arrangements. The *Chicago Tribune*, for example, printed a cartoon of John Bull standing at America's backdoor, saying, "Spare a morsel for a weak, starving man, but make it sirloin medium rare, and if it isn't done just right I won't eat it, and there is no use begging me."[14] The *New York Daily News* published another cartoon of John Bull coming out of a pawnshop, declaring: "Even when I don't pay it back, I don't like it."[15]

Michael Foot, a well-known journalist and newly elected Labour M.P., called the American attitude "a curtain of lies between us and [the] U.S." As early as 1 January 1946, Foot pointed out in his column that: "The iron curtain which was supposed to exist between the peoples of Russia and the West is [a] smaller menace to peace than the curtain of lies, half-truths and distortion which now divides the peoples of Britain and America."[16]

Bevin was also facing revolt from the Labour backbenchers. A number of them joined forces with Conservative leaders to challenge Bevin's passive Far Eastern policy. James Callahan, a Labour M.P. from South Cardiff, launched the attack. According to American Ambassador John Winant, Callahan claimed that, "much of what the United States was doing was not in accordance with what the British would like to see and [he] claimed that the Americans had failed to disarm many of the Japanese and set out on a plan of economic aggression in the Far East." Callahan also said that "The Far East is the powder keg of the world and the problems of Southeastern Europe are insignificant compared with the problems which face the world in the Far East."

R. A. Butler, a leading Conservative foreign policy spokesman, reinforced some of what Callahan propounded by saying: "The problems of the Far East, with which I had the misfortune or fortune to deal with at the Foreign Office, are of immense magnitude and importance." Butler further criticized Bevin for being silent over the Far Eastern issues, arguing that such questions cannot be too ticklish or too delicate to be dealt with on the floor of the House. The Foreign Office had little to say except that Britain was merely "following the American lead" in that part of the world.[17]

Back in China, General Marshall seemed to be working wonders, to everyone's surprise. Within two weeks, he was able to obtain a cease-fire agreement between the Nationalists and the Communists, signed on 10 January. Many people who knew China were skeptical of Marshall's success. Drew Pearson reported a comment made by General Joseph "Vinegar Joe" Stilwell: "It won't last . . . the Gimo has been making and breaking promises for 25 years."[18]

If Stilwell had personal grudges against the "Gimo," Marshall did not. In fact, Marshall was somewhat overwhelmed by his success—the achievement of an overall truce in China that had eluded both Ambassadors Gauss and Hurley over the past four years. In February, Marshall made the personal decision to start the huge China aid program, which had been suspended by the president in support of the Marshall Mission. This quick triumph was indeed too good to be true. Part of the reason for the success was Marshall's personal prestige and integrity. But the most important factor that convinced Chiang to accept a cease-fire lay in Marshall's ostensible power endowed by President Truman to ultimately determine the fate of aid projects. Although Marshall knew that those projects would be carried out regardless of the results of his mission, he concealed this fact from the generalissimo in order to maintain a strong bargaining position. Among the dozen or so projects that Marshall had control over were the Military Advisory Group (MAG) Project, the Export-Import Bank (Eximbank) Loan Project, the extension of Lend-Lease to China, the so-called Eight-and-a-third (Air Force) Project, and the Thirty-nine-Division (Army) Project.[19]

The Communists accepted the cease-fire because they saw it as an opportunity to consolidate their position. However, their suspicions grew as the China aid program restarted, which had virtually nothing to do with them except for a token promise to equip and train nine Communist divisions upon their integration into the National Army. In some cases the Americans used poorly concealed methods to provide combat equipment to Chiang. A report from the British embassy at Chungking in February revealed that "at least fifty American fighter aircraft, i.e., Black Widows, Thunderbolts, and Mustangs" in the Chengdu group of airfields "have been rendered unserviceable by the US Air Force shearing the fuselage with oxyacetylene welders, and have been sold to the Chinese for scrap at $100 each."[20]

On 26 February, General Marshall recommended extending the Eximbank loan to China (valued at $500 million) because he felt that, in view of the president's statement on 15 December concerning China, .the position and actions of the Chinese government now justified beginning the negotiations for a major Eximbank loan.[21] Meanwhile, on 25 February President Truman authorized the establishment of the U.S. Military Advisory Group composed of one thousand officers "to assist and advise the Chinese Government in the development of modern armed forces," an objective that had been pursued since the Roosevelt administration.[22]

Marshall soon learned a hard lesson. Despite the cease-fire accord, sporadic fighting never stopped. Not until he had completed a three-thousand-mile tour of the field in March did Marshall begin to realize the complexity of the Chinese situation. As he reported to Truman on 13 March, the main problem was "a political struggle within the governing Central Committee of the Kuomintang Party—a committee which *rules* China and whose officials and subordinates down the line hold their position of power and personal income by virtue of that Committee's rule, now due to be abdicated to a coalition government."[23]

Cultural differences were no less a problem for the American efforts to be successful. Marshall confided to a British Royal Air Force friend in late February that it was typical of the complexities of negotiation in China that agreement from an English text into a Chinese version that was acceptable to both the central government and the Communists presented "well-nigh insuperable difficulties."[24]

During Marshall's first three-month sojourn in China, before his temporary recall to Washington in March, the Americans had already embarked on an ambitious plan to remake the country. Various economic projects were under way and thousands of military as well as civilian experts flooded into China. Everything seemed upbeat. At one point, General Marshall was pondering how to change the Chinese political system. According to Marshall's British friend, Vice Air Marshal MacNeece Forster, the general told him in February that he thought "the responsibility of Chinese Ministers of the future should follow more closely the British pattern than that of the United States (i.e., responsible both to the Parliament and Cabinet)."[25]

An important cultural project was the establishment in Shanghai of an Operation Center for the State Department Information Service. Directed by Dr. John King Fairbank, the center laid emphasis on feature and background-material magazines and periodicals, as well as on movies, to introduce the American way of life and thinking to the Chinese.[26]

Although the "Marshall Magic" had its limits, it nevertheless bewildered many Americans as well as some skeptical British officials in China. Even General Carton de Wiart allowed himself a momentary feeling of optimism, as he reported to London: "There is such a deep mistrust between the heads of the two parties that I feel, even if an agreement is reached, it will not be of any real value unless it lasts long enough to give some of the Communist leaders time to change their political views . . . I think this is quite a possibility."[27]

While Washington was preoccupied with China, the British Foreign Office began to rethink its Far Eastern policy. As a State Department Daily Staff Officers Summary recorded on 25 February: "Winant learns that the U.K. Foreign Office is now convinced that British territories in Southeast Asia must be handled in conjunction with their relations to other parts of East Asia, and not treated solely as British territories." Winant "has also been informed that the Foreign Office is seriously considering what policy should be followed in China and Manchuria."[28]

Indeed, Bevin had been thinking, along the lines of the December memo on "British Foreign Policy in the Far East," of reorganizing the policy setup in the Far East. In February, Bevin decided to transfer Ambassador Lord Killearn from Cairo to Singapore in order to take over the nonmilitary functions of the deactivated Southeast Asian Command. A veteran China hand, Lord Killearn had been the first foreign representative to present credentials to the Kuomintang government twelve years earlier. Bevin wanted Lord Killearn to reorganize and coordinate British policies in all of Southeast Asia, with the purpose of developing the region into an integrated community to counterbalance the United States and the USSR in Northeast Asia. Bevin was so impatient to transfer Killearn that the latter protested and the two had a falling out. In addition, they had a heated argument over the terms of transfer. First, Lord Killearn bargained for higher salary rates than those he was receiving in Cairo. Then, he started to complain that his family could not join him soon because Bevin wanted him to go to Singapore immediately. At one point, Lord Killearn made a reference to Mrs. Bevin that made the foreign secretary furious.[29]

In April, Bevin made another important move to split the Far Eastern Department into three, i.e., China, Japan, and Southeast Asia. George Kitson was appointed head of the China Department.[30]

Britain's silence over China's internal dispute did not indicate the disappearance of Anglo-American disagreements there. The Foreign

Office managed to refrain from criticizing the American China policy in public, but the competition for influence in that country continued elsewhere. The Anglo-American naval competition came to a head in early 1946. The United States Navy Department was never happy about the Sino-British Naval Program. In February, the Navy Department pushed through the House of Representatives a bill authorizing the president to lease or give to China 271 surplus warships.[31] Then in March, the Americans tried to start a rival project to train Chinese naval officers. The British felt uneasy. The British embassy in China reported that Admiral Charles M. Cooke, Jr., commander of the U.S. Seventh Fleet had recently visited Chungking to discuss with Chiang Kai-shek the question of training Chinese personnel. According to the report, the admiral acknowledged that 1,100 Chinese naval officers and ratings were now being trained by the U.S. Navy at Tsingtao and that negotiations were in progress for the sale or transfer to China of some U.S. naval craft.[32]

But Admiral Cooke was soon frustrated with the Tsingtao project. He attributed his problem in recruiting qualified Chinese for training to the British Navy. As he reported to Washington in October: "I think that the British activity hampers [the] U.S. Naval Advisory Group in that the better Chinese recruits for naval training are lured by the prospects of a prolonged visit to a foreign country, offered by naval training in Great Britain. . . . I am reliably informed that most of the six hundred men awaiting transfer to England are middle school students whereas recruits being furnished to CNTC at Tsingtao are predominantly grade school boys."[33]

The Anglo-American naval competition intensified when, in October, the British government started to transfer a number of naval vessels to China. The Truman administration was furious. Undersecretary of State Dean Acheson sent the U.S. embassy in Nanking a telegram on 31 October, stating, "Our Navy feels that the proposed transfer of U.K. naval vessels to China, including a cruiser, and U.K. arrangements for training Chinese naval personnel in the U.K. will gain for the U.K. a predominant role in Chinese naval affairs." Acheson went on: "We feel that acceptance of the U.K. training and equipment by the Chinese would prejudice the success of the U.S. MAG and would be in effect a violation of the spirit of the draft agreement for MAG" since the generalissimo "had assured us that he desired only U.S.-type organization, training and staff procedure." Acheson concluded that, "We desire that Embassy Nanking take the matter up with the Chinese authorities, and consider possible re-introduction into the draft agreement of an article committing the Chinese not to accept the services of personnel of any third country in connection with the Chinese armed forces." General Marshall rejected Acheson's proposal of pressuring the Chinese on this matter because it would be "impolitic."[34]

Another disagreement between London and Washington was over the future of Manchuria, where the British thought they should be allowed a voice because of the Livadia Agreement, to which Britain was a signatory. In April, the Foreign Office suggested that steps be taken to prevent Sino-Soviet agreements over Manchuria, which might jeopardize commercial interests of other countries there. The State Department emphasized that "we did not believe any further action was called for."[35]

In fact, Washington remained strongly suspicious of any specific steps suggested by the British concerning China. An OSS report dated 20 February summarized the British dilemma this way: on one hand, "A strong China without a democratic system of government would, in the British view, menace Britain's future as a colonial power in the Far East," and "Britain had no more desire to liquidate Hongkong than any other British possession or dependency." On the other hand, "a strong democratic China may well serve as a force to outmode colonialism in the Far East."[36] In other words, the British would stand to lose no matter how China might turn out.

Meanwhile, in Manchuria, the situation was very delicate. Both the Kuomintang and the Communists were struggling for space due to be evacuated by the Russian Red Army according to the understanding made at Yalta. The Communists obtained some Japanese weapons captured by the Red Army. But Stalin soon decided not to continue allowing weapons to fall into Mao's hands because of Western pressure amidst numerous reports that the USSR was arming the Communists.[37]

Ironically, by this time, both Nanking and London seemed to have a common interest in showing toughness toward the USSR in order to appear as a loyal ally deserving of material and monetary aid from the United States. Chiang had always tried to play the Russia card during the American mediation, but without much success because Washington was wary of his motives. At this juncture, Churchill's Fulton speech did both London and Nanking a great service.

On 5 March at Fulton, Missouri, Churchill delivered a sensational speech, calling for an end to the Russian expansion and the forming of an English-speaking alliance against communism. Churchill's speech has since been much quoted and studied in relation to the origins of the Cold War in Europe. However, little attention has been paid to his views on the Far East. Although he was cautious not to criticize the American China policy, Churchill relentlessly attacked Stalin in the Far East by deliberately revising the history made at Yalta only a year before. Churchill implied that he and Roosevelt were tricked by Stalin into signing the Livadia Agreement, thus repudiating the deal for which he was the only other living cosigner. According to Churchill:

> The outlook is also anxious in the Far East and especially in Manchuria. The Agreement which was made at Yalta, to which I was a party, was extremely favourable to Soviet Russia, but it was made at a time when no one could say that the German war might not extend through the summer and autumn of 1945 and when the Japanese war was expected to last for [a] further 18 months from the end of the German war.[38]

Chiang Kai-shek reacted quickly. Encouraged by the speech, the jubilant generalissimo immediately issued an "informal statement" to General Marshall a few days later, saying he was convinced that the Communist Party was loyal to the USSR and that the CCP's intention was to infiltrate government positions primarily to gain control of foreign policy "in order to play the Russian hand." Chiang added that he felt "the outcome of the Manchurian question now depends on the strength of the American stand towards Russia on the subject and that of Iran."[39] The hidden essential point of Chiang's statement was that the U.S. mediation policy was a futile one in the context of the Cold War.

General Marshall was recalled to Washington to confer with the president in March. When he returned to China in late April, he found the situation out of hand. As he reported to Truman on 7 May: "On my return I found the irreconcilable members of the Government Party were firmly in the saddle and the Generalissimo took the line that Communists were in league with the Soviet Government and could not be relied upon to keep any agreements"—in other words "my efforts in the past . . . were based on a false conception as to the dependability of the Communist representatives." What troubled Marshall most was that: "The Government Generals evidently felt that they had far more military power of action than was actually the case" and "influenced the Generalissimo accordingly." Marshall cited the example in Manchuria where "they precipitated themselves into a seriously weak military position of which the Communists were fully aware and seized the advantage accordingly."[40]

Despite his position as a mediator, General Marshall felt compelled to advise Chiang militarily. He told the generalissimo personally on 10 May: "We are confronted with a definite and serious weakness in the Government's military position and a strategic military advantage of the Communist forces." Chiang, however, turned a deaf ear to Marshall's warning, which soon turned into reality when the all-out civil war started.[41]

Marshall realized that the major difficulty came from the Nationalists' side, but he understood his instruction to be to support the generalissimo no matter what resulted from his mission. More importantly, Marshall knew that China would remain within his domain of responsibility when the mission ended. In May, General Eisenhower paid a secret visit to China, carrying a presidential message offering Marshall the position of secretary of state. After Marshall said yes, Eisenhower flew back to Washington and reported to the president. Eisenhower later told Marshall that Truman was greatly relieved, saying, "This gives me a wonderful ace in the hole because I have been terribly worried."[42] Since the American interest lay in preventing the demise of the Chiang regime—a distinct possibility in an all-out civil war—Marshall could not afford to abandon his mission until the very end. As a military man himself, he was fully aware of Chiang's weak military position, a result of both intransigence and stupidity. As a politician, he was convinced that all-out American support for Chiang in a civil war would incur so tremendous a cost that the American political system would never accept it. Marshall decided that providing limited aid to Chiang would give Washington maximum flexibility. Since Marshall's mediation had not yet ended officially, Chiang's urgent military needs could not be met by direct U.S. aid. Thus, Marshall decided that his best option was to sell Chiang large amounts of surplus military materials left on the Pacific islands during the war. On the one hand, the sale could be rationalized as humanitarian aid, while on the other, it showed American commitment and support for the Chinese government. However, the U.S. Foreign Liquidation Commission wanted to make some profits from the sale, which

Marshall thought to be ludicrous, as he wrote Commissioner Thomas McCabe on 18 May:

> I understand that the average price of previous sales has been 37% of the cost. Howard expresses willingness to go down to 30% of cost for China. This to me is too high for these reasons: We have far more than merely a financial interest in the transaction, our position if not our future security in the Pacific is involved.... Such considerations were not involved to any material extent in cases of other countries. Furthermore, in most other cases I believe surplus property was on the ground of country making purchases. China will have to import practically all of her purchases over long ocean distances and at considerable expense from her limited cash resources.[43]

Thus, Marshall recommended that 25 percent of the cost be the maximum amount charged to China for the surplus war materials.

In August, Marshall clearly saw the end of his mediation, but he refused to give up easily. Although fully aware of Chiang's intransigence following Churchill's Fulton speech, Marshall nevertheless concentrated his efforts during what remained of the year in persuading Chiang to abandon the illusion that the U.S.-Soviet confrontation would automatically mean all-out American support for the Nationalists in a civil war. Despite the intensified Cold War environment, Marshall believed that Chiang was wrong to play the "Russia card." For one thing, throughout his sojourn in China Marshall did not detect any substantial evidence of Stalin's meddling in China's internal dispute. Marshall made his point adequately clear during a conversation with Dr. Wei Tao-min, former Chinese ambassador to Washington, when Wei said he did not see how Marshall could succeed in China if Byrnes could not succeed in Europe, particularly when they were both fighting Soviet influence. Marshall agreed that the Russian attitude and intentions did not help the situation in China, but he added that "reactionary elements in the Government had been operating on the belief that the United States would have to support China because of fear of Russia. This was a serious error . . . the United States was not going to be dragged through the mud by these reactionaries." As for Russian activities in China, Marshall pointed out that, "Since the trouble in Manchuria in the Spring of 1946, Russia has been standing off, keeping clear of the situation, apparently so that at a propitious moment in the future she can make a clear case for herself."[44]

In Washington, there was an ascendant view within the military establishment that the Soviet Union was the main culprit in China's internal troubles. In September, General Marshall received a report from his special representative in Washington, Colonel Marshall S. Carter, which stated:

> The Joint Staff planners are now preparing a paper on the serious strategic indications of the situation in China. The feeling throughout is that (a) because of internal discord there is no firm political bastion in China on which to base resistance to Soviet actions, (b) there is no question that Chinese Communists are primarily tools of Soviet policy in China, and (c) current U.S. policy precludes assistance to [the] National Government of China of the sort envisaged for Turkey.

To counter this trend of thinking, Colonel Carter further added, "In the belief that this trend of thinking is premature and overly pessimistic and that its promulgation on JCS level would be detrimental to your efforts, I have been trying to overcome it by persuasion based on limited ammunition."[45]

At the end of 1946, Marshall became quite receptive to views expressed by the State Department's China service. Meanwhile, Henry Luce, founder of the Time/Life enterprises, was waging an all-out China aid campaign. After a trip to China at the personal invitation of Chiang Kai-shek, Luce used all his media tools to attack the administration's China policy. On 8 December General Marshall reported to the president that the most serious complication in the problem and "the one tacitly ignored by Luce is the fact that [the] controlling reactionary group in [the] Kuomintang Government and [the] Kuomintang military clique have upset by indirect action or aggressive military operations whatever success I have had with the Generalissimo."[46]

In London, although the Labour government was silent over China throughout the Marshall Mission, it enjoyed a jubilant mood after the timely Fulton speech made by Churchill. There was a widespread feeling of relief within the Foreign Office. Isaiah Berlin commented a few days after the Fulton speech: "Mr. Churchill is somewhat in the position of a dentist who has diagnosed a severe inflammation and proposes the use of the drill which may have to be followed by actual extraction of the diseased tooth." Berlin went on further:

> Surely the modern medicine has provided more painless methods of cure, and that so brutal a method as that recommended by Mr. Churchill

harks back to old-fashioned practices. But there is no doubt that the speech, more than those of Byrnes, Vandenberg or Dulles, has made it difficult for the U.S. public to ignore the painful choices before them.[47]

Churchill's gift for manipulating American public opinion was greatly admired within the Foreign Office. Paul Mason, in charge of North American affairs, commented in a handwritten note that "The first thing to be said about Mr. Churchill's speech is that he has an almost incomparable sense of the reactions of the United States to a given development or situation. He will be the last person to be surprised at what is now being said about his speech." Mason believed that "Mr. Churchill deliberately chooses to over-stress his claims. He knows as well as everyone that a formal military alliance of the English-speaking peoples is not at this stage practical policy. . . . What he does intend is that when the 'stirring impact' of his speech has died away (as it will) the American people will be prepared . . . to accept the less blatant thought of the closest working relationship with the British Commonwealth with all the joint machine and consultation." He added, "I believe that to have been at the root of Mr. Churchill's intentions. If so the effect of the speech will in the long run prove to be wholly good."[48]

Although publicly denying having had anything to do with the Fulton speech, the Labour government felt extremely grateful to Churchill's personal efforts at smoothing over the difficult loan negotiations. Prime Minister Clement Attlee wrote to Churchill a few days later, thanking him for his efforts to present the British case more forcefully than anyone could have done, stating, "I should like to send you my warm thanks and appreciation for the friendly line you took."[49]

In spite of the fact that Churchill's sensational rhetoric of a bipolar world greatly helped the Labour government's position, neither Churchill nor the Labour cabinet saw the world in a rigid bipolar perspective. The British, after all, were to play the role of balancer. Thus, it is not surprising that as Washington eventually veered toward a bipolar worldview, London began to move in the other direction. As the China experts were being purged in Washington for their hands-off inclination in the Chinese internal dispute, the British Foreign Office was echoing their views regarding the nature of Chinese Communism. George Kitson, newly appointed head of the China Department, stated in a secret paper:

> The Communists derive their power and support from the people, mainly the peasants, to whom the Communist doctrines and political platform have been specially designed to appeal. The Kuomintang derive theirs from the landlords and rich merchants—whom they brought in power and to whom are allied at present the army (most of whose leaders are themselves big landowners) and the labour unions in the big cities, under the control of racketeers loyal to the party and Chiang Kai-shek.

As for the Chinese Communists, Kitson pointed out that they were not really communist in the Marxist-Leninist sense. They became Marxist-Leninist after the split with the Nationalists in 1927, which resulted in the setting up of the Kiangsi Soviet. After the Long March, however, the Communists developed a policy of agrarian reform which, in its application to a rural or peasant economy, should probably be regarded as "not incompatible with social democracy." Moreover, "There has in the past been no proof of any direct connection between Moscow and Yenan or any indication that Yenan takes its orders from or is guided in its policy by Moscow."[50] Such a memo, though mistaken on some points, was very similar to those written by the State Department's China experts.

Thinking along this line of reasoning, the Foreign Office naturally preferred to treat China in the same category as Yugoslavia. In June, Foreign Secretary Bevin made two important appointments. First, Lord Inverchapel was appointed as the new British ambassador to Washington. Formerly known as Sir Archibald Clark Kerr, Lord Inverchapel had served during the war in both Moscow and Chungking; he was thus very familiar with the China situation. Second, Bevin chose a non-China expert, Sir Ralph Stevenson, to replace Sir Horace Seymour in China. Sir Ralph was an expert on Yugoslavia.

Before his departure for Chungking, Sir Ralph Stevenson had a long conversation with Bevin. The foreign secretary explained that "he did not wish, for the purpose of foreign affairs, to deal with the Asiatic countries one by one. Their interests were so closely bound together nowadays that it was essential to treat the area as a whole in formulating British policy." Furthermore, Bevin "foresaw pressure on China by Russia from the North and by America from the Pacific. There was room for us in between and the Chinese would be likely to welcome us as a counterweight."[51]

Bevin's view was strongly seconded by his earlier appointee to Singapore, Lord Killearn, special commissioner in Southeast Asia. After a visit to China at the invitation of T. V. Soong, Lord Killearn made the following report on 11 June: "China is in a mess—politically, militarily, financially and socially. I doubt whether the foundations of the government are broad enough and strong enough to carry the load." He observed with a sharp eye that, "The Soong Dynasty is propped up by the Kuomintang and by the Americans. The Kuomintang seems to have lost much of the driving power and popular appeal it had 15 years ago." Killearn admitted that all this held a special interest for him, as he had been the first foreign representative to present his credentials to the KMT government more than twelve years before. He reported further that "the financial muddle is 'atomic.'. . . American dollars are the standard currency of Shanghai." He added,

> It does not take long in China to learn the dominant role there which America is playing. Nothing new in that—save that during and since the war the Yanks have replaced us as the first power in the land. But what *was* new to me was to note how irritated and impatient the Americans are growing with the Chinese, just as the Chinese are with the Americans. I suspect the honeymoon is wearing thin and a process of mutual disillusionment has set in.

Lord Killearn concluded: "I have always believed that the Chinese had one fixed principle in their foreign policy—namely, to play off the No. 2 of the moment against No. 1. . . . In my day, it was America they were playing against us. Now the process has been reversed—which, if I am right in my analysis, should mean that we *ought* with reasonable skill to have an opportunity to regain our position and trade to some considerable extent." As to America, he confessed, "I am puzzled as to her aims and policy in China today. . . . Is she playing Chiang Kai-shek, even to the extent of sending American troops, in order to hold back Russia?" If so, Killearn conceded, one could understand it, although he personally thought that their action was unwise and that there was no prospect of China "getting together with the bear."[52]

As Marshall was running into trouble in China, there seemed to be a consensus within the Foreign Office that the time had come for Britain to regain the initiative. In November, the Foreign Office received a paper written by Robert Payne, a British Council-sponsored professor in

China. The paper stated: "The Far East is one, the revolution sweeping over China, India, the Philippines, Malaya, Burma and Siam is essentially the same in each country—a socialistic democratic revolution to which Great Britain has everything to offer and everything to gain, by using the movement. The time has come for us to take the lead." Esler Dening, chairman of the Far Eastern Committee, told Ambassador Stevenson that, although he disliked Payne's left-leaning views and considered many of the ideas as impractical, there were "others worthy of careful consideration."[53]

In November the British embassy in Nanking felt that the moment was again at hand for a redefinition of American policy regarding the continuation or abandonment of mediation by General Marshall.[54] Under the circumstances, the Foreign Office instructed Sir Ralph Stevenson to seek a formal conference with Marshall. As the general reported to Washington on 21 November: "The British Ambassador is seeking a discussion of matter with me and [Ambassador] Stuart in a few days . . . I would therefore appreciate advice or instructions for my guidance so that I will be in step with [the] Department's international relationships." While fully aware of British disagreement with the American China policy, Marshall commented that, "Incidentally, [the] British Ambassador told Dr. Stuart that the British now recognize the fact [that] the United States has taken over the position in China previously held by the British."[55]

The reply from Washington was quite illuminating. Signed by Dean Acheson, the long telegram pointed out that although Washington desired to prevent China from becoming an irritant between the USSR and the United States, the State Department did not trust the British intentions because

> There is . . . loose talk about China's inability to fill the "power vacuum" in the Far East created by the defeat of Japan. From chance remarks and attitudes of the British it appears that there is some feeling that Japan might again fill this vacuum, or at least be the "stabilizing influence" in the Far East. From our point of view there is no power vacuum in the Far East. It seems to have been filled by Russia and ourselves. . . . Furthermore, although we welcome the cooperation and assistance of third powers in seeking a solution, we do not intend to relinquish our leadership.

Acheson pointed out further that, "We of course welcome British interest and desire to cooperate in regard to China" and "although there are indications that Britain does not altogether see eye to eye with us on China policy and there are reasons to take with a grain of salt a statement that the British are completely resigned to our having taken over the position they previously occupied in China, ... we feel that the British should be assured that by and large our interests with regard to China are parallel and that we desire to work in the closest harmony with them on matters of common interest." At the same time, "we should bear in mind Chinese proclivity for playing off one power against another and avoid any obvious United States-United Kingdom versus Union of Soviet Socialist Republics development in China." For these reasons, Acheson concluded, "we feel that the British should not be encouraged to intervene actively in the China situation."[56] Upon receiving Acheson's telegram, Marshall decided not to initiate the talk with the British ambassador. The proposed Anglo-American conference was thus aborted.[57]

The American policy to keep the British out had also been consistent in the economic field. For many Americans and the British in China in 1946, the sign of changing wind was not so much the arrival of General Marshall as the change of driving rules on 1 January from the left-hand side (British) to the right (American). There were also talks of a massive project by Westinghouse, an American company, to standardize China's frequency and voltage, because the Americans felt inconvenienced by the old British system of 220 volts and sixty cycles.

The American monopoly in China did not initially deter British business interests. In late December 1945, the powerful Federation of British Industries (F.B.I.) decided to strengthen British business efforts by sending its representative, Asquith, to China. The objective of the F.B.I. was to break the American monopoly in China. As G. A. Wallinger informed the Foreign Office: "Hutchison reports from Shanghai that ... Asquith will shortly proceed to China 'where he will be attached to the Embassy with a view to counteracting in the interest [of] U.K. trade the threatened monopoly of China markets by U.S. trade.' "[58]

Undoubtedly, the determined effort of the U.S. government to intervene in China's domestic dispute was decisive in attracting many American businessmen to the country. Moreover, the prospect of the huge China aid projects sustained the confidence of the American business community. According to an estimate made by the U.S. War Department in April 1946, military-related aid alone totaled $800 million since V-J Day—larger than the amount during the entire war period, which was about $700 million.[59] Furthermore, official American projects were often interwoven with private business activities in China. The Eximbank loan recommended by Marshall was to be used by the Chinese in purchasing American goods. The operation of so many projects would naturally result in a certain degree of economic integration between the two countries, which would inevitably give U.S. business interests an invaluable advantage in terms of privileges and information.

The British believed that American business interests would exert a strong influence upon the administration to retain Chiang Kai-shek's government. This was pointed out in the December 1945 British cabinet memo called "British Foreign Policy in the Far East":

> While demanding equality of opportunities everywhere, America hopes for more than equality of opportunity in China. The war has left her as the only country able to supply the capital equipment which Chinese plans for development require, and America exerts a predominating influence with the Chinese Government. The placing of Chinese orders for reconstruction materials will tend, therefore, to go to America, even for requirements under a forward programme, to the extent that Americans are prepared to risk their capital against such security or trade advantages as they may be able to secure.

Thus, the Americans wanted (a) the KMT to retain the political leadership of China and exert its effective control over the whole of China, (b) Chinese revenues and other assets available as backing for loans to be chiefly earmarked against fresh American advances.[60]

Meanwhile, the Americans were debating about possible long-term development strategies for China, reflecting a desire to integrate the Chinese economy into its new liberal world order. The *Wall Street Journal*, for example, reported that, "American trade experts believe China could sell $500 million of Chinese silk annually if she would set up and enforce standards of uniformity and grading for quality." It was also believed that "Chinese tea could compete successfully with tea from Ceylon and the Netherlands East Indies."[61] As for trade *with* China, the Americans did not foresee any serious competition. The British embassy observed in its *Monthly Report* for February that "American interest continues to be displayed in the China market in which most 'experts' express optimistic opinions." For example, Harrison Wheaton, director of the American Arbitration Association, who was shortly expected to leave for China to assist the Chinese government in establishing commercial cultivation boards, predicted that American exports to China would reach the annual value of between $500 and $600 million.[62]

The *New York Times* reported in late July that trade with China doubled in April, while Arthur Foye, president of the China-American Council of Commerce and Industry, put the total at $40 million, citing 100 companies active in Shanghai.[63] The Truman administration had been anxious to conclude a commercial.treaty with China, reflecting the strong desire of the American business community to venture into the field that had long been dominated by the British, i.e., trade *in* China.

In early 1946, as General Marshall appeared to be successful in the political field, the State Department began to pressure the Chinese to revise the proposed new Company Law. The Americans particularly chafed at Articles 7 and 292, which defined a foreign company as "a company which does business in its country of origin and establishes a branch in China." The proposed law further stipulated that corporations that do not do business in their countries of origin and operate industries and/or commercial enterprises only in China should be incorporated in accordance with local law and treated in the same way as Chinese companies.[64]

The Americans were keen to form companies in the old British "Shanghai style," that is, with guaranteed access to Chinese resources and cheap labor while at the same time retaining privileges as a "foreign company" in matters such as taxation. In early 1946, the British government found a way to circumvent this registration dilemma by encouraging British firms designated as "China companies" to register in Hongkong. The Americans did not have such an advantage; thus, they decided to approach the Chinese alone. American Chargé Walter S. Robertson reported on 3 January that "strong presentations have been made by [the] Embassy to [the] Foreign Minister, [the] President of the Legislative Yuan, and [the] Minister of Economic Affairs for modification of [the] company law with particular reference to [the] definition of foreign corporations." "Confidentially," Robertson added, "as many top officials appear to be sympathetic with our viewpoint, we are still hopeful of favorable action and do not consider it advisable to appeal direct to Gimo except as [a] last resort."[65]

The Foreign Office was greatly disturbed when the British embassy learned that the Americans had approached the Chinese without consulting with them. British Commercial Counselor Leo Lamb found the determined efforts of the American embassy astonishing. As he reported to the Foreign Office on 2 January:

> I am inclined to the opinion that American commercial interests are far more "Shanghai-minded" and insistent upon the maintenance of the protective privileges than the "Imperialistic British." I have no doubt that Americans have succeeded in having some appreciable modifications to meet their *desiderata* effected in the draft law by persistent effort.

Lamb was convinced that "the die, or rather the final draft is now set, so that it is too late to expect any further changes to meet our particular needs and desires."[66]

Although the KMT government was willing to meet the American demand, there was strong protest from Chinese business circles. As General Marshall was riding high in China, the American embassy suggested that he should use his position to intervene in the matter of the Company Law. Counselor Robert Smyth pointed out that, although General Marshall would not be in the position of interfering in an internal public legislative dispute, he could bring the weight of American influence to bear on these larger issues and "could, if necessary, refer to the fact that reasonable progress toward [a] mutually satisfactory commercial treaty is regarded as an essential condition precedent to our Government's consideration of measures for financial assistance to China."[67]

It is not clear how General Marshall took up this issue with Chiang Kai-shek, but the Americans did succeed in deleting the "doing business in country of origin" requirement. Thus, one stumbling block to American business penetration into China's domestic economy was removed. The following months witnessed a substantial increase in American capital flow into China. Arthur Foye, of the China-America Council of Commerce and Industry, declared that, "the record shows that trade does not necessarily have to wait upon establishment of complete political unity."[68]

Among the British, there remained widespread contempt for the American style of doing business in China. A typical observation was offered by British Vice-Admiral Edelston, after a trip to China in May:

"There has been quite a[n] influx of American businessmen, but, in my opinion, they are getting absolutely fed up with nothing doing [and] I think will slowly but surely disappear to leave the field to the 'old established.' " While talking to Wedemeyer at his farewell party, Edelston reported that "at least three of the most poisonous types of [American] businessmen came up and asked him [Wedemeyer] when he thought they might get any business as they were fed up." Wedemeyer replied evasively and the three then went away obviously disgruntled. According to Edelston, these frustrated businessmen then got drunk and burnt holes with their cigars in the carpet. He concluded: "If that type of specimen is going to capture the trade of China, then it is really time we packed up. . . . The Americans, by their abominable behaviour, are antagonizing the Chinese more and more."[69] The Foreign Office was, however, more cautious in judging the American business ability in China. A. L. Scott commented that "Admiral Edelston, I think, underrates American commercial enterprise. The American businessmen will not easily get 'fed up' as long as reasonable prospects of doing business exist."[70]

Despite the difficult financial situation, London took several steps to try to restore British trade in China. One was the decision to send a trade mission to China, the merit of which had been debated for some time. As a Foreign Office briefing recorded in May: "In August 1945, shortly after taking office as President of the Board of Trade, Sir Stafford Cripps came to the conclusion that, 'it would be desirable to give some tangible evidence of our interest in the industrial future of China by sending out a goodwill mission of industrialists.' [The purpose was] 'to create an impression of live interests of British industry in future trade with China despite present supply limitations and generally to counteract as far as possible American penetration." The briefing went on further: "The Treasury was at first opposed to the Mission on the ground that, as we had nothing to offer, it would only raise false hopes. . . . [But] the Foreign Office supported the Board of Trade, and the Chinese Government welcomed the Mission, and suggested September and October this year as a suitable time for the visit."[71]

Another step taken by London was to reorganize and strengthen Britain's consular service in China. Bevin believed that consular services were essential for British business success in China. As Sir Orme Sargent, permanent undersecretary at the Foreign Office, wrote in a memo dated 7 March: "The Secretary of State wished Sir Horace

Seymour's successor to review and reorganize the consular set-up in China with a view to developing and strengthening our trade connexions with China." Moreover, Bevin "feels that Anglo-Chinese trade can thus be used to reinforce our political position in China, which at present, if taken by itself, is none too strong."[72]

During a conversation between Bevin and Sir Ralph Stevenson shortly before the latter's departure for China in June, the foreign secretary pointed out that the Americans were out to capture the China market and that they had great schemes for opening up and developing China, particularly in the matter of communications. As soon as communications were improved, trade was bound to increase. Bevin, thus, emphasized:

> Our consular officers should keep their eyes open, should move about the country and should not fail to report any chance they saw for British commerce, as a result of American development of the country. We ourselves would not be in a position to take our proper share of the China Market for another three or four years. Meanwhile, we must prepare the ground and increase and expand our consular representation wherever possible.[73]

In early 1946, Hongkong once again became an irritant between London and Washington. While discussing the loan impasse, John Allison of the American embassy in London warned the Foreign Office that the American public had not forgotten about Hongkong in considering a loan to Britain, and that it might well become an issue again.[74]

The direct cause of the friction was the State Department's annoyance at reports that the Hongkong government was discriminating against American trade interests in that colony. As one report stated on 8 March: "An increasing number of complaints against the apparent practice of [the] Hongkong Government in favoring sterling bloc imports [and] unduly restricting U.S. imports through exchange control are being received. A survey of the situation indicates that they are justified."[75] In reality, however, since the end of the war, U.S. business interests had expanded greatly in Hongkong, largely lured by the prospects in China. According to a State Department assessment, while about 15 percent of the Hongkong trade was with Britain and the rest of its empire, the American share by 1946 had reached 10 percent of the total trade in the colony.[76]

Meanwhile, commercial treaty negotiations with China were resumed (these had been previously suspended by Marshall in March, while anticipating a reorganization of the Chinese government). However, it soon became clear that the reorganization would not take place. Marshall thus felt that, as an aid to his mission, negotiations for a commercial treaty with China should be resumed as soon as possible.[77]

Under heavy U.S. pressure, the Chinese government agreed to sign the treaty in November, which provided the Americans with some obvious privileges, such as the right of inland navigation, deletion of the "doing business in country of origin" requirement for foreign companies, most-favored-nation status, and so on. The treaty, however, elicited violent reactions from the Chinese press. A British report in November observed that "The Sino-American Commercial Treaty has had so bad a press here, e.g., 'the first of a new series of unequal treaties.' "[78]

Moreover, Washington made great strides in obtaining air traffic privileges in China. In September, the Chinese government was shocked by the draft of an air agreement where the Americans demanded, among other things, the granting of nine traffic points in China. A State Department report stated on 6 September: "The Chinese are concerned at the large number of international traffic points within the Chinese territory requested by the United States"; they felt that granting the nine traffic points might "seriously curtail the feeder-line business of Chinese National Airlines between other points and the international airports."[79]

The Chinese were particularly reluctant to grant the American demand for traffic points in Manchuria. Having been humiliated in front of the world by the the Big Three's Livadia Agreement in 1945, Chiang was determined to avoid any complications the concession of traffic points in Manchuria might bring about. Under the circumstances, Washington informed the American embassy in China on 14 October that, "We agree reluctantly to eliminate Mukden as an international traffic point ... but in exchange, New York is to be dropped from [the] proposed Chinese route."[80]

Washington's vigorous campaign to obtain privileges in China gave rise to widespread anti-American feelings among the Chinese. It is no surprise, therefore, that when William Pearce, an American marine corporal, allegedly raped a Peking University student on Christmas eve, the event immediately caught the tide of a generally anti-American wave throughout the country.

London clearly noted the rapid fall of American prestige in China after the signing of the commercial treaty. By comparison, there seemed to be a general improvement of Sino-British relations near year's end. The British trade mission was warmly entertained in China. Lady Cripps, wife of Sir Stafford Cripps, who was chairman of the wartime British United Aid to China, made a successful trip to China in November. To her delight she found herself popular with both the Kuomintang and the Communists. A State Department report on 17 November showed much irritation at what appeared to be "a pro-British angle in Chinese Communist anti-US propaganda." According to the report, "Chinese Communist publicity organs have taken advantage of the Yenan visit of Lady Cripps . . . to laud 'traditional' Sino-British friendships and U.K. aid to the Chinese people in the liberated [Communist] areas." The report also disclosed that, "These surprising pro-British assertions were contrasted with our alleged violation of international agreements and promise to aid China's 'dictatorial Government' to extend civil war and convert China into a colony of the United States" and a "battleground for World War III."[81]

London was further encouraged by a secret account from Colonel Gordon Harmon, the British intelligence officer who had personal connections with the Communist leaders in Yenan, of his private conversation with Mao concerning Hongkong on 31 December. Harmon quoted Mao as saying:

China has enough trouble in her hands to try and clear up [the] mess in her own country, let alone trying to rule Formosa, for us to clamour for the return of Hongkong. I am not interested in Hongkong; it has never been the subject of any discussion amongst us [i.e., the CCP leaders]. Perhaps ten, twenty or thirty years hence we may ask for a discussion regarding its return, but my attitude is that so long as your officials do not maltreat Chinese subjects in Hongkong, and so long as Chinese are not treated as inferior to others in the matter of taxation and a voice in the Government, I am not interested in Hongkong, and will certainly not allow it to be a bone of contention between your country and mine.[82]

Boosted by the success of the trade mission to China, the Labour government decided in December to form a joint parliamentary goodwill mission to China. The American embassy in London commented bitterly that, as in the case of the earlier British trade mission, the growing demand for a parliamentary goodwill mission to China was probably predicated mainly on the British desire to obtain a larger area of political and economic influence in China, which was regarded in London as being monopolized by the United States."[83]

Upon hearing the news that General Marshall had been appointed as the secretary of state, Sir Ralph Stevenson believed that chances were once again at hand for the British to play a positive role in China. As he reported to Bevin at the beginning of 1947:

> With General Marshall as Secretary of State, we can assume there will be understanding in the State Department for the situation in China but no sentimentality. . . . On the whole, however, I believe that it is the unpopularity of the Kuomintang itself which is the chief cause of the increasing unpopularity of the United States, and that the Chinese now indulge in general criticism of American policy largely because they see America as the backer of the Kuomintang.[84]

Although London had kept a low profile during the Marshall Mission, Bevin was aggressive and energetic regarding Southeast Asia. One major concern of the Foreign Office was the possible impact of Chinese policy toward Southeast Asia. This was complicated by the problem of the overseas Chinese in the region. As the long memo of December 1945 pointed out, the Chinese communities in Malaya and Burma numbered approximately two million and two hundred thousand, respectively. Under the Chinese nationality law, "any person of Chinese race on the father's side is a Chinese national, no matter how many generations his family may have been domiciled abroad." During the last ten years, the report continued, the Kuomintang had been propagating party ideas such as this. "It is an idea of political and economic penetration based apparently on the conception of a restored and enlarged Chinese Empire."[85] In other words, most overseas Chinese in the region might give allegiance to the Chinese government instead of to the colonial administrations in their respective countries. The prospect of a Communist China might pose a nightmare for these colonies, but a KMT-ruled China would not eliminate the same problem.

Malaya was of particular importance to Britain because of its rich raw materials. Most coolies working in the field were ethnic Chinese. Thus, the overseas Chinese issue also had a bearing upon the British neutrality in China's domestic dispute. The American embassy believed this to be the case behind the silence of the British during the Marshall Mission. According to Robert Smyth, counselor at Nanking, "It seems apparent that [the] British, though they have by no means given up hope of reestablishing or even extending their commercial interests in China, have found it necessary and expedient to abdicate their political interest in favor of the United States." Smyth believed that, "The primary importance of China to Great Britain now would seem to be the influence and weight of Chinese policy on the colonial areas of the Far East" and "The most important factor in this connection is the great resurgence of Chinese nationalism which is basically opposed to the continuance or extension of Western influence, except insofar as it may be used by China to advance its own interests." According to Smyth, "This nationalism finds expression in the outspoken sympathy with and support of the aspirations of various Far Eastern colonial peoples for complete self-determination."[86]

On the issue of Siam, Anglo-American relations continued to deteriorate after the Americans succeeded in opposing the rice levy clause imposed by London upon Siam. In January, Lord Mountbatten took his revenge by pressuring the Siamese government to turn the occasion of the Siamese peace celebration into an event honoring the British. A State Department report commented that,

> Energetic British initiative succeeded in partly transforming the enthusiastic Siamese peace celebration of January 18–20 into a state reception honoring Mountbatten and British occupation troops. [Charles] Yost reports British pressure to discriminate against U.S. and other Allied officials in the formal proceedings.[87]

Having failed to impose a rice levy, London demanded that the Siamese surrender "surplus rice" in order to meet the food crisis throughout the region. The Siamese government refused to comply with the British demand and turned once again to Washington for help. As far as the State Department was concerned, the "surplus rice" did not really exist. Charles Yost, American chargé at Bangkok, reported to Acheson on 24 May:

> The British policy was motivated by (1) a desire, which proved wholly misguided in its application, to restore British prestige in Siam and (2) a

feeling that in view of the depressed state of postwar Britain her commercial and financial position must be strengthened by every possible means. The Treasury of course played a vital role in the latter connection and was chiefly responsible for the free rice clause.[88]

Lord Killearn, special commissioner to Southeast Asia, considered the American policy on Siam to be detrimental to British interests. As he reported to Bevin on 17 March: "As regards Thailand, surely it is essential that something must be done immediately and effectively to counteract American infiltration" and "to build up [the] British position which has always been traditional and is in danger of being undermined."[89]

Throughout 1946 the United States was also intensely interested in the Burmese situation and played a strong hand in the Burmese cause of gaining independence from Great Britain. While facing General Aung San's demand for independence, the Labour government tried to solve the problem after the Ceylon and India models. Washington made great efforts to undermine the British position. On 22 April, Glenn Abbey, American consul at Rangoon, reported: "The problem of Burma does not appear to be comparable to that of India and Ceylon. The latter countries have factional troubles," which "are largely missing in Burma. Moreover, a continuing reconstruction program under British control will be difficult" as the Burmese "are extremely chary of what have been termed 'continuing obligations' of the H.M.G." Hence, Abbey suggested that, "It would be a solution acceptable to most Burmese, if the U.S., in pursuance of its interests in expansion of opportunities for foreign investment in Burma and the economic development of the country, . . . should participate in some way with the Burmese and British in the reconstruction of the country, either before or after independence is achieved."[90]

London continued to drag its feet on the Burma issue. In October, the Burmese threatened armed rebellion. American Consul General Erle Packer reported to Washington: "We should undoubtedly gain prestige with [the] Burmese generally and particularly with Aung San and company were we first in the field to arrange exchange of diplomatic representatives with Burma to our advantage in many ways." Packer believed that there would be "unfavorable British reaction" to this move, for Britain "which in post-war period has reversed prewar attitude and has been less liberal (perhaps because pressure was less) in her treatment of Burma than of India might resent our pushing [the] matter."[91]

Nevertheless, American pressure did result in a reluctant decision by London to invite a Burmese delegation headed by Aung San to London to discuss Burma's future. This was tantamount to de facto recognition of Burma's independent status.

Despite many reports from the region asking for action, Bevin, however, was less preoccupied by squabbles with Washington over places such as Siam or Burma. The foreign secretary preferred to think in broad strategic terms by treating the region as a whole and seeking possibilities for collective security arrangements. As he told Sir Ralph Stevenson in June, "the food problem in Southeast Asia was now occupying most of Lord Killearn's time, but the eventual task of the holder of that office would be the coordination of British interests in Asia." This, he hoped, "would grow naturally out of the present short-term arrangement for dealing with the food crisis." Bevin also explained that the special commissioner's functions should embrace the whole of the Far East and that he "had in mind the possible appointment later on of a Minister of State or a similar official, with the authority to undertake these wide powers and advise the Government on general policy in that part of the world."[92]

In July, Bevin made the choice for the position he envisioned. Although not of minister-of-state rank, Bevin's choice was Malcolm MacDonald, son of Ramsey MacDonald. Because Bevin's strategic vision for this region had not been put into a concrete and clearly defined form, there was considerable confusion as to MacDonald's official title. After intense debate over different titles, MacDonald was to become "commissioner general-Southeast Asia," a title that was as vague as its substance and no better than that of Lord Killearn.[93] Nevertheless, despite British preoccupation with Europe, the fuss over MacDonald's appointment indicated deep concern by the foreign secretary over the region's future.

Anglo-American relations in China appeared less in conflict during the Marshall Mission. One reason was that London had kept silent over the U.S. mediation efforts. But their different geopolitical interests and world views continued to separate the two erstwhile allies. The mutual suspicion did not fade away. Near the end of the Marshall Mission, Britain again tried to reenter the China scene, only to receive another rebuff from Washington.

For Washington, the year 1946 was no less frustrating because of the failure of the Marshall Mission. General Marshall, of course, did not fail to live up to his instructions, which set a policy of supporting Chiang Kai-shek in the event of the breakdown of the mediation, no matter who was to blame. However, Marshall did gain considerable knowledge about the situation. The China lesson he learned would become decisive in American China policy for the next few years. The gist of this lesson was that China was a bottomless pit that no American resources available could fill.

Notes

1. *FRUS*, 1945, 7:770.
2. Leonard Mosley, *Marshall—Hero of Our Time*, p. 360.
3. *FRUS*, 1946, 9:119.
4. U.K. PRO, FO Minute by Butler, FO371 53564/F6125/25/10.
5. U.K. PRO, "British Foreign Policy in the Far East," 31 December 1945, CAB 134/280.
6. U.K. PRO, FO800 513/US46/13.
7. U.K. PRO, Berlin to FO, 1 February 1945, FO800 513/US/46/27.
8. U.K. PRO, FO800 512/US/45/67.
9. U.K. PRO, Churchill to Bevin, most secret, 21 November 1945, FO800 512/45110.
10. Ibid., Bevin to Churchill, 29 November 1945.
11. Walter Lippmann, *Collier's Magazine*, 26 January 1946.
12. *Economist*, 20 February 1946.
13. U.K. PRO, Wright to Mason, 25 January 1946, FO371 51639/AN/311/15/45.
14. *Chicago Tribune*, 29 December 1945.
15. *New York Daily News*, 26 December 1945.
16. Michael Foot's column, *Daily Herald* (Labour Party), 1 January 1946.
17. NAUS, Decimal Files, Winant to Byrnes, 14 December 1945, microfilm 711–93/12–1445.
18. NAUS, Daily Staff Officers Summary, 21 January 1946, top secret, box 3.
19. The Eight-and-a-third Project consisted in the formation of eight-and-one-third air groups equipped and trained by the United States, while the Thirty-nine-Division Project involved providing the equipment and training for thirty-nine divisions of the Chinese Army by the United States.
20. U.K. PRO, Seymour to Bevin, 1 February 1946, FO371 53561/1736/25/10.
21. NAUS, Daily Staff Officers Summary, 26 February 1946, box 3.
22. Ibid., 27 February 1946.
23. Marshall to Truman, *FRUS*, 1946, 9:541.
24. U.K. PRO, Note by Vice-Air Marshal Forster to FO, 14 March 1946, FO371 53562/F3824.

25. Ibid.

26. U.K. PRO, Seymour to Bevin, 25 February 1946, FO371 53562/F2919/25/10.

27. U.K. PRO, Carton de Wiart Correspondence, 15 January 1946, CAB 127/28.

28. NAUS, Daily Staff Officers Summary, 25 February 1946, box 3.

29. U.K. PRO, FO Memo, February 1946, FO800 461/FE.

30. U.K. PRO, FO Memo, 26 April 1946, FO371 54069/F6864/61.

31. *FRUS*, 1946, 10:816.

32. U.K. PRO, Seymour to Bevin, 14 March 1946, FO371 53563/F4504/25/10.

33. NAUS, Incoming Classified Messages, Marshall Mission Files, 6 October 1946, box 14.

34. NAUS, Daily Staff Officers Summary, 31 October 1946, box 4.

35. Ibid., 16 April 1946, box 3.

36. NAUS, OSS Report, R & A Report, 20 February 1946, no. 3558.

37. See *Nie Rongzhen huiyilu* (Memoirs of Marshal Nie Rongzhen), p. 393, and *Ye Fei huiyilu* (Memoirs of General Ye Fei), p. 564.

38. Winston S. Churchill, *Winston S. Churchill: His Complete Speeches, 1897–1963*, pp. 7291–92.

39. *FRUS*, 1946, 9:528.

40. *FRUS*, 1946, 9:515–16.

41. Ibid., p. 822.

42. NAUS, Eisenhower to Marshall (private letter), 28 May 1946, Marshall Mission Files, top secret (eyes only), box 11.

43. *FRUS*, 1946, 9:1038.

44. Ibid., p. 604.

45. NAUS, Carter to Marshall, 5 September 1946, Marshall Mission Files, box 1.

46. NAUS, Marshall to Truman, December 1946, ibid., box 2.

47. U.K. PRO, Berlin to FO, 8 March 1946, FO371 51624/AN649.

48. Ibid., 9 March 1946.

49. U.K. PRO, Attlee to Churchill, 13 March 1946, FO800 513/US 1946.

50. U.K. PRO, "British Policy in China," secret paper by Kitson, May 1946, FO371 53565/F7701/25/10.

51. U.K. PRO, Memo of Conversation by Stevenson, 13 June 1946, FO371 53565/F8999/25/G/10.

52. U.K. PRO, Killearn to Sargent, 11 June 1946, FO371 53565/F16334/25/10.

53. U.K. PRO, Dening to Stevenson, 17 November 1946, FO371 53570/F16334/25/10.

54. U.K. PRO, Nanking to London, FO371 53571/F16592/25/10.

55. Marshall to Truman, 21 November 1946, *FRUS*, 1946, 10:557.

56. Ibid., pp. 559–61.

57. NAUS, Marshall Mission Files, 29 November 1946, box 2.

58. U.K. PRO, Wallinger to FO, 16 December 1945, FO371 46186/F11850/57/10.

59. *FRUS*, 1946, 10:737.

60. U.K. PRO, "British Foreign Policy in the Far East," 31 December 1945, CAB 134/280.

61. *Wall Street Journal*, 29 November 1946.

62. U.K. PRO, *Monthly Report* for February from the Nanking Embassy, FO371 53563/F4584/25/10.

63. *New York Times*, 25 July 1946.

64. *FRUS*, 1946, 10:1298.

65. Ibid., p. 1296.

66. U.K. PRO, Lamb to Kitson, 2 January 1946, FO371 53641/F1451/110/10.

67. *FRUS*, 1946, 10:1301.

68. *New York Times*, 25 July 1946.

69. U.K. PRO, Edelston to Admiralty, 7 May 1946, FO371 53641/F1451/110/10.

70. Ibid., Scott's Minute.

71. U.K. PRO, FO371 53565/8984/25/10.

72. Ibid., Note by Sargent, 7 March 1946.

73. U.K. PRO, Memo of Conversation by Stevenson, 13 June 1946, FO371 53565/F8989/225/10.

74. U.K. PRO, 4 February 1946, FO371 54052/F2129/61.

75. NAUS, Daily Staff Officers Summary, 8 March 1946, box 3.

76. NAUS, 19 March 1946, lot files 110, box 10.

77. NAUS, Daily Staff Officers Summary, 14 May 1946, box 3.

78. U.K. PRO, Weekly Summary, Nanking Embassy, 30 November 1946, FO371 53571/F17289/25/10.

79. NAUS, Daily Staff Officers Summary, 7 November 1946, box 4.

80. Ibid., 14 October 1946.

81. Ibid., 7 November 1946.

82. U.K. PRO, Wallinger to Kitson, FO371 63317/F1520/76/10.

83. NAUS, Daily Staff Officers Summary, 7 November 1946, box 4.

84. U.K. PRO, Wallinger to Kitson, FO371 63317/F1520/76/10.

85. U.K. PRO, "British Foreign Policy in the Far East," 31 December 1946, CAB 134/280.

86. NAUS, Decimal Files, Smyth to Byrnes, 5 July 1946, 711–41/7–546.

87. NAUS, Daily Staff Officers Summary, 30 January 1946, box 3.

88. NAUS, Decimal Files, "Evolution of British Policy toward Siam," paper by Yost to Acheson, 25 May 1946, 741.92/5–2546.

89. U.K. PRO, Killearn to FO, 17 March 1946, FO800/FE/46/6.

90. Abbey to Byrnes, 22 April 1946, *FRUS*, 1946, 7:2.

91. Packer to Washington, 30 November 1946, *FRUS*, 1946, 7:7.

92. U.K. PRO, Memo of Conversation by Stevenson, 13 June 1946, FO371 53565/F8999/25/G10.

93. U.K. PRO, Far Eastern Committee, 19 July 1946, CAB 134/279.

4

China Disintegrating?

From the U.S. government's point of view, the most important result of General Marshall's mission to China was a more realistic understanding of the Chinese situation by the administration. Throughout 1947, one salient question was raised in both London and Washington: Would China disintegrate? The policymakers in Washington were faced with a dilemma: on the one hand, the Americans could not afford to let China drift in an undesirable direction; on the other hand, as General Marshall had found out, the costs required to alter the course of events in China were unbearable for the U.S. political system. After General Marshall assumed office at the State Department, American policy toward China was a cautious one aimed at limiting U.S. engagement in the inevitable Chinese civil war. It reflected concerns long maintained by the department's China Service, headed by John Carter Vincent. During the civil war the Marshall-Vincent China policy had the backing of the president and triumphed in each successive debate over China within the administration. The central element of this policy was the judgment that Chiang's regime was a bottomless pit, which rendered an all-out American commitment impracticable. This simple cost-benefit analysis characterized the Marshall-Vincent policy as a middle-of-the-road approach. In other words, it was a policy of overt disengagement but covert support for Chiang on a limited scale. While this policy may have been sound in terms of the American national interest, it inevitably incurred particular political problems in the United States. On the Right, Henry Luce's China aid campaign was vigorous and effective. More importantly, it began to attract sympathizers on Capitol Hill. Republican foes of the administration increasingly realized that China could be used as a strong political card. On the Left, continued support for Chiang was regarded as direct intervention in China's internal affairs. The Marshall-Vincent policy was, thus, unpopular on both ends of the political spectrum. The actual effect was much worse: this limited China policy appeared weak and indecisive. It is not surprising that a major domestic political battle would be fought over China for the next few years.

Abroad, the Marshall-Vincent line could not find many sympathizers in Great Britain, which was becoming the most important ally for the United States to engage the Soviets in a Cold War. This is ironic considering that Britain had traditionally called for a more flexible and realistic China policy—one that was tantamount to letting the Chinese stew in their own juice.

Yet in 1947 Britain began to hope for a more active role by the United States in China as soon as Washington shifted priorities. For London, China's disintegration was nothing new. The worst nightmare was a united China hostile to the West. Active American intervention during the Chinese civil strife could prevent that eventuality. The old British dream of a weak China did not easily fade away.

As civil war began in China, London saw the real possibility of an inconclusive armed conflict, since the Americans were unwilling to pull out of China completely. Thus, the best hope for British interests lay in Chiang's ability to at least hold on to the Yangtze Valley. Whether or not this would mean the actual disintegration of China was not London's immediate concern. As in the case of the Taiping and Boxer Rebellions, the British believed in their ability to make deals with the Chinese who had de facto control over the Yangtze Valley. London deplored the inadequate American aid to Chiang and branded the Marshall-Vincent policy, paradoxically, as letting the Chinese stew in their own juice.

As a matter of policy, there was little evidence indicating that London was actively promoting the north-south division of China. The U.S. administration was, however, alarmed from time to time by reports that Britain was encouraging a "Southern Separatist Movement" in two Chinese provinces adjacent to Hongkong. Upon becoming secretary of state, George Marshall was faced with strong pressure from the powerful China lobby urging all-out aid to Chiang. Within the administration, the China lobby got a strong hearing from the military establishment. It was apparent that both the secretaries of war and the Navy did not see eye to eye with Marshall over China. At a meeting of the State-War-Navy Coordination Committee (SWNCC) on 12 February, Marshall insisted that the most important Kuomintang civilian and military leaders had overestimated their ability to handle the Communist problem. He also said he had been continually pressed for U.S. financial assistance to the central government. Marshall stated further that "it was most difficult if not impossible to convince the Generalissimo that China could only be saved by drastic political and military reforms."[1]

Although Marshall agreed to provide economic aid to China, he was unwilling to give Chiang direct military assistance, which in his opinion would only encourage the KMT diehards to initiate the war. Secretary of War Robert Patterson wrote Marshall on 26 February: "I find it very difficult to distinguish clearly between military aid which might contribute to or encourage civil war, and military or any other type of economic or material aid which would not have such an effect."[2] Marshall replied in a letter drafted by Vincent that, "It would be manifestly unrealistic to withhold arms from National Government forces if such action condemned them to a degree of military anemia which would make possible a successful offensive by the Communist forces." However, "it does not appear that our withholding munitions will result in such an eventuality in the next few months." He added that, "There is a strong doubt in my mind that, even if the United States were willing to give a large amount of munitions and support to the Chinese Government, it would be unable within a reasonable time to crush the Chinese Communist Armies and Party."[3] Apparently, Marshall did not object to military aid to Chiang in principle, but he intended to use the withholding of such aid as a political weapon to press Chiang for the necessary domestic reform.

London was anxious to know what the new American direction in China was to be after the Marshall Mission, but Washington continued to be indifferent to British concerns. In a top-secret brief for Bevin dated 27 February regarding the approaching Big Three conference of foreign ministers in Moscow, George Kitson, head of the China Department, stated: "The Secretary of State will no doubt wish to discuss

China informally and confidentially with General Marshall. . . . It will be useful in particular to try to ascertain future U.S. policy towards China, and whether, e.g., the Americans contemplate giving some measure of material support to the present Government if only to save China from the economic collapse which now threatens it." Kitson went on further: "Our latest information from the State Department suggests that the U.S. may be unwilling to afford any large-scale assistance to China and that they will simply watch development for the time being."[4]

Earlier in February, Bevin tried to invite Marshall to stop by London en route to Moscow. Knowing that Washington was usually suspicious of any suggestion that might indicate to the Russians a "ganging-up" against Moscow, Bevin let George Kitson inform the Americans that China was the only topic on his mind. Everett Drumright, first secretary at the American embassy, reported to Washington after Kitson extended Bevin's invitation on 7 February: "Mr. Kitson said that Mr. Bevin is anxious to have a talk with Secretary Marshall on the situation in China prior to the Moscow Conference if possible" and "I expressed . . . that while Secretary Marshall would doubtless be glad to exchange views with Mr. Bevin on the question of China, I doubted whether Secretary Marshall would come to London for that purpose . . . [because] such a trip . . . would afford the Soviets a further opportunity to level the accusation that the United States and Great Britain were 'ganging up' on the Soviet Union."[5]

At the Moscow Conference, Bevin had a chance to talk with Marshall about China, and he was deeply disturbed when Marshall told him that it was only a matter of time before the Communists were in a position to take over all of China north of the Yangtze Valley. However, Marshall declined to outline what the future U.S. policy would be if such an event took place.[6]

For Marshall, there was good reason to wait and see. In early 1947, Chiang's troops seemed to be meeting with some success. In March, Chiang's seizure of Yenan, long-time headquarters of the Communists, was a pleasant surprise to Marshall when he was attending the Moscow Conference. Although KMT troops seized nothing but an empty city after the Communists had organized an orderly retreat, the Americans saw it as a great boost to Chiang's reputation. Even Ambassador Stuart overestimated its significance. According to Stuart, this victory (a) it would have a salutary effect on "third parties," (b) would discourage adherents of the Communist Party throughout the country, and (c) it would sow dissension between the Chinese Communists such as Mao Tse-tung and the more Sovietized ones such as Li Li-san.[7]

With this victory, Stuart thought that the day might come when the United States would treat China the same as Greece and Turkey. The delighted ambassador told his British colleague Sir Ralph Stevenson "most confidentially" that Marshall had asked him for his personal opinion on the application to China of the policy implied in President Truman's statement on aid to Greece and Turkey.[8] Chiang Kai-shek's government even went so far as to claim that only two more months were needed to defeat and destroy the main Communist armies.

The British, however, did not see the seizure of Yenan as a turning point in Chiang's fortunes. In fact, a London *Times* editorial dated 29 March called the seizure a "Pyrrhic victory." In late February, Bevin instructed Lord Inverchapel, British ambassador to Washington, to seek a meeting with Secretary Marshall in order to ascertain whether the United States meant to wash its hands of China. Instead of meeting Marshall, Lord Inverchapel was received by John Carter Vincent, who explained that the abandonment of mediation did not mean a change in U.S. policy toward China and that "certainly there was no intention of adopting an attitude of 'let the Chinese stew in their own juice.' " However, Vincent explained, General Marshall was likewise unlikely to veer toward a policy of all-out assistance for Chiang Kai-shek. Vincent argued that it would be impossible for the Communists to take over the whole of China and that, in any case, Chiang had never been able to control the outlying Chinese regions. When asked whether the State Department had any indications of increased Soviet activity in China, Vincent replied that he thought the Russians were "well satisfied with the present conditions in China: a state of turmoil was what they wanted."[11]

The Foreign Office was not convinced by Vincent's explanations. A. L. Scott bluntly concluded that "all this amounts to telling the Chinese to stew in their own juice." On 25 March, the British embassy in Nanking sent a long telegram disputing Vincent's thesis. It stated: "We have been thinking a good deal here about Vincent's view on the situation in China. . . . We do not see eye to eye with him . . . that 'the weakness of the Government might lead to loss of control of outlying districts.' We think that this is greatly understating the possibilities. . . . In our view separatism would start much closer to the centre, very probably with the Canton bloc." The telegram went on to say that while it was well beyond the power of the Communists to take complete and immediate advantage of the chaotic state in China, the CCP would obviously set about extending their power wherever they could and in time might be as successful as the KMT. On the other hand, the British embassy noted, it was not to Britain's advantage that the KMT hold undisputed rule over China because fundamentally they were just as hostile to foreign interests as the Communists were to Western democracy. Following this logic, the telegram concluded:

> In all circumstances it seems to us that the best that we can hope for, both from the point of view of the Chinese people and of our own interests, is to secure in China the same kind of balance between the Communists and non-Communists that we hope to maintain in the rest of the world, i.e., an armed peace if nothing better can be achieved— with neither side in the ascendant.

Finally, the telegram suggested: "The first step towards attaining this aim is obviously to stop the civil war. The only country which is physically capable of bringing pressure to bear on both sides in China, and thus tip the scales as required to secure some kind of equilibrium, is the U.S.A." However, "So far as the KMT is concerned this pressure would be in the economic field and so far as the Communists are concerned it would consist of the threat to give material support to the KMT. Such pressure obviously could not be used openly as it would then defeat its own object."[13] Thus, from the standpoint of British interests, Vincent's attitude seemed short-sighted and unconstructive.

In arguing that increased American aid was essential to effect a de facto division of China, this telegram reverted to the old British theory about China's disintegration. As a policy matter, the idea was hardly practicable. London had to realize that the old dream could not become reality unless Washington thought along the same line. Nevertheless, this traditional British inclination to deal with China region by region instead of as a whole had sympathizers within the administration. Dean Rusk, for example, championed international guardianship or trusteeship for Manchuria. As director of the Office of Special Political Affairs, Rusk wrote a memo in October saying that, "it would be reasonably simple to obtain United Nations blessing for a declaration by China proposing the early independence of Manchuria," and then to solve the Manchuria problem by "Great Power guardianship or trustee-ship."[14]

Congressman Mike Mansfield proposed to preserve China's territorial integrity through a "Four-Power Pact," along the lines of the Nine-Power Pact of 1922. The Foreign Office thought this plan highly impracticable. A. L. Scott commented: "Mr. Mansfield's suggestion . . . is entirely unreal. China today is not the China of 1921–22, she is no longer in a state of foreign 'tutelage' and is hardly likely to sit at a conference where she would be outnumbered by 3 to 1."[15]

U.S. Secretary of the Navy James Forrestal went so far as to propose a new "Dawes Plan" for China. In a letter to Marshall dated 27 February, Forrestal suggested that a high-powered economic mission be sent to China headed by another "Jean Monnet"—referring to the French financier who headed the consultative committee organized in China by Chinese Minister of Finance T. V. Soong in 1933.[16]

London, on the other hand, was concerned with the possible aftermath of a physical disintegration of China. In July, there were intense discussions on the subject within the Labour government. The War Department prepared a top-secret paper entitled "Will China Disintegrate?" Dated 7 July, the paper concluded that

(a)   the central government would shortly lose its already precarious hold on Manchuria, which could well become a Russian puppet state;

(b)   Northeastern China, down to at least the Yellow River, seemed likely to come under Communist control as a Chinese Communist state;

(c)   South China and the western provinces might establish their independence under provincial warlords;

(d)   Formosa might make a bid for independence; and

(e)   the threatened loss of territory to the Communists might be a factor intensifying the central government's interest in China's claims to territories bordering Southwest China.

The Foreign Office was more cautious about the War Department's predictions. A. L. Scott, acting head of the China Department, thought that the War Department's theory harked back to Lord Charles Beresford, who at the turn of the century wrote the book *The Breaking Up of the Chinese Empire*. However, convinced that Beresford's well-known view no longer applied, Scott warned that even if China were divided into two, "the inherent Chinese xenophobia will no doubt be played up by both Governments." Moreover, he pointed out that "whereas non-Communist China would largely be under Euro-American influences, the outlook for foreign missionary enterprise and commercial activities in Communist China would be practically non-existent."[17]

Since early May, the State Department had been receiving reports from various sources that the British were encouraging a "Southern Separatist Movement," allegedly led by General Li Chi-shen, a former military leader in Southern China and rival to Chiang Kai-shek. On 3 May, Monnet Davis, American consul general at Shanghai, reported to Washington:

> At [a] dinner given for Tu Yueh-sheng[18] who returned recently from Hongkong, a business associate of his stated that an understanding has been reached between the British Hongkong and General Li Chi-shen, former leader of the Kwangsi Clique, for mutual political and military assistance. The reported arrangement apparently anticipates [the] possible collapse of [the] National Government in which case the Kwangsi Clique would hope to dominate Southern China.[19]

On 2 June, American Consul General Thomas Bowman reported an interview in Canton by consular officer Elmer Newton with General Chang Fa-kuei (Chiang's representative in Kwangtung Province) in which the general complained that "Chinese citizens whom we want to try and imprison can get easily certificates as British subjects in Hongkong," and that "British policy is to delay the recovery of China . . . especially South China, to keep it prostrate."[20]

In May Ambassador Stuart reported that Chiang Kai-shek issued a personal protest against the harboring of Li Chi-shen in Hongkong on the grounds that the latter was engaged in conspiring against the regime in Kwangtung. According to Stuart, "Stevenson apparently replied by defining the British Government attitude towards right of political asylum and mentioned [the] British Government's action in the case of Sun Yat-sen."[21] This was, of course, a clever response to remind Chiang that Republican China's founding father and Chiang's brother-in-law, Dr. Sun Yat-sen, was protected by the British government during his anti-Manchu activities in British territories at the turn of the century.

Meanwhile, the strong American suspicions about British activities in southern China were reinforced in June, when the British government told the Truman administration that, in light of civil disorder in China, the British had to send a naval fleet to protect British nationals and property. Britain's desire to invoke the specter of "gunboat policy" was suggested by Leo Lamb, minister at the Nanking embassy, who reported to London on 24 May that the salient conclusions reached were: (1) with the passing of the "gunboat era" as the result of the 1943 Sino-British Treaty, the British were logically compelled to depend in general upon the Chinese authorities for safety and protection, and (2) at the same time, things could happen so that the British had no alternative but to intervene actively on behalf of their nationals.[22] To Washington, this kind of proposal was preposterous. As Secretary Marshall informed Ambassador Stuart in an abbreviated telegram on 24 June: "Indicating he was acting under instructions [from] his Government [a] member [of the] British Embassy staff [in] Washington has orally informed [the] Dept [that the] British Govt [was] concerned over [the] situation in China, particularly [in] Shanghai, and had authorized its Ambassador [in] Nanking and [the] Consul-General [in] Shanghai with [the] concurrence [of the] Admiralty, to appeal to [the] commander [of the] British Pacific Fleet for warships to be sent [to] Chinese ports in [the] event of civil disturbances [that] endangered British lives and property." Marshall went on to convey that, according to the State Department, the U.S. embassy had given no indication of serious concern over the welfare of U.S. citizens in China and that the department, while concerned over the unrest, had not felt the situation sufficiently alarming to warrant the preparation of such a plan.[23]

As Chiang Kai-shek was anxiously waiting for the American decision on China aid, Ambassador Stuart advised him to make a peace offensive, which would appeal not only to the U.S. Congress but also to the Chinese people. The generalissimo, however, responded by issuing a provocative message condemning the Communists. The reason why Chiang took Stuart's advice lightly was that the China lobby had long convinced Chiang that Stuart, as Ambassador Stevenson reported to London, "was just Marshall's temporary window dressing to be discarded at any moment." Stuart's naiveté was not appreciated in Washington, and even his right-hand man in Nanking, Minister Counselor Walton Butterworth, "thinks any such step would merely result in stiffening the Communist attitude and that Chiang Kai-shek should wait until a sufficiently definite military success has been attained."[24] Apparently, the Americans still harbored great hopes that Chiang would be able to defeat the Communists.

In August, General Wedemeyer was sent on a fact-finding mission to China. He later confirmed that the British were lending moral and possibly monetary support to the separatist movement represented by General Li Chi-shen, who was then based in Hongkong. Wedemeyer suggested that "appropriate agencies be set in motion with a view to clarification."[25]

A few days later, Raymond Ludden, first secretary at the American embassy in Nanking, reported the following to Wedemeyer after a tour of southern China:

> There has been no substantive proof put forth that the British are engaged in any such activity and it is unlikely that any such proof ever will be obtained. However, one must not lose sight of the fact that a strong and united China is not in the immediate British interests vis-à-vis Hongkong, the British will employ delaying tactics for as long as possible and it would therefore be in their immediate interests to have a local regime in effective control of south China friendly to them.

Ludden further pointed out that "It is inconceivable that the British are unaware of the trend of events in north China and Manchuria and therefore they may well be mending their fences in south China with a view to the protection of substantial British interests in the area and the development of overseas trade which they so badly need at [the] present time."[26]

Meanwhile, in North China and Manchuria, Chiang's military fortune deteriorated considerably. Since the U.S. government had previously equipped Chiang's troops with American weapons and supplies, the administration in Washington had no choice but to recommence supplying munitions to Chiang. Thus, the overt American neutral stand, reflected by withholding the provision of military materials to China, officially ended in April 1947 when the State Department decided to lift the ban. Dean Acheson explained this action on 2 April, saying that the complete withholding of ammunition might impair the defensive effectiveness of the Chinese Army.[27] Besides pure military necessity, there was another political objective in the lifting of the ban on ammunition to China. Acheson told Stuart on 15 April that Washington hoped to "seize [the] occasion to demonstrate to [the] Communists that their hostile action merely resulted in [the] release of ammunition to [the] National Government."[28]

The British had grave doubts about any prospect of a KMT victory in view of the limited U.S. aid to Chiang's troops. From London's point of view, China could either be saved by all-out American support, or be left alone to disintegrate. The policy of limited support for Chiang would achieve neither result. Although a Communist victory was still a remote prospect in 1947, London feared that this limited policy would strengthen the Communist hand. Ambassador Stevenson reported to Bevin on 30 April: "It seems very doubtful whether Chiang Kai-shek, unaided, can score [a] sufficiently marked military success over the Communists during the summer, and if he fails, a more or less disintegration of the regime seems likely." Nevertheless, Stevenson hastened to add, "this will not mean a Communist China, it will mean a return to the days of native war lords."[29]

On 26 May, General Marshall decided that the export ban on arms to China should also be lifted. As Vincent recorded: "The Secretary desires that the necessary steps be taken to remove the prohibition established on 29 July 1946, on the issuance of export licenses covering the shipment of arms to China. It is his wish that the Chinese be given normal commercial access to the arms market in this country."[30]

However, Marshall remained reluctant to provide Chiang with large-scale direct military aid. As he told the president in June:

> American military assistance which enables the National armies to defeat the Chinese Communist armies would have to be on a very large scale and would lead to our direct participation in the Civil War. We would probably have to take over direction of Chinese military operations and administration and remain in China for [an] indefinite period.[31]

On 19 June, Chiang Kai-shek summoned Ambassador Stuart, telling him for the first time that the military situation in Manchuria was hopeless; Chiang asserted that he had realized this fact as recently as 16 June. Although the China lobby continued to claim that Chiang's forces could wipe out the Communists in a few months with sufficient U.S. aid, the American government was greatly alarmed.[32] In July, Chiang announced a general mobilization and the civil war officially broke out. Pressured by the pro-Chiang forces in Washington, Marshall had to make it clear that the U.S. government would be on Chiang's side but without an all-out commitment. As a clever political move, Marshall sent Wedemeyer to China on a fact-finding mission. Since Wedemeyer was considered pro-Chiang and trusted by the generalissimo, the mission was aimed at silencing political opposition to the administration's policy. Moreover, Marshall used the Wedemeyer Mission to delay action in supporting Chiang. Back in June, the Joint Chiefs of Staff (JCS) had concluded that U.S. security interests required that China be kept free from Soviet domination; otherwise all of Asia would probably pass into the sphere of the USSR. And unless the Chinese national government was given sufficient military assistance to effectively resist Communist expansion in China, the Joint Chiefs of Staff added, that government would collapse, thus terminating the single unified opposition to Soviet expansionist aims in Asia.[33]

Marshall completely disagreed with the JCS view. As he told Robert Lovett, undersecretary of state, on 2 July: "I felt as did Vincent that the Chiefs of Staff paper was not quite realistic and solutions were offered which were somewhat impracticable, particularly as to implementation in China." Marshall went on to say that, "for about two weeks I have had in mind the probable desirability of sending Wedemeyer to China with a few assistants to make a survey of the situation and to report back [at] as early a date as possible."[34] The State Department directive to Wedemeyer issued and signed by President Truman emphasized that Wedemeyer's task was to find facts, not to make any commitment.[35]

The Wedemeyer Mission came as a surprise to London. Ambassador Stevenson commented on the astonishing way in which the appointment of the Wedemeyer Mission was handled by the U.S. government. But London had no clue as to the real purpose of the mission. George Kitson could do nothing more than speculate that, "It rather confirms what we have suspected for some time, namely that decisions on China are taken by Mr. Marshall himself, usually without consultation with the State Department or the US Embassy in China."[36]

After the British embassy in Washington approached the State Department on this subject, Vincent explained the motivation of the mission in terms of the numerous reports that the Soviet authorities were giving material aid to the Communists. While U.S. foreign service officers had found no evidence that this was so, General Marshall thought an experienced general should ascertain the facts. Moreover, Vincent indicated skepticism about the effectiveness of continued military aid to Chiang because, as he sarcastically commented, "about 50 per cent of the material sent to the forward zones was immediately lost to the Communists."[37]

The Foreign Office did not like the Marshall-Vincent policy, which was regarded as a policy of drifting and indecision. George Kitson pointed out on 27 July that what the Americans did not see was the fact that "large-scale American military and economic assistance is now the only hope of pulling Nationalist China together and enabling her to resist effectively the tide of Communist infiltration."[38] In the long run, London believed, China's disintegration was a "normal state of affairs." Leo Lamb, British minister at Nanking, told Philip Sprouse, political adviser to the Wedemeyer Mission, on 30 July: "The present situation in China seemed hopeless. . . . A study of Chinese history during the past century would indicate that we are perhaps merely returning to a normal situation in China and that comparative peace in the 1930s was abnormal."[39] What Lamb suggested was that the United States should either let the Chinese fight it out themselves or save Chiang with all-out U.S. aid.

General Wedemeyer carried out his directive with vigor. The report of his mission, though recommending military support to Chiang, surprised everyone with its devastating attack on the KMT regime. In fact, Wedemeyer's high-handed manner alienated not only the Nationalist Chinese, but also American Ambassador Stuart. The irritated ambassador confided to Sir Ralph Stevenson that Wedemeyer embarrassed him greatly by canceling a dinner party that Madame Chiang and the Chinese premier were to have attended, only because Chiang himself claimed to be ill. More interestingly, Stuart also told his British colleague about a sensational incident involving a "Wedemeyer list." According to Stuart, during the farewell conversation with Chiang, Wedemeyer accused the central government of not mobilizing large amounts of private Chinese holdings abroad consisting of foreign exchange and gold. This was an extremely sensitive issue, for it was well known that Chiang's family members got enormously rich through the China aid programs during and after the war. According to Stuart, Chiang immediately asked:

How could he be certain that these holdings were not largely imaginary? General Wedemeyer then rather unwisely said that he possessed a list of these holdings in the U.S.A. He was promptly taken by the Generalissimo who asked for a copy of it. Then the General demurred on the ground that he had been given the list in the strictest confidence; the Generalissimo asked "Are you a true friend of mine and of China's? If you are, you will give me the list."[40]

Wedemeyer, of course, refused to comply with Chiang's demand, either because what he told Chiang was true or because he did not have the list. Nevertheless, the Wedemeyer Mission largely fulfilled Marshall's objective of sticking to a policy of limited involvement in China—a policy Vincent and Marshall himself formulated. More importantly, Wedemeyer did not find any evidence of Soviet involvement in China's domestic dispute. As Edmund Clubb reported to Stuart on 30 October: "There has yet been obtained no positive evidence that the USSR is supplying the Manchuria Communists with arms, ammunition or other supplies."[41]

In the meantime, Vincent was becoming a victim of the China lobbyists. In August, under pressure of a Red witchhunt within the administration, Vincent was "promoted" to Switzerland as a minister. The Luce and Scripps-Howard newspapers hailed Vincent's departure and the appointment of Walton Butterworth as Vincent's successor. The New York *World Telegram* gloatingly declared that, "When John Carter Vincent's terms expired as chief of the Far Eastern Office, [and] he was sent to Switzerland instead of China, it was a blow to the Division's anti-Chiang Kai-shek and pro-Soviet clique."[42]

London was also delighted that Vincent was gone. Ambassador Stevenson reported in August: "The appointment of Butterworth, Minister-Counselor of the U.S. Embassy [at Nanking], came as a great surprise. Oxford educated, we certainly have found him an extremely friendly and helpful colleague." Stevenson, however, cautioned against the reports that Butterworth was pro-Chiang: "I should emphasize that despite his acquired continental poise and Anglophile outlook, which induce some of his own colleagues to regard him as somewhat *depayse*, he remains a typical American in his fundamental outlook. . . . I completely disagree with the Scripps-Howard line that he is pro-Chiang."[43]

In May, Marshall decided to create the Policy Planning Staff (PPS), a powerful long-range planning body headed by George Kennan. Ambassador Lord Inverchapel believed that the creation of the PPS might be a healthy development:

> It is unfortunately true that the activities of the State Department have repeatedly suffered in the past from the absence of long-range policy and has thus exposed itself to much criticism on the part of the general public, the press and, most importantly, members of Congress. It remains to be seen whether the absence of any central purpose and proclivity for *ad hoc* decisions on the part of the State Department will be overcome by the Policy Planning Staff.

What interested Lord Inverchapel most were the staff members Kennan brought with him, including John Paton Davies. Lord Inverchapel observed that, "John Paton Davies, Jr., 39, is the Staff's No. 2 expert on Russia after Kennan. He returned to Washington last summer after almost two and one-half years in Moscow. He also doubles as the group's Far Eastern authority." In fact, the British always viewed Davies with suspicion. During Davies's two-and-a-half-year tour in Moscow, the Foreign Office watched him closely. Sir Archibald Clark Kerr (now Lord Inverchapel), British ambassador to Moscow, once reported to London that Davies and his wife "hold left-wing views" but were disillusioned by the Soviet Union. Moreover, Davies was considered vehemently anti-British.[44]

Although wary of Davies, the Foreign Office was delighted to see China hands in and out of the State Department fall from grace one after another. When it came to Owen Lattimore's turn, the Foreign Office had an intense internal debate. Some Asian experts were quite willing to swallow the Scripps-Howard and Time/Life lines in depicting these China hands as traitors and leftists. In January, Sir George Sansom, British minister at Washington, wrote to George Kitson: "Owen Lattimore, whom you no doubt know, has achieved chiefly by prolixity, the position of a leading authority on China and Far Eastern politics. He has a considerable following in the so-called Liberal and leftist circles." Sansom added, "Lattimore, [Theodore] White et al are perhaps not Communists, but they play Communist tunes."[45]

A. L. Scott wholly agreed with Sansom, saying, "I think that Owen Lattimore is a charlatan and that George Sansom's summary up of him is perfectly accurate." George Kitson, however, thought the word "charlatan" was a little strong. H. O. Bryan, a first secretary at Nanking, challenged Sansom's view and stated: "Owen Lattimore is not altogether a 'self-appointed' specialist on China. His views on China are based on considerable experience of that country. . . . If they write about China in a way that can be described as 'playing Communist tunes,' I would say that, even if such tunes may grate harshly on the ear, they may nonetheless be variations on a ground [of] traditional and popular theme—at any rate in China."[46]

Sir George Sansom's reply betrayed how far some senior British diplomats had readily bought into Henry Luce's charges against the China experts in the United States: "The point is not so much whether his views are shared by a great number or even a majority of Chinese, but rather whether he is subversive in his political activities in the United States." Moreover,

> he [Lattimore] has been under strong attack lately here, and is known to be rather embarrassed as he was the chief target in a campaign to purge the Institute of Pacific Relations of fellow-travellers. I used to think that they were just good liberals if a trifle too zealous and idealistic, but I am now firmly convinced that they are dangerous and would sell us and anybody else down the river for the sake of their ideologies.

Sansom then added rather maliciously that Lattimore had achieved his position because "the American public admire big books but don't read them. He has written a great deal about a lot of subjects, and much of it is poor stuff."[47]

Although it is difficult to determine how much this kind of internal debate had affected policy making in London, it confirmed the Foreign Office's suspicion about the misguided American China policy by the purge of the China hands in Washington, who were usually anti-British.

Convinced that the United States was increasingly losing its direction in China, Bevin concluded that Great Britain should not appear, as in 1946, to follow the American lead in China too blindly. At the same time, the Foreign Office should try to ascertain American intentions amidst the purge of the China hands in Washington and, if possible, to redirect U.S. China policy. Bevin was keenly aware that the relatively quiet British attitude during the Marshall Mission had left the impression that the British government in China was lethargic; therefore, he began to look for opportunities to reverse this impression. In late January, Lord Lindsay condemned the American China policy in the House of Lords. Perhaps prompted by his son Michael Lindsay, who was a staunch pro-Communist activist in China, Lord Lindsay asserted that, in view of the "high and honourable failure of General Marshall, it is high time for Britain to have a real policy toward China."[48]

Bevin saw it as a good opportunity to distance Britain from the American policy. The Foreign Office prepared a reply to Lord Lindsay's charge that the United States continued to supply arms to Chiang Kai-shek, the draft of which stated, "I have seen reports that America is continuing to supply arms to China. I am informed that no war materials have been supplied from the United States to China for several months. The position is similar as regards export of arms from this country to China." The phrase "no war materials have been supplied from the United States to China for several months" was, in fact, suggested by the State Department.[49] Bevin personally did not like this passage and changed it to, "Insofar as the supply of arms to China is concerned, certainly I can say that we are sending nothing, and I am also informed that no war materials have been supplied to China from the United States for several months." Bevin explained this change in a handwritten note, saying, "The whole point here is that it should not be put as if we were merely following the American lead."[50]

China was only one of the big issues over which Bevin had been fighting with the Americans. Throughout 1947, he encountered enormous difficulty in a wide range of English and American disputes over such issues as the International Trade Organization (ITO) and the question of sterling. It appeared to Bevin that, despite the intensifying of the Cold War, the gap between English and American approaches to the postwar world as a whole widened. London's key problem was its inability to ascertain the inner thoughts of the Truman administration. In May, Lord Inverchapel telegraphed Bevin a long message entitled "American Approach to the Outside World." In it Lord Inverchapel declared, "The people of the United States are embarking upon an attempt to impose their own 'way of life' on others. . . . Generally speaking, Americans whose *raison d'etre* as citizens of the same republic would take it for granted that, if free to express their choice, the inhabitants of the earth would be found in overwhelming agreement with the conception that 'government of the people, by the people, for the people' is the most acceptable principle of sovereign rule." Lord Inverchapel continued, "Fair-minded Americans are very conscious of the extent to which racial discrimination in the United States and other abuses conflict

[with] these ideals, but few thoughtful Americans would conclude from these shortcomings at home that they should ignore threats to the democratic way of life elsewhere." Thus, "in the light of this mental approach, it would be difficult to persuade Americans that attempts on their part to assure other people's right to decide their own destinies were comparable to Soviet efforts to bully or beguile other countries into handing over their affairs to the undisputed will of a Communist minority." He concluded by saying:

> Our vital political and strategic interest, no less than our financial embarrassments, leave us no practicable alternative than to cooperate closely with the Americans, the question must still be asked whether the risks and burdens of the Anglo-American partnership are not falling too heavily upon ourselves.[51]

Bevin was more than impressed by Lord Inverchapel's exposition, which was very much in line with his own views on Anglo-American relations. He wrote Lord Inverchapel, stating: "I have read with the greatest interest your despatch about America's approach to the outside world. In putting United States foreign policy into proper perspective the despatch should fulfill a most valuable educative purpose and I am giving it wide circulation."[52]

Along this line of thinking, Bevin was particularly annoyed with the lack of frankness on the part of the Americans over many important issues. At the same time, British public opinion and the press were increasingly negative toward the American China policy and the Chiang Kai-shek regime. The London *Times* editorial of 5 July pointed out that "There is no evidence that the Soviet Union is in any way [responsible] for the friction between the Outer Mongolian Republic and the Province of Sinkiang, or for the military reverses which the Nationalist Government has recently suffered . . . the difficulties of the Nanking Administration are of its own making." Everett Drumright reported to Marshall that it was astonishing that the *Times* continued to adhere to an anti-Nationalist government and pro-Communist attitude.[53]

In the second half of 1947 the Americans began to sense that the British government was less and less submissive over foreign policy and international economic issues. Undersecretary Robert Lovett told Lewis Douglas, the new American ambassador to London, on 24 September that "There is [a] growing feeling here that there have been too many occasions of British lack of cooperation in the past few months and there is a tendency to search for the underlying reason." According to Lovett, "Even after due allowance for their discouragement, certain positions taken and several acts appear to be reckless, maladroit and out of character compared with the past." In consequence, "both from the point of view of economic and security interests of this country, some of us here have begun to wonder whether a group in England is trying to rupture [the] relationship so as to make this country the whipping boy for British problems to take the heat off British politicians or to swing Britain further to the left."[54]

If Lovett found the British intransigent, Bevin had stronger grievances against the Americans. At the global level, Britain's financial and political crises in 1947 were widely regarded as the direct result of the American loan policy. At the regional level, it was on matters of the Far East, particularly China, that Anglo-American consultation hardly existed, not even in name. The Foreign Office was deeply concerned about the uncertainty in American China policy. As Esler Dening wrote in a memo on 17 November: "Where does the United States stand in relation to China? We do not know, and I doubt whether the Americans know themselves. Their present tendency to let Far Eastern affairs drift is likely to have the most deplorable consequences."[55]

With persistent efforts, Bevin was finally able to obtain in November Marshall's verbal acquiescence to hold a top-secret Anglo-American conference on Far Eastern issues. Bevin was almost beside himself. He directed the conference preparations personally and advised Prime Minister Attlee that the meeting was to be of enormous value. As he told the latter on 22 December:

> I consider that the talks should cover the political, economic and strategic field for the whole region from Afghanistan to the Pacific, and that we should recommend this to the United States. My reason is that from Afghanistan to Malaya inclusive and beyond to Borneo and Hongkong, British influence at present exceeds that of the United States. In China, Japan, and Korea on the other hand, though our prestige remains high, our economic and financial position does not enable us to enter into any material commitments. Our influence in the Western part of the area I have designated might therefore be used as a counterpoise to American influence in the Eastern part.

Bevin emphasized further that, "Up to now the Americans have shown an apparent reluctance to be frank about their policy towards China,

Japan and Korea, and I feel that these talks might pave the way to a better understanding in the future."[56]

Bevin's enthusiasm also showed in his desire to bring the dominions into the picture. As a top-secret Foreign Office memo recorded, "The Foreign Secretary discussed with the Prime Minister and also with the Secretary of State for Commonwealth Relations just before the Christmas Holidays the question of associating the Dominions with the proposed Top Secret Conversations with the Americans on the Far East."[57]

However, Bevin was a little too zealous, while the State Department, for its part, was less committed. There was hardly any preparation within the State Department for the conference to which Secretary Marshall had given an oral promise. In fact, the conference was postponed until May 1948 and even then, Robert Lovett frankly told Esler Dening, who came well prepared for the conference, that "the difficulties and dangers of holding formal consultations of this nature during this preelection period" were all too obvious.[58]

In the economic field, the prospects of doing successful business in China were shattered by the outbreak of the civil war. The Chinese central government was in a precarious financial position. The war consumed a large portion of Chiang's already diminishing foreign exchange reserves. It was estimated that, by 1947, Chinese external reserves had fallen to the equivalent of four months' imports.[59]

Such a gloomy picture, however, did not entirely scare away private business activities from either the United States or Great Britain. For the Americans, there was a strong belief that their government would not and could not afford to abandon China. For the British, it had always been their traditional strategy during China's internal disturbances to keep a foot in the China market, waiting for better days to come. And, should China disintegrate, British expertise in doing business in a disunited China would enable a return to the good old times.

In any case, the American trade with China had an impressive record during 1946. According to the estimate of J. C. Hutchison, British commercial counselor at Nanking, "for the first seven months of 1946, 53.63 per cent of China's total imports came from the United States and only 4.85 per cent from Britain."[60]

Moreover, the Sino-American Commercial Treaty promised to facilitate trade in China. In 1947, despite the unfolding of the civil war, the American business community remained intensely interested in direct investment in China. In a joint memo dated 13 February, the China-America Council and the National Foreign Trade Council asked the State Department to ascertain the following: (1) which fields of industry would be open to direct investment of American capital, (2) which would be reserved as government monopolies, (3) which would the Chinese government operate alongside private firms, (4) in which fields would there be joint government-private operations, and (5) which would be closed to foreign corporations. Moreover, the two councils wanted to know what assurance did prospective U.S. business interests in China have that (a) new laws, orders, or taxes would not be enacted, preventing operations at reasonable profit; (b) profit would be remittable to the United States and exchange provided for purchase abroad of essential goods; and (c) local regulation would not be imposed preventing operations on a sound basis.[61]

The American embassy at Nanking was instructed to present these questions to the Chinese government, but the Chinese appeared uncooperative. Chiang was desperately preoccupied with the war, and American aid became a question of life and death. The opening up of China to American investment could be used as one of his remaining leverages to induce more aid from Washington. Ambassador Stuart reported on 20 February that Dr. Kan Nai-kuang, political vice-minister of foreign affairs, made the following candid statement: "Unfortunately American businessmen had developed a somewhat unrealistic attitude over the potentialities of [the] China market; that question was not merely one of economics but also, and primarily, one of politics." Dr. Kan further commented that American business interests should realize that the political situation could develop in one of three ways: (1) China may be forced to fight a long civil war during which prospects for American business would steadily decline; (2) the national government at Nanking might be overthrown by Chinese Communists, following which there would be no private business for American and other foreign concerns; and (3) the national government, with outside support, might be able to drive back and confine the Communists (who had very definite outside support) to isolated areas, thereby restoring peace and conditions under which foreign trade might develop.[62] In other words, Dr. Kan was telling the American business community that they must lobby for U.S. aid to China in exchange for special treatment.

In London, the British business community was hoping for a disintegrated China too. A lengthy paper prepared in January by the China Association for the Foreign Office affirmed: "Many informed observers believe that, should America's military support and supplies be withdrawn from the Central Government, the Communists would be able to change their tactics and occupy and successfully defend a considerable part of the North," in which case "it is possible that other groups would break away in the South and Centre and China would once more be divided into a number of small areas under War Lords or petty governments." The China Association emphasized that: "The Americans have to some extent now overplayed their own hand and there is a good deal of antipathy for them among the Chinese People, who dislike the suggestion of patronage implicit in the behaviour of many of the American troops and in a good deal of American policy." Finally, it concluded: "We are old, commercial friends of the Chinese and ... Britain can develop a healthy and friendly relationship with China without involving herself in the very complex internal political disputes."[63]

Meanwhile, in Parliament, the China Association also made its voice heard through its secretary general, Lord Ailwyn. During a debate in the House of Lords on 23 January, Lord Ailwyn complained about the difficulties being experienced by British traders, shippers, and industrialists in China. A Foreign Office minute suggested that these points be noted in the negotiation of the Sino-British Commercial Treaty. The American embassy was annoyed by Lord Ailwyn's activities, reporting to Washington that, "In all probability Lord Ailwyn's reference ... was prompted by the Foreign Office in the hope that a public airing of the British complaints would evoke a satisfactory response from the Chinese Government."[64]

Meanwhile, London began to view the gloomy economic conditions in China from a different perspective: the diminishing British business activities might not necessarily result in gains for Washington. A memo prepared by Esler Dening in February stated cynically that the fact that the United States had virtually replaced Britain in China should not be regarded "too tragically." Though the prewar British position brought many benefits, it also imposed certain responsibilities and burdens from which Britain had been relieved; the political and economic anxieties now fell mainly to the United States as the dominant Western power in China. But Dening still believed that Britain should maintain its position in China. Although China was economically and financially in trouble, and the prospects of conducting successful trade were thus gloomy, Dening thought that Britain should "keep a commercial foothold in China until better days come."[65]

The British Board of Trade began to worry about the unrealistic British business expectations in China. A memo prepared by H. O. Hooper of the Board of Trade in August stated that "British businesses have been doing almost too well in China and in spite of the obstacles, exporters seemed to be showing a greater energy in selling to China than to [a] more desirable hard currency market." In light of Britain's balance-of-payments position—the Board's usual gauge for trade successes—Hooper insisted that "we may have actively to discourage them from doing this."[66]

Neither the Foreign Office nor the British business circle took the Board of Trade's position too seriously. Encouraged by the widespread forecast of China's disintegration, the British business community paid particular attention to the southern provinces adjacent to Hongkong. In February there was talk of a big British project in this area—the Kwangtung Iron and Steel Works Project. But the Treasury, noting Britain's financial weakness, opposed the idea and it was abandoned.

The Foreign Office, on the other hand, continued to concern itself with maintaining Britain's economic position in China. When the United States lifted the ban on arms sales to China in July, George Kitson warned: "A likely consequence of all-out U.S. aid to China (to which strings will undoubtedly be attached) will be Sino-American collusion to exclude British trade from China in the interests of American trade."[67]

British economic activities in southern China caused grave concern in Washington. During a private conversation in October, T. V. Soong, the new governor of Kwangtung, told Ambassador Stuart that he found the British more ready than the Americans to cooperate in industrial and other investment projects. Stuart commented to the State Department that the "Embassy considers this as a natural concomitant of [the] British desire to bolster [the] position of Hongkong in South China."[68]

Throughout 1947, the Truman administration was haunted by the severe financial crisis in China, but there appeared to be no workable solution. Because, as Ambassador Stuart pointed out on 4 February:

The main danger in China, in our opinion, is not one of dramatic economic collapse—as in the United States at [the] beginning of 1933—
but of insidious economic and political disintegration. The process has
already set in, and political, military, economic deterioration mutually
reinforce each other in accentuating it.[69]

While facing this situation, the American dilemma was obvious.
The Treasury Department was unwilling to provide any large-scale
loans to China where the prospect of repayment hardly existed. The
State Department, along with business circles, began to favor some
kind of rescue operation. John Carter Vincent was vigorously pushing
for financial assistance to China, which he believed more important
than military aid. In a memo to General Marshall, Vincent pointed out
that he and the American business community favored a plan to rescue
China financially. He argued that China's "disintegrative force" had
always been stronger than the "integrative force." According to Vincent, Chiang had forgotten two factors that rendered his own unifying
efforts successful: (1) the pressure exerted by Japan and (2) the healthy
financial and economic situation. Thus, "if Chiang goes, the disintegrative trend will be speeded up because there is no strong man or groups
to succeed him. If he stays he may be able, with our assistance, to
improve his position in the Yangtze River area, from a financial and
economic standpoint, and cut some of his liability in outlying areas."[70]
Vincent was suggesting a reduced territory under Chiang's control,
which would enable him to restore financial stability.

London never trusted the American ability to handle China's financial crisis. In February, the British indicated to Washington strong
interest in getting involved in managing China's finances. As Stuart
reported, "The British Ambassador suggested that the U.K. and U.S.
consult together concerning the Chinese financial crisis."[71] The Americans did not even consider this idea. An angry Foreign Office paper
pointed out that the history of the U.S. role in Chinese finance had
hardly been a glorious one: "The raising of the price of silver in the
United States brought about in 1934 a financial crisis of the first magnitude in China." At that time, "His Majesty's Government sent Sir
Frederick Leith-Ross to advise the Chinese Government and under his
guidance the silver currency was abandoned and a controlled currency
at its established exchange level until some six months after the outbreak of the war between China and Japan." The paper concluded,

"From then onward the exchange value has continuously declined until, at present time, it is approximately one-thousandth of its original 'Leith-Ross' value."[72]

More importantly, London worried about the extent to which the United States intended to control China through financial management. The Foreign Office was somehow convinced that the failure of the Wedemeyer Mission was largely due to the American attempt to control China in exchange for aid. Since the Chinese refused to comply with the U.S. demand, Washington also declined to further extend any large-scale support. In late September, the Foreign Office was alarmed by an intelligence report concerning Wedemeyer's alleged three-point proposal made to the Chinese government. According to the report, Wedemeyer placed three alternatives before the generalissimo:

1. For the United States to withdraw all interest in Chinese politics and leave the country to work out her own salvation;
2. For the United States to invite international participation in financial and economic aid to China, foreign experts being appointed to supervise expenditure, etc.; and
3. A combination of (a) United States to appoint supervisors to control U.S. financial and economic aid (to cover all levels down to that of Hsien, or county, magistrates; (b) neither T. V. Soong nor H. H. Kung, or their nominees, to participate in control or disbursement of finances and certain named political leaders to be dismissed from the government; and (c) China to give satisfactory assurances that employment of U.S. supervisors will not provide anti-American demonstrations, articles, or speeches in Chinese universities, newspapers, or assemblies.[73]

It is clear that the Marshall-Vincent policy by no means indicated total disengagement from China. However, it did indicate a strong unwillingness to pay for a policy of all-out commitment. Shortly before his departure from the Far Eastern Office, Vincent elaborated his long-term view about the American China policy to Secretary Marshall: "With regard to general policy on the question of economic aid to China I tend more and more to the belief that, while continuing efforts to contain the spread of Communism in China without becoming directly involved in the civil war, the grass roots and strength of our relations with China over the past 100 years derive from American commercial and cultural activities in the country. . . . With this thought in mind, I believe we should do all that we reasonably can to strengthen American business and cultural enterprise in the country. Specific projects should be considered in the light of their relation to strengthening American business in places [where] we may reasonably expect operations not to be completely at the mercy of the vicissitudes of civil war or of the vagaries of the present National administration." Vincent thus concluded that if the Americans built up enclaves of increasing influence in such places as Shanghai and Tsingtao, the effect could gradually spread and benefit wider areas and perhaps lead to more extensive economic assistance, which the U.S. government could then justify in the eyes of the American people as sound American policy.[74] Vincent was clearly concerned about continued American engagement in China over the long run, which at the time could be ruined by shortsighted anti-Communist fervor in the United States.

The British had similar concerns. In sharp contrast to the silent attitude of the British in 1946, the desire to restore the British position in China was frequently voiced in Great Britain throughout 1947. In April, for example, the *Manchester Guardian* called for a more energetic and comprehensive British policy toward China.[75] During a parliamentary debate on 22 April, Sir Ralph Glyn, a Conservative M.P., asked the foreign secretary whether or not it was still the policy of His Majesty's Government toward China to assist, when conditions improved, in carrying out other projects unrelated to civil strife, to encourage economic reconstruction and reform in China, and thus to promote a general revival of commercial relations. Christopher Mayhew, parliamentary undersecretary, replied, "Yes, sir, but any projects must be considered in relation to H.M.G.'s financial and economic situation." Sensing a revived British activism in China, American Ambassador Lew Douglas was relieved that, "In light of Britain's present stringent economic situation, Mr. Mayhew's qualification may with good reason be taken to mean that Britain is not at present in a position to provide any substantial assistance to the economic reconstruction of China."[76]

Everett Drumright, a leading China expert at the London embassy, commented on the revived British public interest in China in April: "It is admitted on all sides in this country that there is an absence of a positive British policy towards China. What is not so generally recognized, however, is that Britain today has neither the resources nor the power which are required for the implementation of a positive British policy in China."[77]

In October, the Foreign Office was anxiously waiting to see the result of the announced Joint House Parliamentary Mission to China, which had been dispatched on 29 September. Led by Lord Ammon, the parliamentary mission traveled extensively in China and was warmly received. The mission's report, known as the Lord Ammon Report, concluded that, although Chiang Kai-shek boasted that his troops would clear the rebels from within the Great Wall within six or at the most twelve months, the Kuomintang seemed to be losing ground. Another major discovery of the mission, much to the delight of the Labour cabinet, was that American prestige had dramatically declined. As the report pointed out:

> British stock stands very high; in fact it is much higher than that of the United States. The Chinese appear to have a hope that in some way we might intervene in order that this draining of blood and treasure of China might cease. . . . We were assured by the British community that there was very little anti-British feeling in China. There is some feeling against all foreigners, but it is the Americans and not the British, towards whom hostility is primarily expressed.

From a long-term perspective, the report concluded that the real threat to British interests would come from American competition and Chinese nationalism.[78]

In other parts of the Far East, Anglo-American relations remained far from harmonious, despite the fact that London had granted independence to Burma and India in 1947. The most urgent issue at hand in 1947 was the policy toward Japan. London was greatly annoyed by the high-handed approach of the U.S. administration in dealing with issues of reparation and a peace settlement. As far as the first issue was concerned, the Labour government was convinced that American efforts to cut down the British share in the reparation was more than an economic matter. It was a continued effort to belittle the British contribution to the war against Japan. At an Allied Far Eastern Commission meeting held on 12 May, the claims presented by all the member states constituted 176.5 percent of the actual reparation payments. Of this sum, China claimed 40 percent, the United States 34 percent, and the United Kingdom 25 percent, respectively.[79]

Under the circumstances, the American government announced unilaterally its own solution to balance the claims; Britain's share was cut down to 8 percent, while China and the United States reduced their shares to 30 and 29 percent. London felt that the U.S.-China collusion was aimed at discriminating against Britain. Instructed to lodge a strong protest, Lord Inverchapel pronounced on 30 June: "It is difficult to believe that, in proposing the figure of 8 percent for the United Kingdom, the United States Government has given full weight to all the relevant factors." For instance, Lord Inverchapel continued, "the United States Government proposes to give China more than three and a half times the share of the United Kingdom, which cannot be consistent with any just appraisal of relative assets in relation to war effort and [the] holding of Japanese external assets." Thus, only with great reluctance did the American government agree to raise the British share to 10 percent.[80]

Over the second issue, the United States wanted to delay any peace settlement with Japan. The chief objective of this settlement, as pointed out by John Paton Davies of the Policy Planning Staff, was to have "a stable Japan integrated into the Pacific economy, friendly to the United States and, in case of need, a ready and dependable ally of the United States."[81] George Kennan, director of the Policy Planning Staff, thought it would be extremely dangerous for the United States to enter discussions of the peace terms "until we know precisely what it is that we are trying to achieve."[82]

A secret report by Robert A. Fearey of the Division of Northeastern Asian Affairs of the State Department pointed out in October that

1. we need two more years to complete our major reform programs, and they can be better done under a predominantly American control structure than under a post-treaty Allied control structure;
2. we can better supervise cranking-up under the present control structure than under the post-treaty structure; and
3. the economic benefits that a treaty might be expected to confer on Japan can be achieved just as well without a treaty.[83]

Britain's desire to have an early peace settlement with Japan was prompted by concern for the United Kingdom's overall position in the region, especially relating to Commonwealth solidarity. Australia and New Zealand were particularly anxious to conclude an early peace with Japan. In August, the Labour government declined the American invitation for a Washington conference on the issue. Instead, a Canberra conference was held at the end of August to discuss the matter among the Commonwealth countries.[84] This gave rise to grave suspicions in Washington that London was forming a British bloc over the question of a Japanese peace settlement. Moreover, London annoyed Washington by suggesting that Burma and Pakistan participate in the peace settlement process. Walton Butterworth, director of the Far Eastern Office of the State Department, commented on 22 September:

> The British have raised the question of Pakistan's participation in the treaty drafting. This is undesirable because it would (a) increase the "British Bloc" representation to 6 or 50 per cent of the participants; (b) open the door to applications from Burma and Outer Mongolia; and (c) represent a departure from our criterion for determining the participants, namely, membership in the Far Eastern Commission.[85]

The year 1947 was a period of great uncertainty. Despite the differences between the United States and Great Britain over various issues related to China and the Far East as a whole, they had one thing in common: neither side realized the rapid pace of decay of Chiang Kaishek's regime. Both London and Washington expected an inconclusive civil war and believed that they would have time to adjust themselves to the unfolding events. It is, thus, not surprising that when Chiang's fate was sealed in late 1948, the fundamental Anglo-American difference over China would once more be brought sharply into focus.

Notes

1. *FRUS*, 1947, 7:796.
2. Ibid., Patterson to Marshall, p. 800.
3. Ibid., Marshall to Patterson, pp. 806–7.
4. U.K. PRO, Kitson to Bevin, top secret, FO371 63319/F2630/76/10/G.
5. *FRUS*, 1947, 7:36.
6. U.K. PRO, FO371 63320/F3569/76/10.
7. Li Li-san was a Communist leader who returned to China from the Soviet Union, where he had spent over ten years and had married a Russian. At the time, Li was widely, though wrongly, considered Stalin's henchman in China.
8. U.K. PRO, Memo of Conversation by Stevenson, 21 March 1947, FO371 63327/F4117/76/10.
9. NAUS, Daily Staff Officers Summary, 31 January 1947, box 5.

10. *Times* (London), 25 March 1947.

11. U.K. PRO, Lord Inverchapel to Bevin, 15 February 1947, FO371 63318/F2089/76/10/3.

12. Ibid., Note by Scott.

13. U.K. PRO, Nanking to FO, FO371 63321/F4123/76/10.

14. Memo by Rusk, *FRUS*, 1947, 7:320–24.

15. U.K. PRO, FO371 63319/F2715/76/10.

16. *FRUS*, 1947, 7:804.

17. U.K. PRO, Minute by Scott, 7 July 1946, FO371 63325/F9309.

18. Tu Yueh-sheng, known as Big-Eared Tu, was a key figure in Shanghai's underworld and a patron of Chiang in his early years.

19. NAUS, Decimal Files, microfilm 893.00/5–347.

20. Ibid., 893.00/6–247.

21. Ibid., 893.00/5–1047.

22. U.K. PRO, Lamb to Dening, FO371 63324/F7848.

23. NAUS, Decimal Files, Marshall to Nanking, microfilm 893.00/6–2447.

24. U.K. PRO, Stevenson to FO, 29 May 1947, FO371 63323/F7362.

25. Wedemeyer to Marshall, 6 August 1947, *FRUS*, 1947, 7:712.

26. Ludden to Wedemeyer, *FRUS*, 1947, 7:717.

27. Acheson to Bedell Smith, 2 April 1947, *FRUS*, 1947, 7:815.

28. NAUS, Decimal Files, microfilm 893.00/4–1547.

29. U.K. PRO, Stevenson to Bevin, FO371 63322/F5994/76/10.

30. *FRUS*, 1947, 7:833.

31. Ibid., p. 853.

32. U.K. PRO, Stevenson to FO, 20 July 1947, FO371 63325/F9883.

33. Ibid., p. 853.

34. Ibid., p. 653.

35. Ibid., pp. 640–41.

36. U.K. PRO, Minute by Scott, 18 July 1947, FO371 63325/F9732.

37. U.K. PRO, Memo of Conversation, FO371 63325/F9956/76/10/G.

38. FO Minute, 27 July 1947, FO371 63325/F90121.

39. Sprouse to Wedemeyer, *FRUS*, 1947, 7:696.

40. U.K. PRO, Memo of Conversation by Stevenson, FO371 63326/F11861.

41. NAUS, Clubb to Stuart, 30 October 1947, RG 59, microfilm 893.00/10–3047.

42. *World Telegram* (New York), 7 August 1947.

43. U.K. PRO, Lord Inverchapel to FO, FO371 61051/AN331728/45.

44. U.K. PRO, Kerr to FO, November 1945, FO371 46325/F11228/127/G61.

45. U.K. PRO, Sansom to FO, January 1947, FO371 63331/F851.

46. U.K. PRO, FO371 63331/F5201.

47. U.K. PRO, FO371 63331/F6137.

48. NAUS, Incoming Messages, Marshall Mission Files, box 14.

49. NAUS, Memo by Ringwalt, 13 January 1947, lot 110, Division of Chinese Affairs, box 6.

50. U.K. PRO, 18 January 1947, FO371 63317/100599.

51. U.K. PRO, Lord Inverchapel to Bevin, FO371 61047/AN1986/28/45.

52. U.K. PRO, Bevin to Lord Inverchapel, 19 June 1947, FO371 61047/AN2031/28/45.

53. NAUS, Decimal Files, Drumright to Marshall, 25 July 1948, microfilm 893.00/7–2547.

54. NAUS, Decimal Files, Lovett to Douglas, 24 September 1947, top secret, 711.41/9–2447.

55. U.K. PRO, Memo by Dening, FO371 63328/F14773.

56. U.K. PRO, FO800/FE/47/36.

57. U.K. PRO, 29 December 1947, FO800/FE/47/39.

58. *FRUS*, 1948, 7:78.

59. F. H. H. King, *A Concise Economic History of Modern China*, p. 156.

60. U.K. PRO, Hutchison to Bevin, 7 October 1947, FO371 63302/ F1118/37/10.

61. *FRUS*, 1947, 7:1369–70.

62. Ibid., p. 1370.

63. U.K. PRO, China Association to FO, FO371 63317/F76.

64. NAUS, Decimal Files, microfilm 893.00/1–2847.

65. U.K. PRO, Memo by Dening, FO371 63549/F2616/F10250.

66. U.K. PRO, BT 60/83C/42889.

67. U.K. PRO, FO Minute by Kitson, 11 August 1947, FO371 63331/F10250.

68. NAUS, Decimal Files, microfilm 893.00/102747.

69. *FRUS*, 1947, 7:1047.

70. NAUS, Vincent to Marshall, 25 July 1947, RG 59, microfilm 893.00/7–2547.

71. NAUS, Daily Staff Officers Summary, 17 February 1947, box 4.

72. U.K. PRO, FO371 634317/F76.

73. U.K. PRO, Lamb to FO, 29 September 1947, FO371 63327/F13552.

74. NAUS, Decimal Files, microfilm 893.00/7–1847.

75. *Manchester Guardian*, 8 April 1947.

76. NAUS, Decimal Files, Douglas to Marshall, 741.93/4–2247.

77. NAUS, Decimal Files, Drumright to Washington, 741.93/4–1047.

78. U.K. PRO, Lord Ammon Report, 15 December 1947, FO371 69604/F1517.

79. *FRUS*, 1947, 6:395.

80. Ibid., 6:410–11.

81. Ibid., p. 486.

82. Ibid., p. 487.

83. Ibid., p. 487.

84. Ibid., pp. 558–59.

85. Ibid., p. 524.

5

A "Chinese Tito"?

To many Americans, 1948 began on an ominous note. The chill that had come over international politics was matched by the weather: there was a record twenty-five-inch snowfall on the American East Coast. After the failure of the London conference of the Council of Foreign Ministers, tension mounted in Central Europe, and it seemed that the collapse of the American policy in the Far East was only a question of time.

But a new phenomenon had also developed, which showed great promise for the West to crack the international communist monolith. There was an apparent split between Marshal Tito's Communist Yugo-slavia and Stalin's Soviet Union. The fact that Tito, a small-time Communist leader, was able to defy Stalin led many in the West to imagine that a big-time Communist leader like Mao Tse-tung would do the same. For a while, both Great Britain and the United States were intensely interested in such a prospect. However, despite the similarity in objectives, the perspectives and policies of the two countries seemed to move in opposite directions.

Although the New Year's spirit was by no means high in Washington, there was some encouraging news. At the end of 1947, President Truman had urged Congress to approve the first installment of a proposed four-year European Recovery Program (ERP, or the Marshall Plan) worth $17 billion. Having lost the initiative in the Far East, where events were totally out of Washington's control, the State Department was anxious to regain influence and confidence through its European policy.

The idea of "containment" had become a deeply rooted policy, even though the Truman administration had not yet defined the term clearly. In 1948, for the first time since the end of the war, Washington began to set explicit geographical priorities—at least George Marshall and his top aides thought so. Although many scholars have suggested that a "Europe First" strategy was automatically adopted by the U.S. government, the distinction between different geographical priorities was not at all clear-cut at the time. To some extent, the Marshall Plan was conditioned by the failed American attempt at control in the Far East. As late as the end of 1947, some 60 percent of U.S. overseas troops, nearly half of the naval vessels, and most of the military aircraft abroad were stationed in Asia and the Pacific. Apart from the financial burden incurred by the occupation of Japan, the United States had spent some $2 billion in China alone since V-J Day; these funds had virtually been poured down the drain, since as a result the American position in that part of the world had been weakened instead of strengthened. Thus, the inefficacy of the American policy in the Far East prompted Marshall and like-minded "wise men," especially George Kennan's Policy Planning Staff, to shift priorities to Europe where Washington could still control the course of events even though tension was high. This group was primarily concerned with the effectiveness of a "containment" policy.

Based on his own wartime and postwar involvement with China, George Marshall became absolutely convinced that a Europe-First strategy was once again at hand. Having had enormous difficulty in avoiding the image of selling Chiang's China down the river, Marshall tried to convince everyone that this strategy made sense just as it had during the war. In a conversation with M. A. Raymond-Laurent of the French National Assembly, Marshall argued that: "The Chinese had never forgiven me for my part in the decision to fight the war in Europe first and now blamed me for pushing recovery in Europe first. . . . I was endeavoring to convince . . . the Chinese that European recovery was essential to their well-being, whereas sums spent on them would be ineffective in the absence of European recovery."[1]

In November, Marshall told French Prime Minister Henry Queuille that there was a striking similarity between the basic American war strategy and the current one in which Western Europe was given priority.

Notwithstanding the success of wartime precedent, Marshall continued, he was still faced with similar opposition advocating more substantial help for the Far East, especially China.[2]

An important reason for Marshall to openly shift priorities to Europe was the discovery that the Soviet Union was not actively involved in China's internal dispute. Although Chiang Kai-shek desperately sought to tie his war efforts to the overall U.S. containment strategy, the evidence he offered linking the USSR to the Chinese Communists was largely spurious. In one typical case, as Edmund Clubb reported from Peiping in early 1948, KMT generals at the war front claimed that they had captured from the Communists weapons said to be U.S.-made and given to the Soviet Union by the United States during the war. But the generals did not realize that the War Department in Washington could easily trace the origin of these arms. After the American Military Advisory Group asked to see the serial numbers of the weapons, the KMT generals demurred and the numbers never came. Clubb reported that even Sun Li-jen, one of the best KMT generals, readily admitted that these might have been U.S. weapons sent to the KMT. Clubb then recalled a conversation he had with Wu Siu-chuan, a Communist general working at the Cease-fire Executive Headquarters, who remarked that U.S. military aid to Chiang was "of course not without occasional indirect benefits to Communists who frequently captured such arms from the Government troops."[3]

In giving clear priority to Europe, the Truman administration was faced with strong opposition in the domestic political arena. Moreover, the administration needed earnest support from its European allies, above all Great Britain. The American attitude toward Britain was also under transformation. This sentiment was reflected in a pamphlet published in October 1947 by a group of scholars at the Yale Institute of International Studies, which was often thought to be Dean Acheson's "think tank." According to the pamphlet's authors, even if the British Isles could be defended in a new world war, there was still a strong case for immediate large-scale economic aid to the United Kingdom, since "a revived and self-confident socialist Britain could make a better missionary on the European continent for the spread of democratic values than capitalist America."[4]

The precondition for such large-scale aid would be that Britain must become "European." In other words, she must forgo global pretensions—the Sterling Bloc and the Imperial Preference System would have to be abandoned. The Truman administration was pushing Britain back to Europe to play a leading role in the European Recovery Program.

London was thrilled by this rare piece of pro-British exposition. A Foreign Office minute commented, "Fundamentally this excellent pamphlet is a restatement of the ancient doctrine of the balance of power."[5] But the Labour cabinet fully understood the sinister aspect of the Marshall Plan. Paul Hoffman, ERP administrator, seemed more than enthusiastic about a Federal Europe, which was entirely compatible with the Marshall's Plan's original design, emphasizing efficiency and, eventually, diminishing the economic burden on U.S. resources. In the long run, European recovery would provide the American business community with countless opportunities. For Bevin, therefore, the Marshall Plan ought to comprise only straight-dollar transfers without strings attached. The Foreign Office was nervous about the long-term implications of the ERP. In a top-secret "Annual Survey for 1947," the British embassy in Washington pointed out that the American idea of a federal Europe including Britain might indicate the reemergence of a kind of neoisolationist policy—the first step back to Fortress America:

> This new brand of isolationism is based not merely on the fear of an eventual war but the belief that the world will profit little from the U.S. assistance in the way of further financial and material aid if, in [the] course of rendering it, America subjects herself to strains which dislocate her own economy and expose her to the risk of becoming the prey of predatory communism.

The survey went on to argue that, "This neo-isolationism, which is active in the economic rather than the political sphere, differs from its predecessor in being less instinctive and more precious. It should, therefore, be easier to combat."[6]

In a widely circulated handwritten memo in March, Sir Edmund Hall-Patch, deputy undersecretary for economic affairs at the Foreign Office, stated: "Too many Americans still do not understand the political mechanism of the Commonwealth. Still less do Americans (even well-informed ones) understand the mechanism of the Sterling Area. . . . [which] is looked upon in many influential quarters in America as a menace to American economic expansion and as a manifestation of the power of evil." Sir Edmund believed that Washington must be reminded that Britain was not merely a "European" power. He maintained that, "In our present state of dependence upon U.S. money and supplies many Americans will seek, in good faith, to put pressure upon us to 'integrate' with Europe. . . . The political effect of the break-up of the Sterling Area would be far reaching and might well spell the beginning of the end of the United Kingdom as a world power. Our political power is firmly based on an economic foundation: remove the foundation and the political structure totters."

Sir Edmund's forceful argument gained great currency within the Foreign Office. Sir Orme Sargent, permanent undersecretary at the Foreign Office, thought that Hall-Patch's minute was "most certainly worth reading."[7] In order to resist any American attempt to destroy Britain's world position, Bevin began to emphasize Britain's global interest. Hence, British policy in the Far East was given enormous importance, for it was in this part of the world that the United States had turned a stronghold of British global power into a weak link. It is, thus, not surprising that in 1948 as the American predilection for China waned, the British passion waxed. While the State Department was desperately seeking to wash its hands of China, Britain began to reassert its influence there.

Indeed, when the new year came, Bevin was in a "Far Eastern mood." He was determined that the proposed top-secret Anglo-American conference on the Far East be successful not only in solving Anglo-American differences in the region, but also in convincing Americans of the wisdom and necessity of upholding Britain's global position. In London, the British military establishment was puzzled by Bevin's preoccupation with the Far East. The military itself was far more concerned with a European security system. Secretary of Defense A. V. Alexander urged Bevin to take this opportunity to broach the European security question with the Americans, since Washington was not yet willing to commit itself to the defense of Europe. Alexander wrote Bevin on 19 January:

> In the course of examining the problem [the Far East], the Chiefs of Staff threw their net a little wider and took into account the further possibility of discussing with the Americans the situation in Western Europe. [They] felt that discussions on Western Europe are really more urgent than talks on the Far East.[8]

Bevin realized that neither the military nor the secretary of defense understood his true intention. Therefore, he wrote Alexander back a few days later, saying,

I hope in the discussion on the Far East the net will not be thrown wider. The purpose of raising [the] Far East at this time, if other matters can be settled in conjunction with the Dominions, was to let America see that we were interested and not solely with Western Europe.[9]

There was genuine concern in London about the American China policy. Looking back at the year 1947, the British embassy in Washington observed that Marshall's failure in China had demonstrated the futility of a "policy directed towards the establishment of a coalition government." Furthermore, Marshall's first-hand observations about the number of troops required to put the KMT in effective control of the country far exceeded what the U.S. Congress was disposed to authorize.

British embassy officials were dismayed to learn that "the conundrum thus presented to American policy makers has not yet been resolved—throughout 1947 the United States had no China policy worthy of the name." However, in an overoptimistic tone, the embassy predicted changes in American attitudes toward Britain: "Six months ago the alleged liquidation of the Empire was hailed as marking the exodus of British imperialism;" now, "the distinction between imperialism and safeguarding of legitimate overseas interests is coming to be appreciated." Such a tendency, it was thought, ought to be encouraged.

While the revival of British interest in the Far East derived, at least in part, from London's qualms regarding the ERP, the events in the Far East were steadily deteriorating. In early 1948, Chiang's military fortune took so dramatic a downturn that even military experts found it hard to follow. In January it was widely believed that Manchuria was "as good as gone."[10] "For the first time," reported Ambassador Stevenson from Nanking, "Ambassador Stuart is beginning privately to doubt whether Chiang Kai-shek is capable of taking sufficiently drastic and dramatic action."[11]

As the Communists scored one victory after another, debates on both sides of the Atlantic intensified. In Washington, the discussion was focused on the feasibility of continued U.S. aid to Chiang Kai-shek. Outside the administration, the efforts of the China lobby were magnified by the Republican presidential campaign. Although Marshall was able to dissuade Governor Thomas Dewey from making China a serious campaign issue, the China lobby had gained considerable influence during the campaign. The Red Scare went beyond the attempt of ferreting out alleged communist spies from within the State Department.

Within the administration, the division continued to be represented by the State Department, on one hand, and the military establishment, on the other. Inspired by the "Domino Theory," military members of the National Security Council (NSC) insisted on significant military and economic commitment to Chiang. The conflict between the two sides became so severe that, in the top-secret document NSC 6, dated 26 March, different positions over China had to be displayed side by side. The State Department's position was perhaps best summarized in item 8(c), under the subtitle "To Furnish Limited Aid to China in the Form of Military and Economic Assistance." According to this item:

> As it became evident that such aid was inadequate to check the Communists, the limited military aid given would be operated as an obligation necessitating further military, as well as economic, commitments to China. This process could continue indefinitely and lead to deeper and deeper involvement of our national strength in an area of, at best, secondary strategic importance.

The service departments took a totally opposite view. They regarded limited military aid to Chiang as essential and potentially effective. Moreover, such a course of action, it was believed, would not irrevocably commit the United States to further assistance.[12]

George Marshall enjoyed the position of being able to argue against the military and, at the same time, hold the total confidence of the president. While in Bogota attending a conference, Marshall candidly commented on NSC–6: "I favor the State Department position. . . . I consider the military view indefinite as to what is meant by 'limited aid.' . . . The adoption of such policy would inevitably involve us in the drain referred to in the opposite statement of view."[13]

In London, criticism of the American China policy was also gaining momentum. In January, Major Vernon, a Labour M.P., announced in the House of Commons that, "The Americans . . . have intervened with vigor and absolute shamelessness in the affairs of China . . . to bolster up the wrong side in the civil war. . . . The opposition Party are efficient, humane and democratic compared with the Government Party which are tyrannical, inefficient and thoroughly corrupt." He added,

"His Majesty's Government should adopt a policy of friendliness and trade with the Liberated [Communist] Areas."[14]

Another leftist Labour M.P., Konni Zilliacus, went so far as to declare that, "The United States are supporting a feeble Fascist regime in China, a medieval Tyranny in Persia, subsidizing a military dictatorship in Turkey."[15]

Winston Churchill, the Opposition leader, also declared that, "It is not only in Europe that there are those iron curtains and points of actual collision. In China and Korea there are all kinds of dangers which we here in England find it baffling to measure."[16]

Much to Washington's chagrin, the Labour government kept strangely silent when faced with these open attacks on American China policy in the House of Commons. No responsible person within the government bothered to defend the U.S. position. A few days later, Esler Dening told Everett Drumright of the American embassy in London that he regretted that the speakers for the government had not seen fit to refer to China. He said that "the Minister of State (Hector McNeil) had been briefed on the subject of China, but had decided at the last moment to omit reference in his address to China and other areas of the Far East." According to Drumright, Dening tried hard to dissipate the idea that Britain was geared up for a "go-it-alone" China policy by declaring that, "The United Kingdom was too weak economically and militarily to project a positive independent policy. . . . If such a policy were to be undertaken, and he regarded it to be essential as a counterpart to ERP, the United States would have to take the lead."[17]

As Chiang's regime tottered on the brink of collapse, Anglo-American policies toward China began to diverge. The prevailing feeling in Washington was that the Chinese Communists could be coerced into making concessions in dealing with the West. A combination of economic pressure and political nonrecognition would do the trick. In the meantime, partly due to political concerns, Washington was unwilling to sever ties with Chiang by stopping aid, despite the loss of confidence in the generalissimo. From the State Department's viewpoint, continued aid to Chiang would serve the purpose of quieting domestic criticism and getting Congressional approval of the ERP. While the China lobby regarded the passage of the China Aid Bill in April as a major victory, the State Department viewed it in a different light. Continued aid to Chiang was no longer aimed at rescuing a lost cause;

rather, it would serve as a bargaining chip with the incoming Communist regime. It was widely believed that there would be economic disintegration under Communist rule. In such a case, the United States would bring into play its most powerful weapon: economic sanctions. More importantly, as NSC-6 pointed out, this economic weapon could "retard China to be an effective Russian instrument."[18]

Washington's political weapon was nonrecognition of the incoming regime. President Truman, in fact, implied a nonrecognition policy as early as March 1948. At an unsuccessful and highly confusing press conference, Truman declared that the U.S. government did not support any coalition government in China that would include the Communists. The president was immediately besieged by reporters who pressed him to explain his position at the time of the Marshall Mission—a standpoint he found difficult to defend. Secretary Marshall was apparently embarrassed by the confusion. He came out to clarify the president's declaration on the same day, but he dodged the question on whether or not the United States had once had a coalition-government policy that included the Communists. In a clever reply to circumvent the issue, Marshall declared that, "The Communists are now in open rebellion against the Government and that this matter is for [the] Chinese Government to decide, not for the U.S. Government to dictate."[19]

London was puzzled by the contradictory U.S. attitude. On the one hand, every sign indicated that the State Department wanted to wash its hands of China. On the other, the administration was taking a tough stand against the incoming regime. Benjamin Schwartz, a Harvard scholar, wrote a paper in December 1947, warning that a tough policy toward the Communists in China might bring about a stronger Sino-Soviet alliance than otherwise. He admonished that although "the Chinese Communists during the past 15 or 20 years had, in the main, a free hand [vis-à-vis the USSR], external circumstances might easily bring about a sharp revision in the relation between the CCP and the Kremlin."[20] The British embassy in Nanking was thrilled by this argument and reported that Schwartz's paper was "very good stuff and deserved careful study."[21] On 2 February, Ambassador Stevenson sent a long telegram to Bevin asserting that despite American aid to the Chinese government, many competent observers were convinced that the establishment of some degree of Communist control over part, if not the whole, of China, was only a matter of time. Stevenson further pointed out:

Two most obvious points to be made. First, China cannot exclude foreigners by means of an iron curtain for she has too many of her own
nationals abroad. She depends on remittances from the latter. . . . The
process of turning China into an orthodox Communist state would
therefore be extremely slow. Secondly, south China must change her
form of agriculture, but even the purest Soviet doctrinaire will agree
that collectivization is impossible in that land of rice fields at all levels.

Stevenson went on to conclude that as far as British interests were
concerned, there was no reason to suppose that any more hostility
existed toward Britain among the Chinese Communists than toward
any other foreign country, aside from the United States. He noted that,
"Of all foreign commercial interests those of the U.S. are most likely
to be adversely affected. They are not so deeply rooted as are ours, nor
are they of course so extensive. It seems unlikely that they would
persist in trying to weather the storm."[22]

What Stevenson implied in this telegram was a "go-it-alone" policy
for Great Britain, regardless of what the United States did. The Foreign
Office was greatly alarmed by this implication. Although the embassy
became embittered against the Kuomintang from about the end of
1946, the Foreign Office had no reason to believe that Stevenson was
naive about the Communists. In fact, the ambassador reported at the
end of 1946 that, based on his experience in Yugoslavia, the Chinese
Communists appeared to him to be "Communist first, last and all the
time." In a lengthy reply, Dening cautioned against optimism regarding
Britain's position in the event of a Communist victory. He was particularly concerned about the impact of London's unilateral actions on
Anglo-American relations. However, Dening admitted that the question of British relations with a possible new regime had already arisen:

> On previous occasions in China we have sometimes lingered too long in
> our support of a tottering regime and this has complicated our relations
> with the new one when Chiang Kai-shek himself came into power. . . . It
> may well be that if this should occur we should wish to maintain our
> contact with China through our Embassy and consulates as long as we
> can, and that if British merchants can contrive to trade with Communist
> China, we should at any rate not discourage them from doing so.[23]

The view of the Nanking embassy certainly represented the consensus opinion of the British in China. A typical view was expressed by

the general manager of the powerful Hongkong-Shanghai Bank, who told the Foreign Office in June that "the Soong regime [was] becoming ever more unpopular and that it would cause him no surprise to hear of the secession of Kwangtung-Kwangsi."[24] British business circles were eager to establish contact with the Communists. As the loss of Manchuria and North China became evident in the spring of 1948, the issue of whether or not Westerners should remain in Communist-controlled areas came to a head. As early as 29 December 1947, the American embassy had sent out a preliminary warning of evacuation to American civilians in those areas and advised them to concentrate in several big cities.[25] Meanwhile, the State Department retained a few intelligence outposts, especially the consulate general at Mukden. London decided to let the British stay where they were. The American action was viewed as too alarmist. After Leo Lamb made a trip to North China, Stevenson reported to Bevin on 12 February: "We were agreed that premature withdrawal might only serve to antagonise the Communists as a sign of lack of confidence and that in any case, [once] we withdraw it would be unlikely that, the Communists or for that matter, the Central Government, would facilitate the re-establishment of consular posts later on."[26]

In March, the London-based China Association told the Foreign Office in a memo that:

> There would appear to be a real possibility that areas where large British commercial interests are established may shortly fall under the control of an Administration which is not officially recognised by His Majesty's Government and, in such an event, it would seem that special steps, such as have been taken on similar occasions in the past in China, will be necessary to ensure contact with the "de facto" Administration, for the sake of protecting British interests as far as possible.[27]

A few days earlier, the China Association explained the differences between the Americans and the British at a luncheon attended by Bevin's deputy, Minister of State Hector McNeil, and Esler Dening: "The British mercantile interests whose investment in China amounted to £300 million (as compared with £87 million of the United States) had to consider what proposals were and what His Majesty's Government might be prepared to do." McNeil replied that several moves were being considered. On the question of representation with the

Communists, the minister of state "made it clear that in present circumstances we could not contemplate such a step. . . . If the Communist successes were such as to raise the question of whether British merchant interests should trade with them, that was for them to decide."[28]

McNeil was worried about the negative impact of Britain's unilateral move toward the Communists upon the coming Anglo-American talks on the Far East, scheduled for May. Bevin's enthusiasm for the talks remained strong. In January, Dening suggested to Bevin that the Dominions not be included, as preferred by Bevin, lest the already tepid American attitude become even cooler. Bevin readily agreed.[29] As a result, Bevin decided in April to send Dening to the Dominions to sound out London's position before reaching Washington in May for the top-secret Anglo-American conference. Bevin took Dening's trip so seriously that it immediately took on an air of mystery. As a junior officer, Dening was instructed to meet Dominion prime ministers directly. In one case, the British high commissioner in Ottawa reported to the secretary for Commonwealth Relations Office on 10 April that: "I saw [the Canadian] Prime Minister this morning. . . . [He] was somewhat mystified by the cryptic nature of [your] message [but] said at once that he would of course be very ready to see Dening when he arrives here from Australia and New Zealand and to discuss with him."[30]

After several important trips like this, Dening was greatly disappointed in Washington. The State Department was neither well prepared nor willing to disclose what the Truman administration's real thoughts were. The Americans, however, listened while Dening vented his complaints. On the question of aid to China, Dening emphasized the "efforts of the British Government to go along with the U.S. Government during parts of 1946 and 1947 in not permitting the sale of munitions to the Chinese Government." He explained that "his Government had been somewhat embarrassed since it had publicly announced this policy and now found itself in a difficult position because of the constant criticism of aid to China" after the Americans unilaterally lifted the ban. Dening also expressed the British government's serious concern over the dangers to the region south of China, including Hongkong. While refusing to commit himself to anything, Butterworth merely replied that, "The U.S. Government was equally aware of these dangers."[31] Much to Bevin's chagrin, the once-promising Anglo-American conference turned out to be fruitless.

After March, Ambassador Stuart's confidence in Chiang sank deeper still. The China-born ambassador, who had enthusiastically been committed to aiding China, shifted his attention to the so-called Third Forces, which included General Li Chi-shen in Hongkong and the newly elected vice-president and Chiang's rival, General Li Tsung-jen, who was elected against Chiang's will. In his numerous telegrams to Washington, Stuart reiterated his thesis that the United States should stay involved so that Washington would have a chance to influence future developments in China. In one typical telegram, Stuart pointed out that:

> The great majority of Chinese of all classes do not want their country to be communized and I get the impression that the brutal method currently employed in the areas where Communist forces are now operating are intensifying this hostility. . . . We are helping this vast, amorphous population to adjust itself to modern conditions after the shattering of its ancient political and social patterns.[32]

At first, the State Department's Office of Far Eastern Affairs rejected Stuart's recommendation to make a new commitment in China by getting involved with the "Third Forces" to resist the Communists,[33] since this ran counter to the department's policy. Secretary Marshall told Stuart in July to stop any involvement with Li Chi-shen.[34]

But, as Chiang's military position rapidly deteriorated from mid-1948, the State Department began to reconsider Stuart's proposal. Butterworth reported to Marshall on 27 July that given continuing deterioration, there were several possible developments that could occur: (1) the generalissimo might be removed from the scene through a coup d'etat; (2) Marshal Li Chi-shen might establish a provisional government in the near future; (3) in the face of further military deterioration, the generalissimo might be compelled to withdraw to Canton or Formosa; and (4) various provisional groups would establish a rival government. Butterworth believed that, "such groups might actually control a larger part of China than that under the Generalissimo's control at this stage. They might approach the United States for aid, and perhaps recognition, prior to making overtures to the Communists." He thus concluded that: "Failure to give aid or encouragement of any kind would probably lead to the group's coming to terms with the Communists."[35]

In July, Stevenson reported to London that Stuart's faith in President Chiang had "almost reached vanishing point." According to Stevenson, the frustrated ambassador summed up the American dilemma in China by saying, "We cannot get on with the President and I do not see how we can get on without him."[36] As the Chinese Central Bank's resources became exhausted in the summer, Stuart began to embrace the view that China's disintegration into provisional regional governments was both inevitable and desirable.[37] Meanwhile in Washington, the National Security Council was urging that an early decision on China be taken.[38] Paul Nitze, deputy to the assistant secretary of state for economic affairs, recommended strongly in a memo that: "This Government should as a matter of urgent priority consider . . . possible courses of action in the event of [a] collapse in the authority of the present regime in China, . . . particularly with respect to its attitude towards support of other non-communist regimes which may be established in various parts of China."[39]

Thus, there seemed to be a real possibility in July and August that the United States might recommit itself to a role in China through its involvement with the "Third Forces," because, for the first time since the end of the Marshall Mission, this kind of initiative came from the State Department. A consensus on recommitment to China could therefore have been easily obtained within the divided administration.

At this juncture, it was George Kennan and his Policy Planning Staff who stuck to Marshall's original hands-off policy. The PPS produced a timely paper dated 7 September, entitled "To Review and Define United States Policy Towards China." Classified as NSC–39, the paper was soon approved and circulated as NSC–34. The paper argued forcefully that, "The aid which we have extended has been insufficient to check the Communist advance, much less reverse its course. How much more aid would be needed is less likely to be a problem of arithmetic progression than one approaching geometric progression." It went on to explain that:

> All-out aid amounts to overt intervention. Overt intervention multiplies resistance to the intervener. The ramified forces of new nationalism and traditional Chinese xenophobia would likely rally to the Communists, whose ties with the USSR are obscured in Chinese eyes by the Communists' violent anti-imperialism. Open U.S. intervention would, as it militarily strengthens Chiang, tend politically to strengthen the

Communists. Thus, the more we openly intervene in the deep-rooted Chinese revolution, the more we would become politically involved . . . the greater our task would become, and the more the intervention would cost. . . . The American Government cannot rightly gamble thus with American prestige and resources.

The authors pointed out the importance of maintaining a certain degree of flexibility: "The loss of initiative may not be fatal if the tide of events is running in one's favor. In the present situation in China, [however,] the tide is against us and we need the freedom to tack, or perhaps even to lie at anchor until we are quite sure of our bearings." Thus, NSC–34 recommended that the U.S. government pursue the following actions:

(a) to continue to recognize the National Government as now constituted; (b) with the disappearance of the National Government as we now know it, to make our decision regarding recognition in the light of circumstances at the time; and (c) to prevent so far as is possible China's becoming an adjunct of Soviet politico-military power.[40]

The NSC–34 strongly rejected any idea of the United States' recommitment to China on a massive scale. The problem with NSC–34 lay in that it did not specify how the United States could prevent China from becoming an adjunct of the USSR. In fact, the third recommendation could be used by both those who favored U.S. recommitment and those who wanted to get out of China's domestic tangle. This flawed argument was exactly what London was worried about. Within the Foreign Office, doubts were frequently expressed as to the merits of continued Anglo-American solidarity in China, even at the superficial level. As long as the United States kept Britain in the dark regarding China, many in London saw no reason to reject a "go-it-alone" policy. However, the Foreign Office remained torn between the reluctance to antagonize the Americans and the fear of being dragged through the mud in the future by Washington.

Leo Lamb, British minister at Nanking, pointed out this dilemma in a telegram dated 21 May: "We certainly would not think of advocating any olive branch to the Communists." Such a move "would in fact have the additional demerit of antagonising American opinion," and "Anglo-American solidarity is as important in China as anywhere else." According to Lamb, "Any action on our part capable of interpretation as trying to 'cash in' on the present American unpopularity in Chinese Communist circles owing to their active aid by emphasizing that we are not so actively bolstering up the 'reactionary' forces of Chiang Kai-shek would be a crass political blunder." But Lamb quickly added that it was also to Britain's interest to avoid making it too difficult for British nationals and consuls to stay in China. He went on further: "We must nonetheless recognize the practical necessity of dealing with them [the Communists] *de facto* in areas under their control." Lamb, thus, concluded:

> It might in fact be a contribution to the anti-Communist cause if one could ... underline the real need for Sino-foreign trade on a liberal basis (a principle which the present KMT Government has consistently ignored) in the hope that this appeal to the commercial instinct of the Chinese may weaken his faith in the more sterile tenets of Sovietism.[41]

The Foreign Office remained cautious on the issue of dealing de facto with the Communists. Peter Scarlett of the China Department prepared a paper dated in June, stating that the bulk of British interest in China was in territory controlled by the central government and that "expediency alone makes it desirable to maintain friendly relations with the Government. . . ." Scarlett concluded that, "on balance, the time had not come for a China policy independent of that of the Americans."[42]

However, London did not seem to share the American judgment that China would become an adjunct of the Soviet Union. Various reports reached London from sources in Hongkong and elsewhere confirming the view that even if the Chinese Communist Party turned out to be genuinely communist, chances of a "Chinese Tito" still existed. In June, C. B. B. Heathcote-Smith, political adviser to the Hongkong government, was authorized to secretly contact Communist representatives in Hongkong, ostensibly to discuss two British subjects detained in the Communist area. After a lengthy conversation, the Communists intimated to Heathcote-Smith that foreign business would be welcomed in the liberated areas. More importantly, he was informed that Li Li-san, the Chinese Communist leader then widely regarded as Stalin's personal henchman, was not "the most important Communist personality in Manchuria," nor did he enjoy such high status at the national level.[43]

Indeed, Mao's relationship with Stalin was not a happy one—especially in 1948. Mao had never been the Comintern's or Stalin's favorite candidate for the CCP leadership. In the 1930s Stalin had been personally involved in installing CCP leaders and directing policies through his trusted group of Moscow-trained Chinese Communists. Despite the fact that currently available sources from both China and Russia remain inadequate and far from accurate, there is evidence that Stalin was not thrilled by an imminent Communist victory in 1948. The Soviet ambassador, General N. V. Roschin, had always been keen on Russian mediation after the failure of the Marshall Mission. From February throughout the next few months, Roschin continuously offered his services. Ambassador Stuart was ill at ease; he explained Roschin's motives to Washington as being caused by the Chinese Communists' weakness. According to Stuart, there was "a growing body of evidence that the Chinese Communists are weaker than would appear superficially." Moreover, he said, "The Soviets on various occasions during the last 2 or 3 years have been known to express doubts and at times even scorn of the Chinese Communists. Their direct experience of working with them in Manchuria may well have done very little if anything to increase their respect for them." Stuart believed that any such mediation by the USSR in China "will be calculated to advance Soviet interests to the detriment of the U.S."[44]

Secretary Marshall's reply to Stuart on this issue a few days later was illuminating: "[Your conclusion] did not take into account [the fact that the] Sov Amb seemed to fear [the] CCP might follow [a] course similar to Tito. If such anxiety [is the] basis [for the] Sov Amb's apprehension, it suggests [the] USSR may regard [the] CCP as stronger rather than weaker." Marshall's telegram went on further: "It could follow such estimate that the Kremlin seeks political solution now when through mediation it may play Kmt [Kuomintang] and the CCP against one another and exert influence on outcome rather than watch CCP continue [to] gain ground and become more headstrong."[45]

Marshall's judgment seemed closer to the truth. Sources from both the Russian and Chinese Communist sides appeared to confirm the Soviets' fear that the CCP would become stronger rather than weaker. In a memoir written by Ambassador Liu Xiao, Chinese envoy to Moscow in the 1950s, he recalled that: "One late night in December 1954, the Premier [Chou En-lai] invited me to his house for a conversation. The Premier said, 'You are going to work in the Soviet Union, I would like to give you some background story. You should not take any notes, just remember by heart.'" According to Liu, the premier averred:

I am not going to discuss problems between the Third International and the Chinese Communist Party, for it was a long time ago. I will start with the Liberation War [i.e., the Civil War]. In 1948, Stalin sent someone to Xibaipo [then CCP Headquarters] to solicit our views on the situation of the Chinese Revolution. Militarily we were then in very good shape. We were to move southward and cross the Yangtze River. The Soviets disagreed. They wanted us to stop the Civil War. But what they really wanted was two Chinas, or another North-South Kingdoms condition [a historical period of division in China]. The Premier went on further that, "The Soviet objection to our continued fighting derived from their miscalculations of the international situation. They were concerned with the possibility that the Chinese Civil War would disrupt the arrangement of spheres of influence made at the Yalta Conference.[46]

The "someone" sent by Stalin was Ivan Kovaliev, former transportation minister of the USSR, who was assigned by the Soviet Poliburo to go to China in 1948, ostensibly as Soviet representative to the Manchuria Railway Administration. In an interview published in 1991 by the Russian *Far Eastern Studies*, the ninety-two-year-old Kovaliev began to disclose for the first time the nature and operation of his earlier mission to China. Although Kovaliev tried hard to find excuses to defend Stalin's policy toward the Chinese Communists at the time, he allowed us a glimpse into some of the dictator's inner thoughts concerning the Chinese situation in the late forties. According to Kovaliev, Stalin did not, as Chou En-lai had claimed, want the Chinese to stop fighting, but the Soviet leader did suggest that the People's Liberation Army be careful not to disturb areas controlled by the British, French, and Americans when moving to the southern provinces. This suggestion was made in 1949; Kovaliev did not mention Stalin's attitude in 1948.[47]

The Soviet Union was not thrilled by the rapid pace of the Chinese victory. The British Embassy in Moscow noted this in its report to London: "We think it worth drawing your attention to the remarkable reticence of the Soviet press over recent developments in China including particularly the military reverses suffered by the Nationalist side. . . . We are at a loss to account for this state of affairs." The Foreign Office, however, replied by warning that this might simply be a Soviet trick.[48]

Although Marshall's judgment about a possible "Chinese Tito" was not far from Bevin's, Anglo-American policies toward China began to diverge. Their different interests determined the variance in their approaches. While Washington believed that political and economic pressure on the Communists was necessary to hasten any CCP-Soviet split, London was pondering an opposite course—de facto dealings with the Communists. More significantly, London viewed suspiciously the sudden loss of the American initiative in the Far East. The more the Marshall-Hoffman policy in Europe attempted to integrate Britain, the more Bevin wanted to emphasize the Far East. In a private, "off-the-record" conversation with American Ambassador Lew Douglas, Bevin expressed the belief that Russian expansionism in Europe was largely defensive; "once they had obtained such a defensive success in Europe they would, the Secretary of State thought, turn to China and make their main drive there." Douglas, however, expressed his doubts about this theory.[49]

There was another practical motivation behind London's efforts to draw U.S. attention to the Far East. Throughout 1948, the Foreign Office was intensely interested in a Southeast Asian security arrangement. Such a set-up would benefit London on at least two counts. On the one hand, it would ease Britain's anxiety about the Communist rebellions in this region, especially in Malaya and possibly Burma. On the other hand, such a security arrangement would provide Britain with a strong excuse to resume leadership throughout this region. In Bevin's view, 1947 was the year to get the United States involved in Europe because of the economic crisis in Europe. Bevin succeeded in initiating the European response to the Marshall Plan. The British strategy was, as Bevin observed in mid-1947, "the emphasis on Britain's role in European resistance to Soviet expansionism" which "seems the only way of countering American attacks on 'Socialist mismanagement' of the British economy."[50]

Thanks to Cripps's efforts to nurse the economy back to health after he took over the Treasury in 1947, Bevin seemed confident enough to reassert the British role in the Far East. But experience told Bevin that U.S. anti-imperialist sentiment would preclude any positive contribution by Washington to the recovery of the British position in that part of the world. He had no choice but to make his own arrangements. Other European colonial powers were also interested in hooking up with Britain. After the Brussels Pact was signed in March, the Foreign Office was secretly approached by the French and Dutch governments about the possibility of applying the Brussels principle to Southeast

Asia. London took immediate interest in this proposal; Malcolm Mac-Donald, commissioner general for Southeast Asia, strongly supported it. However, after careful consideration, London advised against the idea, fearing the United States would object to any "ganging-up" of the colonial powers.[51]

London's assessment turned out to be accurate, since Washington remained suspicious of any British initiatives in the region. A secret State Department policy statement issued to various embassies in July pointed out that:

> In China the historic roles of the U.K. and the U.S. have been reversed with the U.S. now taking the lead and the U.K. apparently happy to relinquish to us primary responsibility for policy determination as well as the uncomfortable position of chief target for easily-aroused Chinese xenophobia.

The statement added, "In this position as temporary 'silent partner,' it is likely that the U.K. will go along with any fundamental course of action which we adopt." But, at the same time, "there is some sentiment favoring restoration of Britain's formerly preeminent economic position in China and some resentment of U.S. predominance. Aside from intensified commercial competition, the restoration of stable conditions would not be likely to pose any British challenge to the U.S. position in China."[52] Although the general tone of the statement was upbeat, it nevertheless pointed to the possibility that Britain might not remain a "silent partner."

Meanwhile, in London, there were signs pointing to Anglo-American alienation. In August Washington was alarmed by a report from Lew Douglas in London. The ambassador reported on 11 August: "In recent months I have begun to sense an undercurrent of feeling here against the US both in and out of the Government. Sometimes this takes the form of irritation and testiness, but recently it has taken on a much more serious form." Douglas explained that while the British accepted the American assumption of world leadership in the face of Russian aggression, Britain had never before been in a position where her national security and economic fate were so completely dependent on another country's decisions. However, Douglas went on further: "As the British see it, given enough help from [the] U.S. and sufficient time, they will reverse [the] adverse economic damage of two wars."

While the British did not expect to regain their former relative supremacy with help from the United States, they were confident that, in conjunction with the British Commonwealth and Empire, they would again become a power to be reckoned with and, associated with the U.S., could maintain the balance of power in the world. Douglas concluded:

> Thus, one of the objects of U.S. policy, in their opinion, should be strengthening [the] British Bloc, and they regarded as short-sighted and ill-considered any policy of ours which insists on treating [the] U.K. on [the] same basis as other Western European powers, or which weakens or fails to strengthen this bloc.[53]

Douglas was undoubtedly well informed and captured the gist of the British foreign policy in both Europe and Asia.

As the year drew to its end, Washington began to worry that London would not go along with the U.S. China policy at all. Having lost two major battles in Manchuria and North China, Chiang Kai-shek personally directed the massive campaign of Hsu Chou. The Nationalist forces ended up with more than half a million casualties. The capital city of Nanking was exposed to attack as a result. Meanwhile, the issue of evacuation became urgent in Washington. In October an official emergency warning was issued by Ambassador Stuart to American citizens in China, including dependents of officials in North China. In Shanghai, which was still far from the front line, American Consul General John M. Cabot warned Americans on 4 November that, "Unless you have compelling reason to remain, you should consider the desirability of evacuation while normal transportation facilities remain available."[54]

Significantly, American business circles held the same view, as Cabot reported to Washington on 30 November:

> Majority opinion among American business leaders here is that Communists cannot be counted upon to adopt policy permitting their freedom of movement or of continued business operations but instead will sooner or later expropriate or strangle their business. They are therefore loath to take risks to stay behind to protect capital investment unless they have assurance from U.S. authorities. Without such assurances a number of enterprises may decide to move out even if they must abandon property.[55]

The American panic contrasted sharply with British calmness. In London, a consensus was emerging that the British should stay put. In a top-secret brief for the prime minister in October, the Foreign Office pointed out that although Chinese Communists were fundamentally hostile to all non-Communist states, "the programme of the Chinese Government, or rather the Nationalist Party is . . . in many respects not radically different from the modified programme now enforced by the Chinese Communists."[56]

On 11 November, British Consul General Robert Urquhart reported in Shanghai that:

> The General Meeting of [the] British Chamber of Commerce and British Community interests met in my office today to consider [the] situation in Shanghai. It was agreed . . . that it is not politic in view of [the] explosive situation, nor indeed practicable for lack of ships to attempt to remove non-essential British residents.[57]

Two days later, Urquhart sent a long telegram to the Foreign Office, stating that: "We have no intention of adopting evacuation as a policy. This implies no disloyalty to our American friends who are so strongly evacuation-minded." Urquhart further said that, "Although they tend to independent action, we are and must be ready to maintain order, but we could not agree that we must necessarily go down the river with them in any circumstances."[58]

The differing attitude toward evacuation was only the beginning of the Anglo-American divergence. Even the superficial solidarity between London and Washington concerning the incoming regime also began to fall apart at the end of the year. In Washington, conflict between the military and the State Department became increasingly more severe. The hard-line position of the military was reinforced by the fact that the American consul general at Mukden, Angus Ward, had been kept incommunicado by the Communists since November because of espionage charges. Although the U.S. government denied Ward's role in any spying, it was a fact that General Marshall had assigned the consul general at Mukden to be in charge of all American intelligence activities in Manchuria, military or civilian. In August 1946, when Marshall was inspecting the U.S. intelligence organizations in Manchuria, he radically reorganized the whole setup. Marshall found too many U.S. intelligence groups at each other's throats in

China, especially in Manchuria, and, as Marshall told Army Chief of
Staff Dwight Eisenhower, "the American Consul General, a very fine
fellow, was sitting in the middle of this American muddle in the center
of the most delicate region in the world. . . ." Marshall then decided
that all intelligence agencies in Manchuria would be coordinated by
the consul general.[59]

Encouraged by Ward's detention, the military members of the NSC
produced a sensational draft report, stating that:

> After a collapse of the Chinese National Government or its coalition
> with the Communists, the United States should (a) furnish limited polit-
> ical, economic and military assistance to such of the non-Communist
> regional regimes as hold out promise of helping to prevent Communist
> domination of China and to weaken and eventually to eliminate Com-
> munist forces in China, [and] (b) encourage coordination, collaboration
> and eventual unification of the regional non-Communist regime.

With respect to the Communists, the draft report recommended the
following actions: (a) conduct aggressive political warfare designed
to develop and increase strife among the various factions in those
areas, to the end that the popular front be fragmented and the minority Stalinist control isolated; (b) pursue policies toward those areas
calculated to weaken and eventually eliminate Communist control;
(c) not to accord recognition; and (d) not to furnish assistance.[60]
This report was by far the most explicit internal declaration of a
nonrecognition policy toward the incoming regime in China. The
State Department, however, refused to accept this draft. The Department was not so much in favor of recognition as it was unwilling to
pay for this kind of grand scheme suggested by the military. A
top-secret paper prepared by the Policy Planning Staff, circulated as
PPS–39/1, stated: "There is no question but that it is regrettable and
prejudicial to United States interests that the recognized Chinese
Government should be losing ground rapidly. . . . On the other hand,
whether this process will lead to a complete domination of China by
the Communists without at the same time promoting powerful 'Tito'
tendencies within the Communist movement, is doubtful." The
paper further pointed out that it was unrealistic and indefensible "to
assume that we could decisively affect the course of events in China
without taking upon ourselves the major responsibility [and] the

major part of the expenditure of energy and funds and goods which that would involve."[61]

Like NSC–34, the PPS–39/1 avoided the hard question of recognition, perhaps out of fear of political repercussions. The Truman administration, at the same time, rapidly veered toward a nonrecognition policy, though not as militantly and aggressively as the military would have liked. On 26 November, Truman rejected a PPS proposal for the president to announce that, "Information reaching this Government does not indicate that the present course of events in China would have been averted or could now be substantially affected by any measure of aid which the United States could feasibly make available."[62] Such a statement would have meant the open abandonment of the Chiang regime—a step the president was unwilling to take.

The administration was in a dilemma. On the one hand, the State Department's hands-off policy had never been clear-cut and effective; besides, it came too late to have any real impact on events in China. On the other hand, the severance of relations with Chiang was tantamount to a repudiation of U.S. policy since the end of World War II. It was impossible for Washington to deny its overt involvement in China's internal strife because of the Marshall Mission, its economic and military aid, and the presence of a conspicuous group of about a thousand officers who formed the American Military Advisory Group (MAG).

In November, when Chiang attempted desperately to save his regime through an appeal to the United Nations "exposing" an alleged Soviet plot behind China's civil war, the State Department promptly rejected the idea. As Undersecretary of State Robert Lovett reported to Marshall, who was in Paris, there was no tangible proof of Soviet intervention, while American aid to Chiang was so obvious that the appeal would certainly "boomerang to Soviet advantage."[63]

London fully understood the American dilemma. A lengthy cabinet paper prepared by Dening on 10 December stated that:

> The State Department are in a dilemma since if they were to issue some statement calculated to assist Chiang Kai-shek, they would be concealing the true facts from the American public and being dishonest with Congress. If, on the other hand, the State Department revealed the true facts to the American public, they would, in Mr. Lovett's words, "pull the rug from under Chiang Kai-shek's feet."

Dening analyzed the consequences of a Communist victory in great depth. As far as political impact was concerned, the paper noted that, "Mao pays at any rate whole-hearted lip service to the Kremlin and the Moscow press has avoided comment on his success with such scruple over so long a period as to suggest that it is in the interests of Soviet policy not to trouble the pipe dream of the complacent." Thus, "It would . . . be highly dangerous to assume that this initial honeymoon period would be likely to ripen into any enduring bond." Dening also listed several economic areas that would be affected by the Communist victory, such as commercial property and investment, as well as shipping and the China-Hongkong trade, since the economy of Hongkong depended largely on entrepot trade with the mainland. Dening believed that the retention of Hongkong as a British colony, in the absence of strong British naval and military forces, depended on whether or not the Communists found the existence of a well-organized British port convenient for their trade with the outside world. Southeast Asia was another major concern. According to Dening, Communist control of the whole of China posed a grave danger to Malaya as the Chinese would stimulate Communist movement throughout the area. Therefore, there was an urgent need for Britain to build up resistance in the surrounding countries and improve the economic position of Southeast Asia as a whole. On balance, Dening concluded:

> As far as the United Kingdom is concerned our best hope probably lies in keeping a foot in the door. That is to say that, provided there is not actual danger to life, we would endeavour to stay where we are, to have *de facto* relations with the Chinese Communists. . . . In short, it would be unwise for us by our own action to close the only door which remain to us to keep behind the Iron Curtain.[64]

It is clear that the policy of "keeping a foot in the door" required de facto dealings with the Communists that ran counter to Washington's nonrecognition stand. Under the circumstances, London was worried that the confusion in Washington's policy toward China would be prejudicial to British interests. From late November onward, the British embassy in Washington was instructed to keep close contact with the State Department concerning China, but to no avail. As Counselor Hubert Graves reported bitterly to London, "We keep almost daily touch with the Chinese Division and like you, get a lot of waffle from the spate of telegrammes but very little indication of policy."[65] Ambassador Sir Oliver Franks was instructed to talk with Butterworth directly, who appeared to be as elusive as before. Only at the end of the talk did Butterworth intimate that the president and the secretary of state would soon discuss China. Upon receiving Franks's telegram, one Foreign Office official commented, "The only part of this telegramme of interest is the last para. For the rest it only shows how far Mr. Butterworth keeps us in the dark."[66]

Frustrated by the American attitude, London decided to clearly present its own position on the China situation with Washington. In December, Dening informed Ambassador Lew Douglas that London was prepared to keep a foot in the door. On 9 December the irritated Douglas apprised Washington that he had

> discussed China situation with Dening who stated Chinese Ambassador urged Bevin recently to use British influence with U.S. to have more aid sent to China. Foreign Office opinion, however, is that no amount of aid which it would be possible to send China now would alter situation appreciably as rot in National Government too deep. Western powers now must face fact that any government emerging from the present chaos in China will be entirely Communist or will be coalition which will soon be dominated by Communists.

Douglas went on to say that the British Foreign Office believed foreigners could continue to do business with such a government because of many "holes in [the] Chinese economy (for example, shortages of rice, cotton goods and petroleum) which Communists even with Soviet help cannot fill. Therefore [China] must rely on [the] goodwill of Western powers." In Dening's view, Douglas reported, the main thing was for Britain to keep a foot in the door and "consequently [the] Foreign Office will retain British diplomatic and consular offices at posts and is not urging essential British businessmen to leave."[67]

In fact, London at this juncture was prepared to abandon Chiang. When the Chinese ambassador asked to see Bevin in December, a Foreign Office minute for Bevin stated, "Expediency alone seems to dictate that the Secretary of State's answer to these appeals (support Chiang) should amount to a negative . . . but this bitter pill should be coated with what little sugar we can scrape together." The minute also made it clear that, "No purpose can be served by supporting Chiang Kai-shek publicly if, as we believe, he and his clique have little or no support at home, nor do we wish to prejudice such chances, as our business communities in China may have of maintaining themselves under a new regime."[68]

As London was abandoning Chiang, President Truman was communicating with and assuring him of continued U.S. recognition and aid worth $400 million.[69] The British position was made clear to Washington at a time when the State Department was contemplating "concerted action" by the Atlantic Powers to force the incoming Communist regime to make concessions. One such action that Washington was considering involved utilizing trade weapons against the Communists. However, there was considerable anxiety that Britain would break the ranks by not going along with such policies. At a joint State-Commerce conference on 1 December, Commerce Department representatives pointed out that export control for Communist China alone would be ineffective since controls between non-Communist and Communist China were probably nonexistent. Thus, it was "imperative to reach agreement with the British on similar policies, not only to prevent the British from replacing U.S. business in China, but also to control transshipment through Hongkong."[70]

On 30 December, the State Department formally took up this issue with the British. During a conversation between Philip Sprouse, chief of the Chinese Division, and J. F. Ford, first secretary at the British embassy in Washington, the American position was presented in the following terms: "It would be desirable to have concerted action on the part of the British, French and the United States Governments," since "all three had interests in China which could be served advantageously in this connection." Ford promised to convey the gist of their conversation to London.[71] Through dialogue at this level, the Foreign Office noticed that, for the first time since the end of the war against Japan, the U.S. government was asking for "concerted action" in major policy issues regarding China. Bevin was personally impressed. He thought that 1949 would be a crucial year in the Far East and that it was high time for Britain to play a positive role in that region again. This sentiment was reflected in his appointment of Sir William Strang as the new permanent undersecretary at the end of the year. Strang, a veteran expert on Central European affairs, was a key architect of the 1935 Anglo-German Naval Treaty.[72] Bevin was, however, worried about his lack of knowledge and experience concerning the Far East; thus, Bevin wrote Prime Minister Attlee:

I think it would be very useful for Sir William Strang to visit Asia next month before he takes over his duty as Permanent Undersecretary at the Foreign Office. Strang has not had previous experience of the Far East and personal contact not only with our people there but also with local leaders. [The trip] will, I am sure, be most helpful to him and the Foreign Office.[73]

Throughout 1948, events outside the Far East, such as the Czech coup and the Berlin crisis, tended to strengthen Anglo-American solidarity vis-à-vis the Soviet Union. At the same time, fundamental differences had developed over policy toward China. These differences had their deep-rooted causes and had been kept dormant for a long time. The question remained whether the United States and Great Britain would openly split over the issue of dealing with the incoming Communist regime in China in 1949.

Back in 1945, Bevin had accepted the fact that Britain's dire economic position would not permit it to play an important role in the Far East. He had predicted that it would take three or four years before London could restore her position there.[74] Bevin's vision was not totally off base. The British economy seemed to be on the way to recovery, with a trade surplus possible for the first time after the war. Under the circumstances, Bevin resolutely began to reassert British influence in the Far East, even at the risk of antagonizing the United States.

Notes

1. Memo of Conversation, 15 July 1948, *FRUS*, 1948, 3:469.

2. Ibid., p. 678.

3. NAUS, Clubb to Marshall, 23 January 1948, Marshall Mission Files, top secret, box 14.

4. U.K. PRO, Copy dated 21 January 1948 in FO371 68103B/AN156/6/45.

5. Ibid., FO Minute by Rundall, 21 January 1948.

6. U.K. PRO, Washington to FO, Annual Survey for 1947, 14 February 1948, FO371 68103B/AN667/6/45.

7. U.K. PRO, Minute by Hall-Patch and Attached FO Minutes, FO371 68103B/AN517/45/G.

8. U.K. PRO, Alexander to Bevin, 19 January 1948, FO371 68041/ AN517/ 45/G.

9. Ibid., Bevin to Alexander, 23 January 1948.

10. U.K PRO, Stevenson to Bevin, 5 February 1948, FO371 69527/F90.

11. U.K. PRO, Stevenson to Bevin, 21 February 1948, FO371 69528/ F2769/13/10.

F2769/13/10.
12. *FRUS*, 1948, 8:48.
13. Ibid., Marshall to Lovett, p. 53.
14. U.K. PRO, FO371 69528/3288.
15. NAUS, Decimal Files, Gallman to Marshall, 31 January 1948, microfilm 893.00/1–3148.
16. Ibid.
17. NAUS, Decimal Files, Drumright to Marshall, 5 February 1948, microfilm 893.00/2–548.
18. *FRUS*, 1948, 7:49.
19. Ibid., pp. 141–43.
20. U.K. PRO, FO to Nanking, FO371 69528.
21. U.K. PRO, Nanking to FO, 19 April 1948, FO371 69531/F6466.
22. U.K. PRO, Stevenson to Bevin, 22 February 1948, FO371 69527/F2535.
23. Ibid., 8 April 1948.
24. U.K. PRO, Memo of Conversation, 20 June 1948, FO371 69534/F8106.
25. *FRUS*, 1948, 8:809.
26. U.K. PRO, Stevenson to Bevin, 12 February 1948, FO371 69528/F3295.
27. U.K. PRO, 17 March 1948, FO371 69529/F4310.
28. Ibid., F4392.
29. U.K. PRO, 7 January 1948, FO800/FE/48/9.
30. U.K. PRO, 10 April 1948, FO800/FE/48/18.
31. *FRUS*, 1948, 7:77–79.
32. Stuart to Marshall, 22 March 1948, *FRUS*, 1948, 7:164–65.
33. Ibid., Memo by Butterworth, pp. 178–79.
34. Ibid., p. 363.
35. Ibid., p. 380.
36. U.K. PRO, Stevenson to FO, 8 July 1948, FO371 69536/F9585.
37. U.K. PRO, Stevenson to FO, July 1948, FO371 69537/F9883/10/G.
38. *FRUS*, 1948, 7:122.
39. Ibid., Memo by Nitze, 2 August 1948, p. 131.
40. Ibid., pp. 146–55.
41. U.K. PRO, Lamb to FO, 21 May 1948, FO371 69527/F8032.
42. U.K. PRO, Paper by Scarlett, 24 June 1948, FO371 69527/F10028.
43. U.K. PRO, Lamb to FO, 7 June 1948, FO371 69535/F8675.
44. Stuart to Marshall, 15 July 1948, *FRUS*, 1948, 7:361.
45. Marshall's Reply, 21 July 1948, ibid., p. 374.
46. Liu Xiao, *Shi Jie Zhi Shi* (World Knowledge), no. 3, pp. 3–18.
47. "Stalin and Mao Tse-tung: Interview with I. Kovaliev," *Far Eastern Studies* (Russian), no. 6 (1991), quoted from translation in Chinese, *Min-Pao Yueh Kan* (Hongkong, August 1992), pp.64–69.
48. U.K. PRO, Moscow to FO, 12 November 1948, FO371 69542/F16093.
49. U.K. PRO, Memo of Conversation, 26 February 1948, FO800/515/US/48/18.
50. Watt, *Succeeding John Bull*, p. 56.
51. U.K. PRO, FO Minute, 25 June 1948, FO371 69702.
52. *FRUS*, 1948, 3:1101.
53. Ibid., pp. 1113–14.

55. Ibid., p. 901.

56. U.K. PRO, FO Brief for Attlee, 11 October 1948, FO371 69540/F14397.

57. U.K. PRO, Urquhart to FO, FO371 69541/F15742.

58. U.K. PRO, Urquhart to FO, 13 November 1948, FO371 69542/F15977/G.

59. NAUS, Marshall to Eisenhower, 2 August 1946, Marshall Mission Files, top secret, box 2.

60. *FRUS*, 1948, 8:185–87.

61. Ibid., p. 208–11.

62. Ibid., p. 220.

63. *FRUS*, 1948, 7:589–91.

64. U.K. PRO, Paper by Dening, 10 December 1948, CAB 134/285.

65. U.K. PRO, Graves to Scarlett, 22 November 1948, FO371 69542/F15920.

66. U.K. PRO, FO Minute, 23 November 1948, FO371 69542/F16491.

67. Douglas to Marshall, 9 December 1948, *FRUS*, 1948, 8:683–84.

68. U.K. PRO, FO Minute by Scarlett, December 1948, FO371 65546/F17745.

69. U.K. PRO, Franks to FO, Conversation with Butterworth regarding Chiang-Truman Exchange on 23 November 1948, FO371 69542/F1649.

70. Name Files, Clayton-Thorp Papers, box 16, Truman Library.

71. *FRUS*, 1948, 7:703–4.

72. Lord Strang, *Home and Abroad*.

73. U.K. PRO, Bevin to Attlee, December 1948, FO800/FE/45/49.

74. U.K. PRO, Bevin to Seymour, 17 September 1945, FO800/FE45/49.

6

Open Split

The Anglo-American conflict in 1949 was largely a replay of the one in 1945, for it affected all aspects of the two countries' relations in the Far East: world views, economic policies, and political objectives. However, the 1949 conflict culminated in an open split between London and Washington. The split was not, as many studies seemed to believe, based on misunderstandings and lack of communication. In fact, for the first time since the war, the two governments consulted frequently with each other. But the more they made their respective positions clear, the more the two were driven apart. This suggests that the conflict may have had deeper roots than many scholars tend to think.[1]

By 1949, events in China were obviously reaching a decisive phase. At the start of the year, it appeared to everyone that Chiang's cause had already been lost. While commenting on Chiang's New Year Message, Ambassador Stuart stated in a telegram to Washington that: "It was much a literary composition in grand manner." Stuart further described that, "In this it ignored unpleasant realities: the virtual collapse of military capacity, the failure of [the] latest monetary measures, the almost universal drive for peace and [the] impossibility of it as long as he [Chiang] stays in office."[2]

In Washington, Chiang's message came as an ominous note. Before his departure from the State Department, General Marshall made a last effort to wash his hands of China. A top-secret paper known as NSC–34/1 emphasized that flexibility was the only viable choice. The paper, in fact, merely reiterated NSC–34 in a more succinct form.[3]

The new secretary of state, Dean Acheson, adopted a very different style, which would greatly enhance the role of the White House in foreign affairs. Like Marshall before him, the new secretary enjoyed the total confidence of the president. However, there were some subtle changes in foreign-policy decision making. The Department was increasingly subject to President Truman's personal sentiment. One senses the change even in the language used in the department's outgoing messages. In the case of China, the word "commie" became the standard expression for the Chinese Communist regime. Acheson's views may not have been radically different from those of General Marshall, yet he was in quite a different personal position from his predecessor. On the one hand, Acheson could not defy effectively Capitol Hill's pressure exerted through the White House. On the other hand, Acheson was not always able to keep the military establishment at bay. More importantly, Acheson was far more concerned with congressional politics and his contribution to President Truman's political fortune. This was largely due to his personal style, which was excessively smooth and supple, often ending up with an image of weakness and indecisiveness. Perhaps the best observation about Acheson's appointment at the time was made by Sir Oliver Franks, British ambassador to Washington. In a long telegram dated 11 January, Franks pointed out that:

> There must always be the possibility in this country of differences of opinion between the President and his Secretary of State over questions of foreign policy and given the absence of any system of Cabinet responsibility as we know it, there must often be the risk that such differences become public and that as you suggest the administration gives the impression of pursuing a dual policy. So much must always depend on the relationship between the President and the Secretary of State and on their respective personalities and strength of character.

According to Franks, "Both Marshall and Lovett were men of strong character with no domestic political ties, supported by the bipartisan idea in Congress and in close touch with certain Republican leaders such as Vandenberg and with no great personal anxiety to remain in office." He also said that neither Lovett nor Marshall was afraid of saying "no" to the president. Although the president had a high personal regard for Marshall, Truman was not in a strong political position in the United States or vis-à-vis Congress and, thus, was hesitant to assert himself in matters of foreign policy. Because of this, Marshall and Lovett were generally able to either reject the president's ideas altogether or considerably tone down his views. Franks believed that Acheson's apointment would "make such a duality of policy between the White House and the State Department considerably less likely." As far as the implication for Anglo-American relations was concerned, Franks cautioned against the notion that Acheson was a known Anglophile and that, therefore, the relationship between the two countries would be much easier than before. According to Franks:

> Although as a result of better coordination with the White House it may be easier for the U.S. Administration to stick to an Anglo-American policy once it has been agreed between our two Governments, it may equally be more difficult for us to reach firm agreement with them on the details of any such policy—having regard to the increased personal influence of the President, Acheson's suppleness and responsiveness to American public opinion, the doubtful future of the bipartisan idea, and the probability that under the new regime the State Department will be less influenced by strategic considerations and we may find that when we do reach agreement with the State Department on a policy, this policy is less in line with our own ideas than would have been in the case with Marshall and Lovett.[4]

By the end of 1948, Anglo-American policies toward China had deviated from each other so much as to be bound for an open split, though neither side wanted to see such a result. While Washington still harbored some hope of changing the nature of the coming regime, London was prepared to deal with the reality on a de facto basis. The first NSC document under Acheson's direction, NSC–34/2, attempted to revise the ideas contained in the original NSC–34. It was believed that NSC-34 had underestimated the administrative and economic problems confronting the Communists. Although, as in NSC–34, it was admitted that continued aid to Chiang would be ineffective, NSC–34/2 contemplated alternatives: "to discover, nourish and bring to power a new revolution, a revolution which may eventually have to come to a test of arms with the Chinese Communists, . . . if it cannot in the meantime so modify the composition and character of the Chinese Communists that they become a truly independent government, existing in amicable relations with the world community." Since such opposition forces hardly existed in China, NSC–34/2 recommended that, "We should avoid military and political support of any non-Communist regimes in China unless the respective regimes are willing to actively resist Communism with or without US aid. . . . [and] we should continue to recognize the National Government until the situation is further clarified."[5] With this document, Dean Acheson clearly conveyed his line of thinking: to "wait until the dust settles."[6]

An accompanying paper, NSC–41, further recommended that a system of controls be established on U.S. exports to all of China. NSC–41 did not believe that the time had come for economic warfare against the Communists, for it was thought that limited measures would be sufficient to influence the Communist behavior.[7]

Trade control, thus, became the first step in the nonrecognition policy toward Communist China. At the same time, President Truman decided not to stop aid to Chiang, who had already resigned his position as president of the Republic of China. Partly because of congressional pressure, Truman told Acheson in February that he would continue aid to Taiwan, where the KMT regime retreated after fleeing from the mainland.[8]

Despite his long-time personal distaste for Chiang, Acheson agreed with the president that political expediency justified such a move. In February, fifty-four Republican members of Congress wrote a joint letter questioning the American China policy. In his typical conciliatory manner, Acheson advised Truman that there were three ways of answering this letter: (1) to make a noncommittal reply; (2) to formulate a vigorous reply setting forth the facts, which would inevitably hurt the Chinese government; and (3) for Acheson to get in touch with the letter signers and try to have a frank off-the-record discussion with them. The president was naturally persuaded by the third option.[9]

Acheson's excessively propitiatory style was further reflected in a conversation he had with General Marshall S. Carter, a China policy-making insider who was General Marshall's top Washington liaison officer during the Marshall Mission. Acheson told Carter that he preferred the third option, since telling the true facts to Congress would "definitely pull the rug out from under the Nationalist Government." Carter was puzzled by this statement and replied that, "It looked to me like the rug had already pretty well slipped on all four corners and in the middle." Acheson retorted that, "Pulling the rug now without some other hook on which to hang our hat would appear to leave the Communists in complete ascendancy."[10] There is, thus, little doubt that Acheson at this stage still harbored some hope of being able to soften, if not prevent, a Communist regime in China.

London did not share this American sentiment. Bevin believed that the time had finally come for Great Britain to resume her position as a positive player in China, a country where the Americans seemed to be losing influence day by day.

Bevin's energetic foreign policy throughout 1949 rested on a relatively sound economic base. For the first time since the end of the war, Great Britain began to register a trade surplus. But the foreign secretary did not want to flaunt this fact. Bevin was especially angered, as the *Daily Express* reported on 27 February, when his trusted aide, Parliamentary Undersecretary Christopher Mayhew, blurted out to the Americans during a United Nations meeting that "we were very near to an overall balance of trade. This was not quite the moment to say that when we were hoping for the second installment of European aid."[11]

The U.S. Senate reacted quickly and urged the reexamination of aid allocation to Britain. Mayhew was panic-stricken. Angry though he was, Bevin sent Mayhew a sympathetic telegram, stating, "Don't worry too much: when you get into a tangle like this we old ones have to get you young ones out of trouble." The Foreign Office then issued a statement, stressing that the British government would have to achieve "not only an arithmetical balance on our spendings but a balance on our dollar earnings, since not only had we to earn for ourselves but for the whole Sterling area if we were to maintain our place as the bankers for the Sterling area and the Commonwealth."[12]

Behind this tangle, there was sharp disagreement between London and Washington over Europe. In spite of the successful formation of the North Atlantic Treaty Organization (NATO), Bevin was strongly concerned about American objectives in Europe. To him, NATO should not become a step toward "satellization of Western Europe" by the United States. Although his health was failing, Bevin's mind remained sharp and active. In a top-secret telegram to Sir Oliver Franks at the end of the year, when he had made up his mind to recognize the Communist regime in China, the ailing foreign secretary said: "On my instruction Strang has written to you a letter expressing our anxieties about certain recent manifestations of American policy towards Western Europe. . . . These anxieties have been sharpened by recent events in Paris in connexion with [the] Organization for European Economic Cooperation and Atlantic Pact organizations." Bevin pointed out further that there was growing talk everywhere that the U.S. policy was one of "satellitization" and that the United States was building up for itself "a fund of resentment and resistance which may be disastrous for us all."[13]

Under the circumstances, distrust between the two countries further intensified, especially in China. In the economic field, London disagreed with both the rationale and method of utilizing trade weapons against the Communist regime. According to NSC–41, "It is in the field of economic relations with China that the United States has available its most effective weapons vis-à-vis a Chinese Communist regime." It was admitted, however, that an economic warfare against the Communists was impracticable. On the one hand, the Chinese economy was largely autarkic. On the other, the U.S. government desired continued trade between China and Japan in order to lessen the enormous burden of financing an occupied Japan. In Acheson's words, Japan should not remain "a permanent pensioner" of the United States.[14] Thus, NSC–41 recommended a middle-of-the-road approach: limited export controls to China through a mechanism known as the "R-Procedure," which stipulated that, in addition to munitions, various export items to China would be classified as 1A and 1B categories, depending upon their strategic values as deemed by the United States government.[15]

To implement this procedure, the U.S. government needed cooperation from its allies, but Washington was soon dismayed to find that the British were not interested in it at all. In January, the Foreign Office furnished the State Department with a report contending that, "Unless it is prepared to face widespread suffering and discontent, any Chinese Government must foster at least enough foreign trade to pay for essential imports of which rice, food-stuffs and raw materials form a high percentage."[16] This report implied that the Chinese should be encouraged to trade with the outside world.

During a formal conference between Hubert Graves and Walton Butterworth on 10 February, the Americans officially raised the issue of putting Hongkong trade under the control system. Graves emphasized the difficulty Hongkong was facing as a free port: "the imposition of controls at Hongkong would be an extreme measure." Graves suggested that the Philippines could be used as a point of transshipment to China, and he asked Butterworth why the United States was less enthusiastic about imposing controls on Japanese trade with China. Butterworth sensed the British reluctance to cooperate with the Americans. In a somewhat threatening tone, Butterworth emphasized pointedly that, "If Hongkong could not control its exports, the United States would, in his opinion, have to treat the island as part of the China area in applying US export controls."[17] This would, symbolically at least, reopen the question of Hongkong's sovereignty.

The British position on this issue was also a result of a widely held belief in London that the true American motive for trade control was one of selfishness—cutting its losses as early as possible. A February meeting of the Interdepartmental Far Eastern Committee pointed out that, "The Americans had smaller commercial interests in China than the United Kingdom, and there were signs that they wish to cut their losses there at an earlier stage than we should and to proceed at once to a policy of economic warfare against the Communists. . . . We should discourage other governments, particularly the Americans, from doing anything to wage economic warfare."[18]

On 22 March, the State Department informed London about "'R-Procedure,'" a legal device to ensure that all export shipments to a given area would require licenses. The Americans again raised the issue of the Hongkong trade. British Counselor Hubert Graves countered that "it would be useless to close up the loophole of Hongkong so long as other nearby available transshipment points were available."[19]

Moreover, London took the view that the alleged mistreatment of the Americans in China by the Communists was largely the result of the American policy over the past years. The British, after all, did not fare badly, as Dening reported to the Far Eastern Committee: "The indications were that, at the moment, the Communists were leaving British commercial interests reasonably unmolested."[20]

At the first meeting of the Ministerial Committee of China and Southeast Asia chaired by Prime Minister Attlee in March, it was decided that the Hongkong and Shanghai Bank ought to accept the Communist invitation to act as foreign exchange agent in North China. This was a significant move, especially since the American banks in China were not invited to attend the meeting. The Foreign Office noted that the American banks were, in this case, "left out on a limb."[21]

In late March, the State Department decided to use American shipping and trade as a lever to induce Communist authorities to permit

U.S. consulates to function. British Ambassador Sir Ralph Stevenson warned that Great Britain and the United States seemed to approach this matter from different angles. Stevenson continued: "The U.S. Government regarded the ignoring of their Consulates as derogatory while we do not attach so much importance to that aspect. They are thinking of using their commercial interests to strengthen the position of their Consulates while we consider the maintenance of our Consulates as being important primarily to assist our trade interests." A common policy in this matter therefore seemed difficult to attain. He concluded that, "In any event I do not think that we should risk damage to our own following a possible American lead in this matter either by attempting any kind of economic pressure and withdrawing our Consulates."[22]

Stevenson's plea for a "go-it-alone" policy was echoed in London. In fact, before the Foreign Office received the ambassador's telegram, the Labour cabinet had already reached the decision not to use economic weapons against the Chinese Communists. The Foreign Office had also instructed the British embassy in Washington not to act along the American line. Patrick Coates of the Foreign Office was delighted to read Stevenson's telegram, commenting: "It is good ... to see ... that H. M. Ambassador is of the same opinion, although he has not yet rec'd a copy of our dispatch to Washington."[23] The dispatch mentioned by Coates put it clearly: "As we see the picture, an attempt to bully them [Chinese Communists] now is unlikely to produce the result desired and may well slam the door in our faces."[24]

As the Communists continued to ignore the official status of Western diplomatic missions in Nanking, pending recognitions accorded to China by their governments, Washington became increasingly restless. The State Department thought it was time to pressure the Communists through economic means. But the Americans were also concerned that Britain, their major ally, might not go along in this matter. Britain's position was clarified in a memo to the State Department dated 5 April, in which the British objective was defined as "to reach agreement with other powers to take no positive action for as long as foreign interests remain reasonably unmolested."[25]

The State Department was not too happy. During a private conversation with Hubert Graves, Butterworth complained that "the cream is being skimmed at Hongkong" by the British trade with China, as a result of the unilateral measures taken by the United States to control its trade with Hongkong.[26] Dean Acheson was determined to have Britain join the control system. In a memo to the National Security Council dated 14 April, Acheson emphasized that the effectiveness of the American policy would depend on multilateral cooperation.[27]

A week later, Acheson urged Ambassador Douglas in London to secure formal British cooperation in the control matter. After several persistent approaches to the Foreign Office, Douglas reported in despair that the British were deliberately delaying a reply. In late April, the British warship *Amethyst* engaged in a gun battle with the Chinese Communists on the Yangtze River. The ship was severely damaged and there were many British casualties. The Amethyst Incident had caught both the Communist and the British government by surprise, since neither side was keen on provoking any incident. At first, tension was high and, because of the Amethyst Incident, Washington waited anxiously for the British to become more cooperative in getting tough with the Communists. However, the British did not change their mind; in May, in reply to Ambassador Douglas's approaches a month earlier, the Foreign Office sent a memo that stressed various difficulties in implementing the "R-Procedure." The true effect of the measure, according to the memo, would be the "diversion of trade away from Hongkong and Singapore."[28] During an official conference with the British, Butterworth lamented that, "The present memorandum did not seem to be much of an advance over our previous discussions; . . . we had been discussing the China problem with the [British] Embassy since February in anticipation of the fall of Shanghai; . . . now Shanghai had fallen, while we had made very little progress in reaching agreement on a policy for handling trade with Communist China."[29]

The British, however, only agreed to hold a conference in London on technical aspects of the trade control issue. The State Department immediately seized the opportunity and notified London that E. M. Martin, acting director of International Trade Policy, would be sent there in June.

The Martin Mission was ill-fated from the start. As Acting Secretary of State James Webb pointed out, the problem was that, since London had not "addressed itself to [the] desirability [of] controls in principle," and there was no prior agreement on the chief objective, any success resulting from such a conference would depend on Martin's ability to persuade the British to cooperate on this issue.[30] In London, Martin soon realized that the British intended to delay, if not eliminate, the

R-Procedure. To his dismay, as he reported to Washington, the British often raised the issue of trade control in Tokyo and Manila, as soon as Hongkong or Singapore was mentioned.[31] In Hubert Graves's words, this tactic was effective to "keep the Americans at bay."[32]

Besides the Martin Mission's failure, the State Department was further irritated by the immediate leak to the *New York Times* of what was supposed to have been a secret mission. The accurate, insightful, and damaging report by the newspaper disclosed serious disagreements between the two countries. An earlier cabinet paper prepared by the Board of Trade actually recommended that Great Britain should "do a bare minimum" in the matter of trade control.[33] Thus, Ambassador Douglas was prompted to believe that the British Treasury and the Board of Trade were directly responsible for the untimely leak.[34]

After the Martin Mission, the Foreign Office concluded in a top-secret paper prepared for the cabinet on 25 June that

> The scheme which the Americans had in mind for China may be summarised as follows: (1) The U.S. Government (who are prepared to go ahead on their own if necessary), the U.K. Government and the Governments of Hongkong and Singapore should institute a system of control over the exports of goods which would be of strategic or of political importance to the Chinese Communists. . . . The system of export control would differ from that imposed by the U.K. Government in respect of Eastern Europe.

The paper stated the British position in a forceful way: "We had doubts about the concept of export controls being used as political bargaining counter and we thought it possible that the imposition of such controls might only precipitate Chinese Communists' action against our established commercial interests in China. . . . It would be undesirable to impose controls which would be ineffective and damaging to our trade and to the Hongkong and Singapore entrepots if these controls merely resulted in the re-routing of exports via other entrepots in the Far East."[35]

In a message to the State Department along similar lines, the Foreign Office categorically pointed out that, first, the 1A items in the American R-Procedure could not be effectively controlled unless the Supreme Commander Allied Powers (SCAP) at Tokyo exercised the same control. Second, the British were not at this stage prepared to institute a control system over the selected list of 1B items, as suggested by the Americans.[36] Acheson described this message as "very disappointing."

He immediately urged Ambassador Douglas in a telegraphic message to tell the British that "failure [to] demonstrate effective Western control [over] selected exports of key importance to China's economy would represent abandonment [of the] most important single instrument available for defense [of] vital Western interests in China and [the] Far East generally."[37]

The Anglo-American difference in trade policies was further widened in June, when the U.S. government tacitly approved an action taken by the KMT government, now based in Taiwan, to bomb and blockade important port cities along the coast of the mainland, which included Shanghai. London reacted strongly to the KMT move and suspected that Washington was behind this action. Although there was no proof that the Americans had initiated the blockade, the U.S. government did receive prior notification and did nothing to oppose the blockade. On 6 June, Lewis Clark, American minister counselor in China, reported that a vice-minister of the Chinese Foreign Office told him that the bombing and blockade plan was under way. The American government reacted to this in a suprisingly mild manner. Acheson merely instructed Clark not to interfere, as long as the KMT government was prepared to pay for any damages done to Americans in these port cities.[38] London, however, was outraged by both the blockade and the American attitude. When the British ship *Anchise* was bombed by KMT troops while trying to break through the blockading line, Bevin refused to acknowledge Chiang's right to do so. In a strong protest to the Chinese ambassador in London, Bevin maintained that "the Chinese Government had never claimed belligerent rights. In default of such a claim we could recognize no blockade."[39]

Washington, of course, had good reason to sit back and enjoy the blockade. Since Chiang's objective was to paralyze the coastal economy under the Communists, especially in Shanghai, it served as a good opportunity to test the thesis contained in NSC–41, which argued that limited economic pressure would suffice to influence the Communist behavior. As John M. Cabot, consul general in Shanghai, reported a few days before the bombing: "While [the] blockade might intensify [the] anti-foreign movement, [it] might also eventually impress on the Communists [the] extent [of] Shanghai's dependence on foreign imports, facilities and personnel for survival as [the] most important center [of] modern economy in China especially if [the] blockade [were] prolonged much beyond [the] month's time limit assumed, when Shanghai might well approach economic chaos."[40]

In July, Bevin was angered by the American refusal to cooperate with London in ending the blockade, which had produced enormous difficulty for the British in the coastal cities. When the State Department finally agreed to the joint action of sending "relief ships" to Shanghai, the Foreign Office was dismayed to discover that the American objective was to withdraw its citizens from there.[41]

At a meeting of the Far Eastern Committee on 11 August, Esler Dening reported that "it appeared as if the United Kingdom and the United States views on this subject were taking divergent paths." Dening believed that the policy adopted by the U.K. to date had been to avoid any "incidents." He continued: "Now we were faced with the possible necessity of going to the Americans and telling them that we intended to continue trade with China, even though Communist-dominated, and that in order to do this we intended to break the blockade, which would almost certainly provoke 'incidents.' " The Board of Trade representative at the meeting stated that he could not understand "the naive and childish outlook of the Americans on this issue." The Far Eastern Committee concluded that, "Up to now we had kept quiet in Far Eastern affairs since the war and had deliberately not interfered with American policy in spite of the latter's shortcomings. [However,] our roots and interests in China were far older and more extensive than theirs. . . . It seemed that the time had come when Ministers should be asked to agree that we should play so clearly and unequivocally and take our own line."[42]

Although the KMT blockade did not bring the Communists to their knees, it worsened the U.S.-Chinese Communist relations steadily. To Washington, the blockade's lesson was that limited economic measures against the Communists did not work. Thus, it is not surprising that after August 1949 the administration, particularly the White House, veered quickly toward a more comprehensive economic blockade against the Communists. A memo dated in August, written by Livingston Merchant of the Far Eastern Office, recorded that, "Mr. [Dean] Rusk indicated to me this afternoon that the President is moving rapidly toward an attitude and policy with respect to Communist China which will result in an abandonment of the thesis contained in NSC 41."[43]

On 16 September, Secretary Acheson noted a conversation he had with the president during which Truman, with a copy of NSC–41 in his hand, said he thought it was out of date and should be revised.[44] In the meantime, the State Department was putting more pressure on London and urging for concerted action. In a U.S. aide-mémoire dated 9 August, it was pointed out to the Foreign Office that, "It is difficult for the Department of State to understand what 'political and administrative difficulties' would be so great as to outweigh the importance of solidarity in the adoption of a strategy for the maximum protection of U.S.-U.K. mutual, vital long-range interests."[45]

Washington seemed anxious to start the trade control. On 1 October, the day the Communists declared a People's Republic in Peking, President Truman instructed the State Department "to do nothing of assistance," to British vessels trying to run the blockade and being harassed by the KMT troops. He also told Acting Secretary of State James Webb that he expected strict adherence to his policy on this matter. Two days later, Webb told Truman that, "Our general policy was to ignore the strictly legalistic approach and, in effect, permit the Nationalists to take the kind of action that would make the running of the blockade unprofitable for those engaged in it."[46]

Contrary to common belief, London did not harbor any illusions about maintaining commercial interests in a Communist regime in China. A cabinet memo prepared by the Foreign Office in August made clear that the British recognized that foreign economic interests were likely to be faced with the threat of expropriation sooner or later. Provided that the normal commercial channels were still open, the Communist desire for trade with the West could conceivably be strong enough for trade to go on, The memo thus concluded:

> It is of the first importance to maintain for as long as possible the maximum Western contact and influence behind the Asiatic Iron Curtain, particularly bearing in mind that it may conceivably prove that one of the tasks most beyond the powers of the Communist regime may be that of regimenting and controlling the deep-rooted trading propensities of the individual Chinese.[47]

In September Bevin was invited to Washington. Urged by Acheson, China was one of the top issues on the agenda. A day before the talks, Acheson held an inner conference preparing for the meeting with Bevin. Butterworth reported that the British China policy "represented an unusual alliance between the City, which was interested in the commercial stake, and the Left, which wish to normalize relations with the Communists." George Kennan commented that, "the British are suffering from a policy of disunity between themselves and the United States. The important point is on whose terms trade is carried on."[48]

The next day, during the Anglo-American conference, Bevin insisted that the imposition of controls on 1A items had already "left a nasty taste in Europe." Butterworth countered with: "The point is are we going to have China's trade under control or not." Under the American pressure, the British finally agreed to control 1A items on the condition that the United States would exercise similar controls in Tokyo and Manila.[49]

Having achieved this, Washington could not wait to implement the R-Procedure. On 14 October, two weeks after the founding of the People's Republic in Peking, the American government decided to accept the British position. Acting Secretary of State James Webb informed Secretary of Commerce Charles Sawyer that, "Mr. Bevin and his advisers informed us . . . that they would be unable to go further than their offer last August." For their part, the Americans deemed it advisable to accept the offer, but hoped that the British would be able to reconsider their future position with regard to the export controls on 1B items.[50] On 4 November, Acheson submitted a revised version of NSC–41, as requested by the president. The new document, NSC–41/1, recommended that the R-Procedure be promptly extended to China and adjacent areas. The administration's prompt action was brought about by two unforeseen developments that had "consequences of considerable significance." One was a series of natural disasters, while the other was the Chinese government's closure of the Shanghai port, which effectively reduced its industrial and commercial activity. The Americans believed that the cumulative effects of the two would undoubtedly mean severe economic hardship in China for a long time. However, NSC–41/1 complained that:

> It is clear from the outcome of our negotiations with the British that the Chinese Communists would frequently be able to find a ready substitute in the markets of Western Europe for such American or Japanese exports as might be denied. . . . The net effect of such action would be to penalize American exporters and demonstrate the impotence and dis-

unity rather than the power and solidarity of Western governments in the field of economic relations with the Chinese Communist regime.[51]

In December, London raised a sensitive issue with Washington: the regulation of 1A items to the KMT-controlled Taiwan. The Foreign Office believed that the American intention to exempt Taiwan from any embargo of 1A exports would represent a serious breach in the common policy that could "well undermine its basic structure." Washington was outraged by the British position made at the time that the American government was contemplating methods to deny the island to the mainland. The State Department stressed in an angry memo that the embargo "almost certainly would lead to the collapse of Chinese Government resistance" and "a prompt surrender of Formosa to the Chinese Communists—an event which surely would be in the interests neither of the United States Government nor of the British Government."[52]

The Anglo-American dispute over trade control was, thus, not merely a limited conflict of parochial economic interests in China. On the contrary, it embodied the long-time rivalry in the Far East between the two countries. The trade control controversy went hand in hand with the dispute over diplomatic recognition of Communist China, a dispute that culminated in an open diplomatic split over a major foreign policy issue after the war.

By early 1949, the U.S. administration had reached a consensus over the issue of getting tough with the triumphant incoming Communist regime. While the military establishment continued to urge for a nonrecognition policy through military intervention and total economic embargo, the State Department preferred economic and diplomatic means, even though, influenced by the White House, it was no less hostile than the military to the new regime in China. This was clearly reflected even in the thoughts of more pragmatic diplomats such as John Paton Davies and George Kennan. While commenting on Chiang Kai-shek's last desperate efforts to induce a "Four-Power mediation" to end the civil war, George Kennan pointed out that no mediation would work in dealing with the Communists, since "We have no reason to believe that Chinese Communist leaders would be inclined to pay any serious heed to the views of the United States people, whose motives and aspirations they have been maliciously maligning and distorting for years in their press and radio."[53]

If George Kennan sounded like an ideologue, John Paton Davies began to sound like General Claire Chennault, the legendary commander of the Flying Tigers and a staunch pro-Chiang figure. Ironically, as Davies's personal loyalty was becoming an issue outside the State Department, this China-born diplomat was contemplating a kind of strategic bombing against the Chinese Communists, an idea that preceded a similar proposal made by General MacArthur during the Korean War. In a top-secret memo dated 24 August, Davies commented that: "The Communist victory over the Nationalists armed with American weapons, their humiliation of the British Navy in the lower Yangtze and their ignorance of the real significance of air power have resulted in the thesis that the United States is a 'paper tiger.'" He admitted, however, that Americans had done little to belie the role attributed to them. Advocating a policy of educating the Chinese by force, Davies recommended punitive action by air on the industrial installations in Manchuria.[54]

Walton Butterworth was in favor of a tough nonrecognition policy on the ground that accommodating the Communists in China might have a negative impact on Europe and Japan. He said, "The U.S. Government would be placed in the position of responsibility for seeking to form a coalition government with the Chinese Communist participation which would inevitably mean Communist domination." Butterworth went on further, "This would have extremely undesirable repercussions particularly in France and Italy as well as Japan and other areas in the Far East and would affect the European Recovery Program and Western Union."[55]

Thus, from the White House to the State Department, the predominant mood in Washington toward the Chinese Communists was utter hostility. It would be wrong to argue that the American mood in 1949 changed primarily because of the Communist behavior in such cases as that of Mukden Consul General Ward. In fact, a report from Shanghai by the Millard Publishing Company pointed out in November that the Americans were actually using the Ward Incident to delay recognition of Peking as long as possible. The report confirmed that "most political observers here agreed that American recognition would not have been forthcoming irregardless of the Ward incident."[56]

The American attitude contrasted sharply with that of the British. To London, the recognition issue arose as soon as Chiang Kai-shek resigned as president of China in February. On 1 February, Legal Adviser Sir W. E. Beckett triggered an intense debate within the Foreign Office over the recognition question. According to Beckett's memo, "It is both legally wrong and in practice leads to every conceivable difficulty, to refuse to accord any sort of recognition to a government which in fact effectively controls a large portion of the territory. . . . The Communist Government in China is already in a position where it must be recognized as *something*." The legal adviser further pointed out that by granting recognition, the British would be adopting a similar attitude to that which they adopted toward General Franco during the Spanish Civil War, and they should then have a basis on which to talk to the Communist Government.

Esler Dening, who was among the "hawks" within the Foreign Office in his attitude toward Chinese Communists, did not like the Franco analogy. As a leading expert on Japan, Dening countered that

> With all respect to Sir W. E. Beckett's view, the Spanish Civil War is not the only parallel, and there was another one very much closer to the present scene, namely the puppet state of Manchukuo, . . . we neither recognised it *de facto* nor *de jure*, and nevertheless continued to maintain our Consulate-General at Mukden and Harbin and even, as I myself well recollect, to exercise extraterritorial jurisdiction.

Dening went on to admit, however, that this was only possible because the Japanese, for reasons which had never been clear to him, decided to tolerate the British presence. He, therefore, proposed that Britain follow the same tactics for Communist-occupied China. Beckett retorted on the same day that he was aware of the Manchukuo precedent and that, in legal circles, it was considered one not worth emulating precisely because its success was so inexplicable. Beckett went on further to say:

> In fact, the non-recognition of Manchukuo was about the most patently dishonest and contradictory policy that was ever followed. On paper we did not recognise, but all our actions contradicted everything we said on paper. . . . Anyway, the question is whether the Chinese Communist Government are going to take the same line as the Japanese. So far there is every indication that they won't.[57]

The debate clarified the international scope of the recognition issue. The Foreign Office's standpoint was based on Beckett's position that the Chinese Communist regime must be recognized as *"something,"* which ran counter to the American position that Peking should not be recognized at all. The United States, therefore, became a formidable obstacle to the British position on this issue. In January, Butterworth asked the British government to help induce the release of Consul General Ward by "bringing pressure through Communists in Hongkong." The Foreign Office did not like this idea at all. As Patrick Coates pointed out, "It is easy enough to bring pressure to bear on the Communists in Hongkong, by cutting off their wireless facilities, deporting them, etc., but I do not understand how we can bring pressure *through* them."[58] To London, the American request reflected the same mentality as in the case of the trade controls: bullying Mao into a Tito—a strategy London thought would not work. Deporting Communist representatives in Hongkong such as Chiao Mu (Chiao Kuan-hua), who was Chou En-lai's right-hand man, would only worsen the situation by angering Peking while, at the same time, cutting off the only existing channel of communication between the British and the Chinese Communists.

In fact, the Foreign Office at the time was seriously considering the feasibility of establishing some kind of secret contact with the Chinese Communists in Hongkong. The idea was first put forward by Ambassador Stevenson, who recommended Colonel Gordon Harmon, then attached to the Hongkong government, to play the liaison role. Colonel Harmon had established personal ties with top Chinese Communist leaders during the Yenan days. But since he was a British official working for the colonial government of Hongkong, any such contact would be regarded as official recognition of the Communist regime. Despite grave concern about possible American objections and the U.S. pressure for concerted action, Bevin approved Stevenson's plan in March. Before its implementation, however, the Hongkong government presented a forceful case against the move. Assistant Undersecretary Dening seized the opportunity to urge Bevin to abandon the plan because of the Hongkong government's worry that, once leaked, such an action would stir up chaos in the colony. Instead, Dening suggested substituting Harmon's personal contact with impersonal "open-air mail" to the Communist-occupied territories. It was thought that the Communist authorities would surely open these parcels, which would reveal Britain's intentions in dealing with them.

Dening's argument prevailed. However, in April, the cabinet decided to delay for the time being the recognition of the Chinese Communist regime mainly because of heavy pressure from Washington, although there were other practical considerations as well. A cabinet paper on this subject clarified that the British were aware that to refuse recognition to a government that, in fact, effectively controlled a large portion of the territory not only was legally objectionable but also led to practical difficulties. However, the paper continued:

> In spite of these arguments we feel that some time must still elapse before we shall be in a position to consider according any form of recognition to the Communists, our reasons . . . are (a) the North China People's Government must be regarded as an interim regime which is now in process of converting itself into something else; . . . (b) on general grounds, we do not wish to appear unduly precipitate in recognising the Communist regime; and (c) we are anxious to proceed to recognition only on the basis of full consultation with the other powers concerned.[59]

In April, the Communist troops occupied the capital city of Nanking. The American government, at the same time, decided to close its consulate general in Mukden. The British, however, started the "open-air mail" as an unofficial means of communication with the Communists. The difference in policy between London and Washington became increasingly more evident. At a meeting of the "Atlantic Group" in Nanking after the fall of the capital, Ambassador Stuart found most of his colleagues less than enthusiastic about his "concerted action" or "united front" policy. "Support for a common front," reported the ambassador, "came only from the French."[60] It was widely believed in Washington that the British were largely responsible for this tepid attitude of the allies.

London was gradually less willing to follow any American lead in China. On 7 April, Ambassador Stevenson argued against his own early withdrawal from Nanking. Permanent Undersecretary William Strang reported to Prime Minister Attlee that, "American prestige has declined as a result of recent events and our information is that the prestige of the United Kingdom is higher than it has been for some years." In consequence, "we may expect that more will turn upon the action we take than upon the action taken by other powers. We have therefore to weigh very carefully the probable result of any action we may take and must feel free to make our own decision." Commenting on Stevenson's report, Strang said, "We are inclined to support Sir Ralph Stevenson" on the question of staying put in China.[61] Washington became very nervous in the spring that London would make a unilateral move toward recognition, which would destroy the basic assumptions of the American policy. In late April, Washington approved Stuart's plan to remain in Nanking after the Communist takeover. Apparently one important purpose for Stuart's staying put, often neglected by scholars, was to continue the effort of building up the "united front." Shortly after the Amethyst Incident, the State Department thought that the chance had come for inducing the British support in both the trade and recognition issues. Thus, in a message from Washington, Stuart was instructed to intensify his efforts to secure a "common front":

> We strongly oppose hasty recognition of any Chinese Communist regime, either as the *de facto* or the *de jure* authority in China by any power and that we favor continuance of our efforts to obtain full agreement of the foreign powers, particularly the United Kingdom, to a common front. The U.K. has remained noncommittal to our approaches on this question. We pointed out that "recognition should be based on *de facto* control of territory and administrative machinery, ability and willingness to discharge international obligations and general acquiescence of the people of the country."[62]

The conditions outlined by the U.S. government, especially those concerning international obligations and political legitimacy based on Western democracy, were obviously not obtainable. This tough position taken by Washington was reflected in the handling of Stuart's personal initiatives at contacting the Chinese Communists. Throughout the ambassador's three-month stay in Communist-occupied Nanking, Washington vetoed almost all the moves Stuart proposed in response to Communist overtures in Nanking and elsewhere aimed at winning official recognition from the U.S. government. The most important veto was perhaps that of Stuart's acceptance of an invitation to Peking in his capacity as ex-president of the Yenching University—an invitation that could have resulted in personal contact with top Communist leaders such as Mao and Chou. The only exception to Washington's vetoes was a case involving an alleged demarche from Chou En-Lai, in which the Chinese leader supposedly asked for help in the matter of Western recognition so that he and his "pro-Western faction" could defeat the militant "pro-Soviet faction" within the CCP. Formally addressed to the American and British governments, the "Chou Demarche" was a highly questionable document. The sources were dubious and the contents unimaginable, especially since after it became publicly known later, it hardly affected Chou's remarkable career.

It is interesting to note that Washington did react to this demarche. The White House authorized a reply that was sent to an intermediary, but drew no further results. That Washington reacted to the demarche may be explained by the fact that its pleading tone suited President Truman's sentiment at the time. This humble attitude was what the administration wanted to see.

Although the British cabinet took the demarche seriously, the Foreign Office dismissed it summarily. Thus, in contrast to the Americans, the British did not even attempt a reply. The British embassy in Nanking believed that in sending a demarche like this, Chou could scarcely have expected to receive a response. The embassy went so far as to suggest that Chou's motive may have been either to assure the West that all the pro-Soviet propaganda about China was not genuine, or that Chou himself was preparing for political asylum in Hongkong or Japan.[63]

Back in May, Washington had calculated that the Amethyst Incident would prompt London to become more congenial regarding trade control as well as a common front vis-à-vis the Communists. The British were thinking, however, in the opposite direction. Although outraged by the loss of prestige and human life, the Labour government handled the incident with considerable calmness and constraint. In the first place, the Labour cabinet immediately realized that it was a mistake. As a top-secret memo prepared for the prime minister stated,

> The intelligence report that Communist forces were likely to cross the river on 21st April was issued probably on the 19th. It has not been possible to establish at what precise time this report was received by all concerned but Amethyst was already well up the river and fairly close to her destination before effective action could have been taken to cancel her passage.[64]

On the Chinese Communist side, the incident was no less a surprise. The gun battle between Communist troops and *Amethyst* personnel took place amid enormous confusion. The Communist field commander at first thought it was American naval intervention. The general responsible for the gun battle in the field, Ye Fei, recalled in his memoirs that he and the others were not even sure that the *Amethyst* was a British ship. General Ye asked, "Why should it be a British ship? If it is American, I will understand."[65] Nevertheless, the fact that the

Amethyst was inactivated symbolically marked the end of Gunboat Diplomacy. The Communists lost no time in capitalizing on their victory over imperialism; it was now a different China. Interestingly enough, Britain seemed to have less trouble adjusting than did the United States. London's sober attitude toward the incident reflected the mindset of an old China Hand. It may be interesting to speculate on what could have happened had a similar incident occurred between the United States and Communist China.

Contrary to expectations of a rapid deterioration in Sino-British relations, the incident's effect was to hasten, rather than delay, the British decision to recognize Communist China. A Foreign Office minute clearly pointed out that the incident "might well never have occurred had we been [in] day-to-day contact with the Communists." Therefore, "It is of the greatest importance that we should establish contact with them as soon as possible, but our ancestors in China found that it took two parties to establish relations."[66]

Back in Nanking, Communist authorities refused to recognize any foreign mission whose government had not accorded recognition to the new regime. Under the circumstances, a "common front" policy became even harder to achieve. In May, Ambassador Stuart reported to Washington that, "We have had several recent indications that our colleagues are, under present inactivity of ill-defined status, becoming restless and would welcome opportunity to recognize Commie central regime." He insisted that the United States should "reserve recognition as a bargaining lever, and to press for detailed agreement along [the] lines [of the] 1937 Litvinov Agreement with [the] USSR."[67]

The American embassy in Moscow shared Stuart's view completely, as Chargé Kohler reported to Acheson: "I cannot support too strongly Ambassador Stuart's conviction. . . . [The] Embassy [is] disturbed at [the] anxiety for quick trade with [the] Communists seemingly prevailing certain U.S. and British circles."[68]

In June, Ambassador Douglas reported from London that the Foreign Office vehemently denied the State Department's allegation that pressure from British economic interests in China had played a decisive role in the issue of recognition.[69] The Foreign Office was not lying. Throughout the postwar years, the British business circle related to China had generally been accommodating and in agreement with the Labour government's China policy. Its chief representative in London, the China Association, had seldom given the Foreign Office serious headaches; this contrasted sharply with the strong political influence of the China lobby in the United States.

Having failed to obtain active British cooperation on the trade issue, Secretary Dean Acheson was very anxious to confront Bevin in person. On 20 July, Acheson instructed Douglas to see Bevin immediately and to urge him to come to Washington, saying:

> You can remind him that on two occasions he spoke metaphorically of taking a "trip around the world" in order to see whether our two countries could not have a common policy. I now want to have through you a frank exchange of views with him regarding the Far East in a "matey sort of way" as he expressed it in Paris when we discussed Hongkong, before either Govt has finally crystallized its position.[70]

Acheson was now preoccupied with the efforts of forestalling a British decision on the recognition issue. One day after Douglas had conveyed the message to Bevin, Dening wrote a long memo to the foreign secretary, stating that, "For the past three years we have been trying to get the Americans to be frank with us over China and Japan and all our efforts have failed. The Americans have gone their own way, with unhappy results for everyone." Dening continued: "Now they are asking us to discuss China and Japan, I think we should welcome this as the best way in which to try to keep American policy on the right lines. . . . It will not involve us in any wider commitments. It will merely mean a more active diplomacy by us in Far Eastern affairs which we are well equipped by past experience to conduct."[71]

Washington's desire to obtain British cooperation was also reflected in a long and secret mission to London by George Kennan, who was considered by the British to be a key policy insider. During a conversation with Minister of State Hector McNeil, Kennan expressed strong American interest in "resistance elements in China." He intimated that the State Department was "expecting shortly to publish a White Paper on past events in China which they hoped would confound their critics." More importantly, Kennan emphasized that the State Department's preliminary reaction to the new regime was that "on a governmental level we should make no concessions to the Chinese Communists unless they recognize and adhere to the principle of reciprocity. The State Department have not much sympathy with the American community in Shanghai whom they regarded as hostages."

Moreover, Kennan indicated that Washington was interested in a two-China policy (referring to Taiwan and the mainland), although the American government did not believe in Chiang's ability to hold on to the island despite continued aid from the United States. However, if the Formosans were to "revolt" against the mainland Chinese, the U.S. government would support them.[72] Kennan's mission was by far the most frank and informative one on the Far East from the Foreign Office's point of view.

Shortly before Bevin's trip to Washington, the Foreign Office prepared a memo for cabinet approval, in which it was pointed out that, even though the Chinese Communists were orthodox Marxist-Leninists, "to display a general and avowed hostility to the new regime is calculated to drive it further into the arms of Moscow." The memo concluded that "the only hope of encouraging the emergence in China of a less anti-Western tendency is to give the new regime time to realise both the necessity of Western help in overcoming its economic difficulties. . . [and] the natural incompatibility of Soviet imperialism with Chinese national interests (e.g., in Manchuria)." From the British point of view, the recognition question was likely to become acute in the next few months, although there were still too many undetermined facts to be considered. The memo concluded that,

> At the worst, the relations of the British Commonwealth and North Atlantic Powers with a Communist Chinese Government after recognition may follow the pattern of their relations with Soviet satellite states in Eastern Europe. There is, however, the possibility that the pattern will eventually develop along the lines of our present relationship with Yugoslavia and it is therefore considered that the Western Powers should be careful not to prejudice future possibilities by developing an openly hostile attitude towards a Communist regime from the outset.[73]

Clearly the British position on this issue ran counter to that of the Americans, and Washington was anxious to change Britain's standpoint. In August, the State Department reiterated the desire to discuss China with Bevin, as Ambassador Franks reported to London: "[Llewelyn] Thompson of [the] Office of European Affairs of the State Department enquired whether we thought Mr. Bevin was likely to be coming prepared to discuss China during his visit to Washington. . . . The present divergence between the British and U.S. policies in China was clearly a matter of concern from the point of view of [the] Anglo-American community."[74]

Meanwhile, Ambassador Stuart formally left China at the end of July, coincident with the publication of the White Paper on Chinese events. Although this long public document was a devastating blow to the KMT regime, there were many ambiguities. The British ambassador continued to stay put. Even if his personal position was becoming increasingly awkward because of Britain's failure to recognize the PRC, Stevenson strongly recommended that in case he could not hang on in Nanking, the embassy must remain there. Bevin was also vehemently against the early withdrawal of the ambassador. As Washington was eager to build up a "common front" in China, Bevin was thinking of forming a united front within the British Commonwealth. In June, during the Council of Ministers Conference in Paris, Roderick Barclay, one of Bevin's top aides, often wrote Dening on the issue of China, indicating the foreign secretary's grave concerns. On 3 June, Barclay wrote:

> The Secretary of State remarked to me this morning that he had been thinking about the situation in China and had reached the conclusion that it would be a good thing to try and get an agreed policy between the various Commonwealth Governments on the question of relations with the Communists in China, the position of recognition and other connected questions. He thought that it might be possible to organize a meeting, something on the lines of the Delhi meeting about Burma.

Dening's reply cautioned against such a meeting because it would attract unnecessary publicity. Bevin wrote a note on Dening's letter to Barclay, saying, "I have had no previous papers on withdrawal [of Stevenson], I am against this." A few days later, when Bevin was back at Blackpool for the Labour Party conference, Tomkins, another top aide of the foreign secretary, wrote a note to Dening stating that, "The Secretary of State told me yesterday in Blackpool that he thought the Chinese Communists were anxious to do business with us," and that "he, for his part, was anxious that Sir Ralph Stevenson should remain at his post so as to make the best of any opportunities for establishing trade relations which might arise."[75]

As Bevin became increasingly anxious to establish relations with Communist China, London was less and less enthusiastic about the KMT regime. In fact, London was prepared to abandon the Chiang government altogether. In June, the Chinese embassy in London handed a strongly worded memo to the Foreign Office, warning about the consequences of recognizing Communist China. Peter Scarlett, head of the China Department, angrily reported that he received it "with due solemnity." Dening simply dismissed it as "a rather impertinent document."[76]

With such fundamental differences between the two governments over China, Bevin's trip to Washington had no chance of obtaining fruitful results. During the talks on China on 13 September, Acheson hit hard and expressed his strong desire that, "the Atlantic Pact countries will consult fully and carefully and concert policies on recognition of the Chinese Communist Government." Bevin countered by saying that Britain was not in the same position as the United States was; the British did not want to get out of China. Furthermore, Bevin did not think that by staying, the British would complicate the recognition problem any further. The Americans insisted on China's "honoring international obligations." Butterworth pointedly reminded the British that it was "possible that denunciation of the treaties might include denunciation of those respecting Hongkong." In addition, Acheson kept raising rhetorical questions such as "Have the Communists consulted their own people?" "Do the Chinese think that the Communist Party controls them?" Bevin admitted he was afraid that "by being too obdurate we will drive the Chinese into Russia's grip." Acheson rejected this idea by saying, "We doubt if recognition is a strong card in keeping China out of Russian hands and they will be there any way."[77]

Thus, despite an amicable atmosphere, the Anglo-American conference did not go well. In the meantime, Sir Ralph Stevenson's continued stay in Nanking caused great concern in Washington. American Counselor John Jones reported from China on 9 September that, while the French and Dutch ambassadors were prepared to leave by the first available transport, the other Western European representatives were torn with indecision, awaiting the move of the British ambassador. Jones added, the latter had become a key figure in the plans for the general exodus of chiefs of mission from Nanking, and he showed no inclination to leave.[78]

Washington was further embarrassed by London in October, when the Communists declared a People's Republic in Peking. From the British viewpoint, the establishment of a central government by the Communists indicated that the issue of foreign recognition had now become de jure, rather than de facto. Chou En-Lai, the regime's new premier, formally asked foreign missions for official recognition on 1 October. Although Chou's message deliberately avoided the official titles of foreign chiefs of mission, the British reply addressed the new regime by its official title: the Central People's Government. Washington was furious when the French embassy disclosed the text of the British reply a few days later.[79]

Acheson sent a strong paraphrased protest to Bevin on 14 October, stating "I was concerned by the text of [the] msg [message] from [the] Brit Govt to [the] Chi Commie auths [in] Peiping. The phraseology of the note ... appears to imply *de facto* recog although the FonOff [Foreign Office] has assured us that such was not the intent."[80] The American embassy in Moscow bitterly commented on this event, saying, "We feel it impossible to avoid the impression that [the] British have deliberately taken [a] strong step toward recognition. . . . British action in sending [the] note may indicate British determination not to be maneuvered by us into [the] position of sharing our current unpopularity in China through participation in what [the] British may consider to be unnecessary and undesirable pressure activities." The Moscow embassy further predicted the grave consequence would be that: "British action seriously compromises highly desirable and previously agreed upon policy of coordinated Western action towards CPG [Central People's Government]."[81] President Truman was even more angry with the British action. He told Acheson that he thought the British "had not played very squarely with us on this matter."[82]

Bevin later apologized for such a unilateral action without prior consultation with Washington, although the Labour government had already made its decision about the recognition question before the Communists had declared the Central People's Government. On 30 September, one day before Mao announced that the "Chinese people have stood up!" in the Tiananmen Square, Dening reported to the Far Eastern Committee that, "As the Committee are aware, there had been considerable danger of United Kingdom and the United States views on the policy to be adopted in China diverging, and the Cabinet had decided that in the event we should go our own way. The American policy had been one of full retreat and verged on panic."[83]

Bevin was deeply concerned about Anglo-American relations over China. In his opinion, the United States lacked a proper historical perspective when dealing with China. Shortly before his departure for Washington, Bevin had a private conversation with Lew Douglas, in which he told the American ambassador that, "The whole problem of China was much influenced by past history. We believed, too, that the Chinese Communists were first and foremost Chinese and they were not capable of becoming Russians overnight. . . . It seemed to me that the American White Paper had effectively dismissed Chiang Kai-shek as being unworthy of any further American support, but the U.S. Government did not seem to have any alternative to put in his place."[84]

The State Department's argument that China must honor its international obligations was badly received in the Foreign Office. Ambassador Stevenson believed it was absurd to insist on deferring recognition,

> until we had obtained an undertaking that the new regime would carry out international obligations which the Kuomintang signally failed to observe. Nor would it really be reasonable if the rest of the non-Communist world were deprived of diplomatic relations with China because the new regime refused to abide by e.g., the Sino-American Commercial Treaty.

Stevenson further emphasized that he presumed "international obligations" meant multilateral agreements such as the Hague Conventions and the UN Charter, and that nothing would be gained by unduly delaying recognition.[85]

The British business community was also anxious to accord recognition to Peking. On 14 October, the London-based China Association told the Foreign Office that recognition of Communist China was inevitable.[86] A week later, Dening reported to Bevin that the question of recognition had now become de jure rather than de facto.[87]

Meanwhile, a report from Nanking seemed to reinforce the British view that recognition might widen the Sino-Soviet distance. According to the report, Huang Hua, head of the Communist Alien Affairs Office in Nanking, criticized "with unusual vehemence" the American assertion that China was controlled by Russia. Huang had recalled the desertion of the Chinese Communists by the USSR twenty years ago and how "Chinese Communists fought their own fight single-handed and beholden to none." Although the Foreign Office was somewhat skeptical, A. A. E. Franklin of the China Desk reinforced Huang's argument by providing his personal account of events in Tientsin in 1948 after the Communist takeover. Franklin noted that the Russian consul general expressed "undisguised contempt of the 'alleged Communists' " and that the Russian Chamber of Commerce in Tientsin "associated itself with other foreign Chambers of Commerce."[88]

In late October, the Labour government decided to notify various countries of the British intention to recognize Communist China. Meanwhile, a meeting of the chiefs of British missions in the Far East, known as the Bukit Serene Conference, was held in Singapore. On 29 October, the Foreign Office notified various British embassies abroad that, "If we decided to recognise the Chinese Communist Government, we are under no illusions that this will confer any great benefits on us. . . . It is rather that if we do not recognise them, we shall be in no position to take advantage of developments or to protect our interests."[89]

Three days later, the Foreign Office handed a memo to the State Department, stating that, "The Communist government of the People's Republic of China is the only alternative to the Nationalist Government and the Communists are now the rulers of most of China." Moreover, "Mr. Bevin is advised that recognition of the Communist government as *de jure* government of China in present conditions cannot be held to be contrary to the principles and practice of international law."

While presenting the memo, Hubert Graves explained to Butterworth that, "it was the British Government's view that the disadvantages of nonrecognition were so great as to outweigh any possible advantages to be obtained from securing Chinese Communist assurance of respect for international obligations."[90]

To London, the "international obligations" the U.S. government insisted on primarily referred to the Sino-U.S. bilateral treaties the Americans wanted to preserve, for the negotiated Sino-U.K. Commercial Treaty had not yet gone into effect. Butterworth strongly suspected that the British had struck a secret deal with the Communists, as he asked Graves "if the British had had any preliminary conversations with Chinese Communist authorities either in Hongkong or in Shanghai through intermediaries such as John Keswick (head of Jardine-Matheson)," which would "provide some common ground and make the British approach to the question of recognition seem less of a 'bolt out of the blue.' "[91] A few days later, London received the final report from Singapore that the Bukit Serene Conference favored the earliest possible de jure recognition of the PRC.[92]

The State Department refused to give up its efforts to forestall formal British action. A long memo prepared for the Secretary of State recommended that Acheson continue to press for a "common front." Significantly, the memo also drew up a somewhat bizarre list of more than thirty treaties specified as China's "international obligations." These included the General Agreement on Tariffs and Trade (GATT), the Nine-Power Pact of 1922, and, of course, the Treaty of Sino-American Friendship, Navigation, and Commerce of 1946.[93] It is doubtful that the State Department expected these obligations to be honored in the first place.

In November, Acheson endeavored to keep the French in line on the issue of recognition, by offering Robert Schuman U.S. support for his position on Indochina.[94] In November, Washington made another attempt to prevent London's action by proposing a UN resolution on China. Sir Alexander Cadogan, U.K. representative to the UN, reported on 26 November that,

> The Americans are pressing us very strongly to reconsider our attitude . . . . The U.S. Resolution called upon all states: (1) to respect China's territorial integrity; (2) to respect the right of the Chinese people to choose freely their own political institutions; [and] (3) to refrain from seeking to acquire [a] sphere of influence or to create foreign controlled regimes within the territory of China. This proposed resolution, though aimed at the Soviet Union, was provocative enough from the Chinese Communist point of view, for it implied a puppet regime in Peiping. The State Department thought that was not enough.

A few days later, a principle of "international obligations" was added to the proposed resolution.

Bevin was greatly disturbed by the American action. He told Cadogan that, "I am at a loss to understand why the Americans should insist on opening up the China question in this way. . . ." He pointed out further, "American initiative has already landed us with an embarrassing resolution on Libya in this session . . . [and] their present initiative bids fair to do the same over China at a time when I am working strenuously and with reasonable hope of success to bring Commonwealth and Western Powers towards joint recognition of the Chinese Communist towards the end of the year."[95]

London was now prepared for the open split with Washington over China. Peter Scarlett pointed out in a Foreign Office minute that, "the U.S. Government feels strongly that as long as there is any opposition to the Communist regime, it would be a stab in the back if recognition were to be accorded."[96]

In late November, Bevin could not wait any longer, especially as the Foreign Office had learned that India might accord recognition to China before Britain's action. The pros and cons of advance recognition by India were carefully analyzed by Peter Scarlett on 22 November. As for the advantages, Scarlett believed that India's action would "break the ice on recognition as far as US opinion was concerned and ... make subsequent recognition by us and others easier." On the disadvantage side, it would "add Communist prestige in Southeast Asia. It might be interpreted as recognition by Asiatics as distinct from Western 'imperialism.' " Bevin decided that London should follow India's lead immediately.[97]

On 8 December, Acheson made a final attempt to dissuade Bevin from according the recognition. During a conversation with Sir Oliver Franks in Washington, Acheson reiterated the American government's viewpoint on the matter, again emphasizing China's international obligations. According to Acheson: "It seemed to us that the inclinations of the Chinese Communists were to follow the Russian example of considering themselves not an evolutionary regime which had sprung from the previous one which, therefore, entailed that they assume both the rights and obligations of the former regime, but a revolutionary one which would seek to assume all the rights and only those obligations they choose to undertake. . . ." Acheson went on: "Secondly, it was important to have evidence of how they propose to conduct themselves with respect to the outer world. . . . Thirdly, we did not believe that hasty recognition would confer any permanent benefits on those who undertook it. Fourth, as respects the United States, it was important for us to bring Congress into our deliberations so that, at any rate, the problem would be fully talked at and the issue clarified." Franks could only reply that, in any event, the cabinet would make a decision before the year was out. Acheson strongly urged that the Americans be given "as much advance notice as possible."[98]

On 16 December, the British cabinet decided to take action on recognition, but the exact timing was left to Bevin to determine. In a personal message to Acheson, Bevin pointed out that,

> We have deferred a decision on this matter as long as we felt able, but having taken into account all the circumstances and all the views expressed by other governments, we nevertheless feel we must now proceed to recognition. There are some factors which affect us specially,

not only our interests in China, but also in Southeast Asia where there are vast Chinese communities. We advised that continued non-recognition is liable to cause trouble there which we cannot afford to risk, and we have had to bear this in mind.

Bevin emphasized further that "to withhold recognition indefinitely is to play straight into the hands of the Soviet Union. . . . We feel that the only counter to Russian influence is that Communist China should have contacts with the West and that the sooner these contacts are established the better."[99]

In a belated and unhappy reply, Acheson "hoped that although we are adopting different courses in this instance our two governments can follow a common course in all other important matters of mutual concern in the Far East."[100]

Acheson had good reasons to worry about the Far Eastern region as a whole. Throughout 1949, Washington and London were often at loggerheads on regional issues. On the one hand, London believed that the collapse of American power on the Asian mainland was largely the result of a wrong and obstinate policy. On the other hand, traditional Anglo-American rivalry in the region had by no means disappeared. One of their disagreements was over a containment plan in Asia. Bevin was attracted to the idea of a regional organization in Asia for both political and security purposes. On 2 April, Bevin wrote Acheson a memo, stating that, "While strategic necessities of Europe and Middle East are greater and should have priority, the requirements of South East Asia, though in a different category, are of vital importance." According to Bevin, "We should do our utmost to encourage a spirit of co-operation and self-reliance of a common front against Russian expansion in that area."[101]

The Americans remained strongly suspicious of any British move of this nature. Washington insisted that initiative be taken by the local peoples, among whom the Filipinos seemed to be on the top of the list. Earlier in the year, President Elpidio Quirino of the Philippines proposed a "Pacific Pact," modeled after NATO. Quirino insisted that the United States provide money and leadership. Washington watched this development with considerable interest.[102] A top-secret paper prepared by the PPS, later circulated as NSC–51, stated that, "It is our continuing objective to encourage the SEA region to develop in harmony with the Atlantic Community and the rest of the Free World." NSC–51

continued: "We should avoid at the outset urging an area organization.
... [But] if Asian leaders prematurely precipitate an area organization,
we should not give the impression of attempting to thwart such a move
but should go along with them while exerting a cautiously moderating
influence."[103]

In July Washington was embarrassed when only Chiang Kai-shek
jumped on Quirino's bandwagon. The rest of the Asian countries remained cool, if not hostile, to the Quirino plan. The Truman administration backed off immediately after the signing of what was quickly
dubbed as the "Chiang-Quirino Pact."[104]

In London, Bevin was contemplating the possibility of a regional
conference sponsored by Britain. The failure to obtain American support in Southeast Asia prompted Bevin to build up his own regional
organization. In April, Bevin made an attempt in Washington to ascertain American opinion on a containment plan in Asia. He deliberately
chose to overstate the case. During a conversation with Acheson,
Bevin maintained that the United Kingdom "intended to stand firm [on
Hongkong], making it, if necessary, a sort of 'Berlin of the East.' "
Acheson immediately replied that, "The thought of another Berlin . . .
filled me with considerable distaste."[105]

Returning to London, Bevin wrote Prime Minister Attlee, who was
presiding over a Commonwealth Prime Ministers' Conference, saying
that, "We do not know if the Commonwealth Prime Ministers will
agree to a meeting of Foreign Ministers in Ceylon next year, and I am
by no means sure that it would be safe to wait until then to consider
Southeast Asian problems." Bevin added that if the British waited too
long, they might find themselves unable to influence the situation,
since a tendency was already developing (led by Pandit Nehru) to issue
invitations to international conferences without asking the United
Kingdom. Thus, Bevin concluded:

> There are so many political difficulties in South East Asia that a purely
> political approach may meet with no success. It seems desirable, there-
> fore, to approach the problem more from an economic angle since in the
> economic field, there is a good deal which the West has to offer to the
> East, thus providing a solid basis for cooperation.[106]

The "Chiang-Quirino Pact" came as a great shock to London. The
Foreign Office suspected an American hand behind the deal. Guy Bur-

gess, a Soviet spy at the China Desk, described it as "another attempt to involve other powers in the Civil War." Dening agreed and called it a "fantastic idea."[107]

Bevin's approach met with little success in Washington, however. The Americans were primarily interested in a regional defense arrangement that preferably excluded the United Kingdom. John Paton Davies of the PPS suggested a Three-Power Pact to be signed by the United States, Australia, and the Philippines.[108]

During the September conference between Bevin and Acheson, Butterworth emphasized that, since the West was not very popular in the area, the United States took pains not to initiate a regional pact. Washington viewed Bevin's economic approach with enormous suspicion, considering it another effort to bolster the Sterling Bloc. At a dinner party in September, Acheson told Ambassador Franks bluntly that, "There was real anxiety on the American side whether the British wished to work towards a free world in which exchanges between dollars and sterling areas were at high level or whether they wished to build up a soft currency world centered around the sterling area and cut themselves off from North America."[109]

At a State Department inner conference held on 13 September, Butterworth commented on Britain's motives for a regional arrangement in this manner: "The British are reluctant to have a rival to the Empire in this part of the world; that they consider the Asiatics will be reluctant to do much unless pressed from behind and they consider the Empire the proper instrument of pressure." Butterworth, thus, recommended that,"the Secretary of State point out to Bevin that we believe a Pacific Union should have indigenous roots but that we also believe we should encourage it."[110]

While working toward a regional arrangement, Bevin was faced with another stumbling block: the peace settlement of Japan. Since all countries around the Pacific were still worried about Japan, Bevin realized that the success of his proposed Colombo Conference would be seriously compromised if the peace with Japan was not settled before the meeting.

In September, Bevin told Acheson that "the people who live near the Japanese are anxious about the settlement." Acheson merely replied that the U.S. government "did not want a treaty, the main principles of which might be dictated by other powers in circumstances which give them no right of veto." Bevin complained that he had made

an effort at the 1947 Canberra Conference to get an agreed Commonwealth policy but the U.S. government had appeared to be somewhat
suspicious of his attempt.[111]

The State Department was always worried about any British initiative that was based on Commonwealth consensus. In November, Joseph Satterthwaite, director of Near Eastern affairs, wrote an
interesting memo titled "Suggested Technique in Dealing with the
British," in which he pronounced that, "Hardly a day goes by that the
United States Government does not ask the United Kingdom to do
something which it isn't doing and which in many cases it does not
want to do." According to Satterthwaite, "In every case of any importance the British consult [the] Commonwealth before deciding whether
or not to accede to our request." Thus, "The greater the degree of
United Kingdom resistance or dislike to a given request, the more
certain complete consultation with the Commonwealth will be made."
Convinced that the United States should start dealing with the Commonwealth countries directly, Satterthwaite concluded: "I believe that
in the past we have not taken enough trouble to explain our views to
the Commonwealth and the reasons why we make this and that request
of the British. . . . [Therefore] the Commonwealth gets our position
presented through a British filter and slanted in whatever direction the
British want to take."[112] Satterthwaite was apparently seeking an effective way to actively counter the British influence within the Empire.

As the date of the proposed Colombo Conference drew near, the
Foreign Office became impatient with the American attitude toward
the peace settlement with Japan. On 8 December, Sir William Strang,
permanent undersecretary of state, reported to Attlee that, "Mr. Acheson fears that the Americans will not be ready with their proposals on a
Japanese peace treaty before the Commonwealth Conference meets in
Ceylon on 9th January. You will also see from the Foreign Secretary's
message that he is very perturbed at this development." Bevin then told
Ambassador Franks: "I am sure if this matter is not dealt with at the
Colombo conference the chances of success later on will be very
doubtful. I am very anxious both for his sake and mine not to miss the
boat." After a fruitless reminder from Franks, Acheson vaguely
blamed Defense Secretary Louis Johnson for the delay.[113]

Under the circumstances, Bevin had to go to Colombo without an
Anglo-American agreement on Japan. Nevertheless, Bevin carefully
timed his decision to recognize the PRC. As he reported to Attlee on

23 December: "I have come to the conclusion that we should notify the Chinese Communist Government of our intention to accord *de jure* recognition on 6th January, 1950."[114]

As the New Year approached, Anglo-American relations were on the verge of an open split over China. While London prepared for its historic announcement on China, Washington became even more hostile toward the new regime. On 30 December President Truman approved NSC–48/2, which recommended, among other things, continued recognition of the KMT regime now based in Taiwan and nonrecognition of the Communists until it was clearly in the United States' interest to do so. Not surprisingly, the degree of American hostility toward Communist China was surpassed only by U.S. hostility toward the USSR itself.[115]

Washington was now well on the collision course with Communist China. There is little evidence that the Truman administration had actually considered recognition as a serious alternative to hostility in its efforts to induce a "Chinese Tito." What the United States found difficult to stomach, however, was not so much the loss of the China market as the forfeiture of its influence on the Asian mainland. As Acheson told Truman in a July memo entitled "United States Interests in China," it was the loss of U.S. influence that was of utmost importance: "Throughout the past one hundred years, American influence has grown steadily in China and, notwithstanding setbacks during the past year or so, it remains one of our most valuable assets in that country."[116] In short, there was no "lost chance" for compromising with the Communists, although the loss of American influence was real. NSC–48/2 was not a turning point but a continuation of American policy in China since 1945.

Notes

1. Typical studies that underestimated Anglo-American divergences can be found in *Uncertain Years*, edited by Dorothy Borg and Waldo Heinrichs, and in Nancy B. Tucker's *Patterns in the Dust*. Tucker, in particular, believed that Acheson's policy was much influenced by his Anglophile outlook, p. 191.

2. Stuart to Washington, *FRUS*, 1949, 8:13.

3. *FRUS*, 1949, 9:870–71.

4. Franks to Bevin, 11 January1949, FO 371 74174/AN/135/1023/45/G.

5. *FRUS*, 1949, 9:434.

6. Dean Acheson, *Present at the Creation*, p. 307.

7. *FRUS*, 1949, 9:826–34.

8. Ibid., p. 486.

9. Memo of Conversation with the President, 15 February 1949, *FRUS*, 1949, 8:132.

10. Ibid., pp. 123–24.

11. *Daily Express* (London), 27 February 1949.

12. Bevin to Mayhew, FO800/UN/49/11.

13. Bevin to Franks, 23 December 1949 FO 800/516/1949.

14. Acheson's Speech at the Joint Chiefs of Staff Meeting, December 1949, *FRUS*, 1949, 9:466.

15. *FRUS*, 1949, 9:832–37.

16. Ibid., p. 819.

17. Ibid., p. 825.

18. CAB 134/286 FE (O) (49).

19. *FRUS*, 1949, 9:839.

20. CAB 134/286 FE (O) (49).

21. 26 March, 1949 CAB 134/669 S.A.C. (49).

22. Stevenson to Bevin, 23 March, 1949, FO 371 75810/F4314/1023/10.

23. Ibid., Minute by P. D. Coates, 25 March 1949.

24. FO to Washington Embassy, 26 March 1949, FO 371 75810/F4314/3343.

25. *FRUS*, 1949, 9:839.

26. CAB 134/286 1949.

27. *FRUS*, 1949, 9:844.

28. Ibid., pp. 847–49.

29. Ibid., p. 850.

30. Ibid., pp. 853–54.

31. Ibid., pp. 854–60.

32. Graves to Scarlett, 22 April 1949, CAB 134/286/49 FE (O).

33. 16 May 1949, CAB 134/287/F6965/1121/10.

34. *FRUS*, 1949, 9:864.

35. 25 June 1949, CAB 134/287/FE (O) 49/41.

36. *FRUS*, 1949, 9:866.

37. Acheson to Douglas, 29 July 1949, ibid., pp. 867–68.

38. *FRUS*, 1949, 9:1098–99.

39. FO Memo to the State Department, ibid., pp. 1109–10.

40. Cabot to Acheson, ibid., pp. 1109–10.

41. CAB 134/286 FE (O) 49.

42. Ibid.

43. *FRUS*, 1949, 9:870–71.

44. Ibid., p. 878.

45. CAB 134/287/FE (O) 49.

46. Name Files, Clayton-Thorp Papers, October 1949, box 16, Truman Library.

47. CAB 134/287 FE (O) 49.

48. *FRUS*, 1949, 7:1202–8.

49. *FRUS*, 1949, 9:81–85.

50. Ibid., pp. 878–79.

51. Ibid., pp. 878–79.

52. Ibid., pp. 890–96.

53. *FRUS*, 1949, 8:26–27.

54. *FRUS*, 1949, 9:535–40.

55. *FRUS*, 1949, 8:28.

56. *Monthly Report*, Millard Publishing Company, 30 November 1949, FO 371 83243 FC1019/921.

57. FO Minute, February 1949, FO371 75785 F1533.

58. FO Minute, 14 January 1949, FO371 75785 F667.

59. 18 March 1949, FO371 75870 F3305.

60. NAUS, Daily Staff Officers Summary, 25 April, 1949, top secret, box 7.

61. Strang to Attlee, 8 April 1949, FO800/FE/49/4.

62. NAUS, Daily Staff Officers Summary, 16 May 1949, box 7.

63. Nanking to FO, 1 September 1949, CAB 134/288 (1949).

64. U.K. PRO, Memo for the Prime Minister, 21 April 1949, *Amethyst Files*, PREM 8/944.

65. Ye Fei, *Ye Fei huiyilu* (Memoirs of General Ye Fei), p. 626.

66. FO Minute by P. D. Coates, 29 April 1949, FO371 75785 F5972.

67. Stuart to Washington, 24 September 1949, *FRUS*, 1949, 9:23–24.

68. Ibid., p. 35.

69. Ibid., pp. 47–48.

70. Ibid., pp. 50–52.

71. Dening to Bevin, 23 July 1949, FO371 75183/F10976/23/10/G.

72. Memo of Conversation, July 1949, FO800/FE/47/21.

73. FO371 75813/F11653.

74. 13 August 1949, FO371 75813/F12678.

75. Correspondences of 3 and 10 June 1949, FO371 75812/F8543.

76. FO Minute, 3 June 1949, FO371 75812 28351.

77. *FRUS*, 1949, 9:81–85.

78. *FRUS*, 1949, 8:825.

79. *FRUS*, 1949, 9:103.

80. Ibid., p. 128.

81. Ibid., p. 130.

82. Ibid., p. 132.

83. 30 September 1949, CAB 134/286 /FE (O) (49).

84. Ibid., Memo of Conversation.

85. Stevenson to FO, 8 October 1949, FO371 75817/F15141.

86. FO371 75817/F15516.

87. Dening to Bevin, 20 October 1949, FO371 75818/F16028.

88. FO Minute by A. A. E. Franklin, 10 November 1949, FO371 75818/ ·F16882.

89. FO371 75818/F16370/1023/10.

90. *FRUS*, 1949, 9:151–54.

91. Ibid., pp. 149–51.

92. 4 November 1949, FO371 75819/F16589.

93. *FRUS*, 1949, 9:168–72.

94. Ibid., p. 189.

95. Bevin to Cadogan, 26 November 1949, FO371 75823/F17675.

96. 14 November 1949, FO371 75822/F17266/G.

97. Ibid., Memo by Scarlett.

98. *FRUS*, 1949, 9:219–20.
99. Bevin to Acheson, *FRUS*, 1949, 9:225–26.
100. Ibid., p. 189.
101. *FRUS*, 1949, part 2, 7:1137.
102. Ibid., p. 1125.
103. Ibid., pp. 1129–30.
104. Ibid., pp. 1151, 1170.
105. Ibid., p. 1139.
106. Bevin to Attlee, 21 April 1949, FO800/FE/49/5.
107. 26 July 1949, FO371 75799/F11076.
108. *FRUS*, 1949, part 2, 7:1148–51.
109. 19 September 1949, FO800/516/US/49.
110. *FRUS*, 1949, part 2, 7:1207–8.
111. 13 September 1949, FO800/FE49/24.
112. NAUS, Decimal Files, 711–41/11–349.
113. December 1949, FO800/FE/49/37.
114. Bevin to Attlee, 23 December 1949, FO800/FE/49/42.
115. *FRUS*, 1949, 9:1215.
116. Acheson to Truman, July 1949, Truman Papers, President's Secretary's Files, China General, box 173, Truman Library.

7

The Korean War

Nineteen fifty was perhaps the most hectic year since the end of World War II. The Cold War suddenly turned hot in the Far East where it was not expected, rather than in Europe where it was. The outbreak of the Korean War brought about a direct armed confrontation between Peking and Washington. For the first time in history, the two continental powers were at war. If the outbreak of a war in Korea was largely an accident, the basic Sino-American conflict was not.

It has often been argued that President Truman made two fatal decisions in 1950 and that these had led to a tragic end that could have been avoided. The first decision was to mix up unnecessarily the problems of China and Korea by neutralizing the Taiwan Strait in response to the invasion. The second was to authorize the UN forces to cross the Thirty-eighth Parallel. From the viewpoint of Sino-American relations, the first decision was certainly fatal, but many in the American government thought it was inevitable at the time. Originated by John Foster Dulles, the idea to neutralize the Taiwan Strait had encountered virtually no opposition within the administration. It was, in fact, proposed at a cabinet meeting by Dean Acheson himself. The Korean conflict provided, in effect, a perfect opportunity for Washington to implement its two-China policy aimed at denying the island to the Chinese Communists. Undoubtedly, U.S. involvement in Korea was a key step toward further entanglements on the Asian mainland, resulting later so disastrously in the Vietnam War. Yet this involvement had been consistent with U.S. Asian policy. A few years before 1950, the United States came close to becoming the dominant power not only in the Pacific, but also on the Asian mainland proper. The international environment for *Pax Americana* in Asia was hardly unfavorable. Soviet opposition was ambiguous. Stalin clearly had a vested interest in maintaining the Yalta system in Asia. It is hard to define Stalin's China policy, other than to describe it as passive opportunism. It seems, therefore, unfair to attribute the U.S. failure in Asia to the Soviet Union. If the U.S.-USSR conflict in the Far East was more imaginary than real, the clash of interest between Britain and the United States was definitely real and consistent with long-term patterns reflecting interest and policy.

During the six months before the Korean War, London and Washington quarreled constantly over Truman's two-China policy, a policy the British believed would lead to disaster. As Bevin was endeavoring to capitalize on his policy advantage after recognizing Peking, the Truman administration was seeking a way to minimize this advantage by justifying its two-China policy. The Korean War, thus, came at a fateful moment for British hopes in China.

The beginning of 1950 witnessed an open split over China between London and Washington. The Labour government declared its de jure recognition of Peking on 6 January. The Truman administration was, however, preparing to withdraw all its official representation from China. A few days before the British recognition was announced, Sir Oliver Franks reported from Washington that, "The shadow boxing that usually precedes the return of Congress has on this occasion largely concerned China and Formosa" and "the Army department has done its bit in embarrassing the Administration over the defense of the island. The atmosphere is less favourable than it was a month ago and we shall be in for a sticky patch immediately after our recognition of Communist China." Sir Oliver believed that "The President and the Secretary of State are against military intervention in Formosa and the despatch of military missions. . . . [But] the President might, for political reasons have to bow to Congressional pressure over measures designed to throw a defense screen around Formosa or in some way keep this island out of Communist hands."[1]

Sir Oliver's comment was somewhat off the mark. What he did not realize at the time was that the Truman administration was genuinely interested in denying the island to the mainland. The only prohibitive factor for U.S. military commitment was the prospect of overwhelming cost—a fear fresh from the Chinese civil war. On 5 January President Truman declared that the United States would not commit itself militarily to the defense of Formosa, but there is no evidence that this declaration was designed to please Peking. As Acheson explained to Senators Knowland and Smith on the same day, the island was indefensible without a full-scale military commitment by the United States. Besides, the island's strategic value was greatly diminished by its equal distance from mainland China, Okinawa, and the Philippines.[2] On 12 January, Acheson made his well-known speech at the National Press Club. Although the Secretary of State indicated that both Taiwan and South Korea were not included in his "defense perimeter" concept in Asia, he promised continued economic aid to these areas.[3]

London was greatly concerned by such declarations, which seemed to contradict actual policies of the United States. Two days after Truman's pronouncement on Taiwan, Sir William Strang reported to Attlee: "We welcome this realistic decision, as we have always felt that any attempt to bolster up the discrete Nationalists must be doomed to failure and would have dangerous implications." But Strang added that,

> The State Department had however previously made it plain to us that they hope that Formosa will be denied to the Communists for as long as possible and that they will not (repeat not) take steps to prevent the Nationalists from completing their purchases of war material under the Military Aid Programme, or from using whatever funds may be available to them to purchase such material in the United States. . . . We are not at all pleased that the Nationalists should get further supplies of war materials.[4]

Millard's *Monthly Report* from Shanghai, dated 31 December 1949, pointed out that the United States, "despite the melting away of KMT rule on the Chinese mainland, steadfastly continued its policy of sticking with the Kuomintang [and] shying away from even the possibility of recognizing the new Chinese Government." It added that although "Chiang's ability to hold Taiwan was a foregone conclusion, the U.S. Government was apparently bent on going through the fiction that a regime set up on an island in the Pacific . . . is the 'legal government' of all of continental China."[5]

In January, U.S. interest in Taiwan's defense was further highlighted when American military and naval attachés were sent to Hainan—an island in the South China Sea about the same size as Taiwan and the last ditch of Chiang's defense—as an indication that Washington was interested in defending a similar island. London dismissed the American move as "more U.S. wishful thinking."[6]

Besides continued support of Taiwan, the State Department remained interested in sabotaging the Peking regime at every opportunity. One occasion was during Mao's visit to Moscow in early 1950. When Washington heard of the difficulties encountered at the Mao-Stalin negotiations, which dragged on for several months, Secretary Acheson immediately instructed David Bruce, American ambassador in Paris, to "plant some highly speculative stories" into the European press in order to discredit the PRC government by emphasizing the treacherous nature of the Chinese Communists.[7]

London, however, saw this unusually prolonged negotiation as a golden opportunity to drive a wedge between Moscow and Peking. Bevin believed that British recognition of Peking actually strengthened Mao's hand in dealing with Stalin.[8] Indeed, Mao did not have a happy experience in Moscow, recalling a few years later that to negotiate with Stalin was "like to take meat from a tiger's mouth."[9]

While attending the Colombo Conference in January, Bevin decided to have another talk with Acheson in London. In a letter to Sir William Strang, Bevin confided: "As you know I have been anxious to get Acheson to London in [the] fairly near future. I believe such a visit would provide [the] best possible opportunity for clearing up some difficulties." Bevin continued, "It will also make it possible to review perhaps together with Schuman, many outstanding European problems as well as those of the Far East and South East Asia."[10]

Bevin had many good reasons to be worried. At the same time as Anglo-American differences in the Far East became increasingly intractable, their quarrel over the European Recovery Program grew more intense thanks to the efforts of Paul Hoffman, director of the Marshall Plan agency ECA, to create a European Payments Union (EPU). In January, Julius Holmes, American minister in London, reported to Washington that "British leaders feel they are now fighting a last-stand battle for survival as a world power." During an inner conference held by William Averell Harriman, special representative in Europe for the ECA, it was mentioned that Chancellor of the Exchequer Sir Stafford Cripps was very petulant and arrogant toward the

American European policy. Cripps actually criticized the policy to create an EPU as a "schoolboy lecture manner in the settlement of European problems."[11] In February, Cripps sent Hoffman a strongly worded letter, stating that, "What I want to ask you and your people to do is to realise that we as 'bankers' for the Sterling Area have a great responsibility to others besides ourselves, . . . that we cannot rush headlong into a scheme which may depreciate the value of sterling to the rest of the Sterling Area and to the whole Trading Community of the world." In equally strong language, Hoffman replied that, "I am quite aware of the specific difficulties faced by the United Kingdom in its relationship to the proposed Payment Union. . . . May I express the hope that the United Kingdom will find a way fully to implement the decisions taken at the O.E.E.C. council meeting on 29 November 1949."[12] Unless this was done, warned Hoffman, the restoration of a cordial relationship between the U.K. and the U.S. would be difficult to achieve.

It was in this difficult atmosphere that the Truman administration was desperately seeking new ideas to justify and give coherence to its global policy. The NSC–68, a manifesto-like document embodied as a National Security memorandum, was a major intellectual result of this probe. As befitting the Truman-Acheson worldviews, authors of NSC–68 headed by Paul Nitze began to see the world through a strictly bipolar perspective. The Marshall-Kennan pragmatism was out. According to the document, the United States, having "witnessed two intense revolutions . . . and [the] collapse of five Empires," was called upon to save the world in a Wilsonian fashion but with iron teeth. More significantly for actual policy, the NSC–68 provided a strong Keynesian rationale for the huge government spending it believed necessary to finance the Cold War. By using the Keynesian underconsumption arguments developed as a cure for the prewar depression, NSC–68 concluded that whatever was spent on defense would simply mean that production would soon catch up with demand. Defense spending would be a way to ensure growth. That, of course, had largely been the American experience in World War II. Applied in entirely different postwar circumstances, it eventually became a recipe for the perpetuation of inflation and budget deficit. Unlike Marshall and Lovett, who were always concerned with costs, the free-spending Acheson seemed quite comfortable with NSC–68's conclusion, which called for massive defense spending.

British Ambassador Sir Oliver Franks was conscious of the difference in fundamental thinking between Acheson and Marshall. Although Franks did not know that NSC–68 was in the making, he felt something was going on within the administration. He reported to London on the mysterious atmosphere in which the top-secret document was being formulated, saying, "The Americans seem to me to be groping desperately for ideas on foreign policy, both as regards Europe and South East Asia. . . . [If we have ideas,] their minds are wide open to them. I think in the next few weeks we have the opportunity to take advantage of this attitude of combined eagerness and frustration." With a sharp eye, Franks went on to say that,

> We have been compelled so often recently to bring questions of cost and make it clear that what we could do and how far we could go along with the Americans turned on the question of expense. Acheson is, I think, a little inclined to treat the economic consequences of foreign policies in their effect on the national economies of America and Britain as secondary in importance and to say that, if only we could get satisfactory and effective policies in the foreign field and applied, other matters would in a large measure look after themselves. Unless a successful foreign policy can ensure a more peaceful world, counting the cost of particular operations has little point.[13]

Sir Oliver Franks undoubtedly captured the mood and the mindset of those who were formulating NSC–68.

To be sure, NSC–68 reflected the fact that American power had reached its peak in 1950. To the architects of the project, past lessons of U.S. foreign policies were nothing more than indications that resources available had not been adequately utilized in the Cold War, which was bound to escalate at a certain point in history.

The simple and dramatic language used in this document suited the taste of the administration, above all the president. However, its revolutionary tone in U.S. foreign policy incurred some severe criticism. One critic was, understandably, William Schaub, the NSC member representing the Bureau of Budget. According to Schaub, the main weakness of NSC–68 was that it did not put the past American experience in foreign affairs into proper light, so the real danger lay in the possibility that past mistakes might repeat themselves. Schaub particularly emphasized the example of the U.S. experience in China, where the gap between cost and benefit had become largest in recent years. He lamented:

> A revealing commentary on NSC–68 is that it does not basically clarify or utilize the Chinese experience in the discussion of issues and risks, nor does it point toward a course of action which can effectively deal with probable repetitions of that experience in the future.[14]

Schaub's prediction was soon proven true in Korea. The irony is that the fallacious assumption on which NSC–68 was based appeared absolutely correct when the Korean War validated NSC–68's thesis that the Cold War would intensify because of Soviet proxy attacks.

Under the circumstances, the Korean War was a godsend for the NSC–68 formulators. Shortly before Acheson's trip to London in May, the authors prepared a paper entitled "The Current Position in the Cold War." They concluded that in Asia, the Communist victory in China was probably a greater loss for the West than it was a gain for the Soviet Union.[15] Ambassador-at-Large Philip Jessup, Acheson's trusted aide, also reported to the secretary in April that there was a lack of coordination among the Western powers in Asia.[16] Acheson was, thus, advised to go to London to patch up Anglo-American differences over Asian policies, but was counseled to avoid the unresolvable divergence over China.

China, however, was one of the major topics in Bevin's mind. Throughout the spring, Anglo-Chinese negotiations on establishing diplomatic relations had run into difficulties. Peking refused to move until the United Kingdom voted in favor of its seat at the United Nations Security Council, then still occupied by Chiang's representative from Taiwan. Without American consent on this issue, Bevin felt all Britain could do was abstain, since Britain had, after all, recognized Peking. As the United States was bent on using the UN to antagonize the new regime, Bevin found this position increasingly more difficult. In a long cabinet memo dated 13 April, Bevin pointed out that,

> This is not the only instance where action by the United States or its nationals has been to the detriment of our common interest. To some extent it can be said that several adverse factors in the present situation in China are attributable, not so much to any conscious policy on the part of the United States, but because of U.S. military aid to the Nationalists on the one hand and actions of the Administration in antagonising the Chinese People's Government on the other.

Bevin recalled bitterly: "As regards the U.S. attitude towards the Chinese People's Government, there has without question been considerable provocation from the latter." However, Bevin continued, "as early as 30th July, 1949, when this provocation was in no way serious, Mr. Acheson, in his letter of transmittal to the President of the American White Paper on China, stated that the attitude of the United States 'will necessarily be influenced by the degree to which the Chinese People come to recognize that the Communist regime serves not their interests, but those of Soviet Russia,' [and] that the United States 'should encourage all developments in China which now and in the future work towards throwing off the foreign yoke.' " Bevin concluded that the American China policy was erroneous and that Britain should continue its current strategy despite hardships, as well as "make every effort to bring the U.S. into line with that policy, . . . to the extent that internal political considerations permit."[17]

With these thoughts in mind, Bevin received Acheson in May. Both Prime Minister Attlee and Secretary Bevin tried every means to convince Acheson of what they considered to be sound China policy, but they soon found it impossible to influence their guest's crusading NSC–68 mindset. At a luncheon, Acheson discoursed about the U.S. destiny and responsibility to the world: "In the old days the British fleet by a show of force had been enough to maintain the peace of the world." He added, "[it] is just as essential now to be able to demonstrate to the peoples of Asia, and also to the satellite powers, that the West is strong, organized and determined to maintain its way of life." According to the British record, Acheson then elaborated his thesis on the "position of strength" and spoke particularly about Southeast Asia. Moreover, Acheson refused to be persuaded by his British hosts to settle relations with Communist China—a move London thought essential to British interests in all of Asia and the Pacific. The day after the luncheon with Acheson, Bevin reported to Attlee that he thought his meetings the previous day had been a little disappointing in that they were not very precise. As far as China was concerned, Bevin reported that he had endeavored to get Acheson to agree at least "not to criticize each other."[18]

Although little had come out of Acheson's visit regarding China, Bevin continued working toward establishing full diplomatic relations with Peking. Sir Esler Dening, the newly knighted key architect of the British Far Eastern policy throughout the postwar era, was appointed as ambassador to China.

Acheson, for his part, remained highly interested in a general containment plan for Asia. Washington was disappointed by the lukewarm reaction from other Asian nations to the Philippines' plan, also known as the Chiang-Quirino Pact. Even after President Quirino had dissociated himself from the unpopular Chiang Kai-shek, no other Asian country expressed interest in signing such a security pact. Acheson then began to ponder the possibility of getting other Western allies involved in a containment scheme for Asia. At a top-secret-level conference held in March, Acheson suggested that "NATO discussions need not be limited to specific problems of the Atlantic area but might cover such things as South East Asia and the Far East as they bore upon the situation of the member countries."[19]

At the end of 1949, Acheson sent Ambassador-at-Large Philip Jessup to fourteen Asian nations on a fact-finding mission. After a four-month tour in Asia, Jessup concluded that "the situation in the Far East is bad but not desperate. The area cannot be written off. We are committed."[20]

Amidst the NSC–68 atmosphere, there was growing talk within the State Department of "drawing the line" at Taiwan. Dean Rusk, who became assistant secretary for Far Eastern affairs in May, was particularly keen to do so. During a conference with Nitze, director of the Policy Planning Staff, Jessup, and others, Rusk pointed out that public opinion in the United States and around the world was generally unhappy at the lack of forthright action in the Far East by the U.S. government. Furthermore, he said, Formosa presented a plausible place to "draw the line" and was important politically, if not strategically, for what it represented in continued Communist expansion.

Rusk was perhaps the first person to suggest the expediency in "packaging" the three problems in the U.S. China policy: (1) Formosa; (2) recognition of Communist China; and (3) the Chinese representation in the UN.[21] Rusk did not specify how to "package" these three difficult problems, but his thinking indicated a simple-minded solution perfectly compatible with the NSC–68 mood: how to perpetuate de facto two Chinas now separated by the Taiwan Strait. Ever since Chiang fled to Taiwan, the Truman administration had found it hard to keep these three issues within one coherent policy framework. First, because it was agreed to at Cairo and Yalta, the United States could not challenge China's sovereignty over Taiwan, whose future imminently lay in Communist hands. Second, the administration found its position of denying China's UN seat to Peking increasingly more difficult to sustain; perpetuating a seat occupied by a regime that had no control over its claimed territory was not feasible both in front of world public opinion and in practical policy. Refusal to recognize Peking might give coherence to the policy embodied in the first two positions but was, in itself, increasingly less popular and practical due to the fact that the Taiwan-based rival regime was thought to disappear soon.

As the administration was seeking a way to package the three problems, John Foster Dulles came up with a policy advocating the "neutralization" of Formosa. In his capacity as State Department's special adviser and bipartisan liaison, Dulles submitted a memo a month before the outbreak of the Korean War, which argued:

> If the United States were to announce that it would neutralize Formosa, not permitting it either to be taken by Communists or to be used as a base of military operations against the mainland, that is a decision which we could certainly maintain, short of open war by the Soviet Union.[22]

The "Dulles Formula" immediately drew attention. It was so attractive that Dean Rusk signed his name to it before submitting the memo to Acheson.[23] Many studies claim that the Korean War drastically changed the administration's China policy, especially regarding Taiwan, which, it is said, the U.S. was prepared to abandon. The fact is, however, the Korean conflict greatly facilitated Washington's strategy to implement a two-China policy embodied in the "Dulles Formula." The cards were already on the table, waiting for opportunities to play themselves out, because the option of neutralizing the Taiwan Strait had already been broadly accepted before the sudden outbreak of war on the Korean peninsula.

By sharp contrast, the British, who clearly preferred to deal with the three problems regarding China one by one, adopted a policy that appeared reasonable, convincing, and practicable. Bevin was painfully aware that the West would have to pay a heavy price if China were to be excluded from the international community. In the face of Peking's continued intransigence over conditions for establishing diplomatic relations with London, which was also complicated by other minor issues such as the ownership of airplanes in Hongkong previously belonging to the KMT regime, Bevin was prepared in early June to end the quarrel by changing the United Kingdom's vote on seating Peking from an abstention to a "yes." The foreign secretary became impatient with the slow pace of Sino-British negotiation in Peking. In June Bevin even thought of replacing Britain's chargé d'affaires, John Hutchison, with a more experienced and higher ranking official. Kenneth Younger, minister of state at the Foreign Office, wrote to Sir William Strang ten days before the Korean fighting broke out, stating that the foreign secretary, "after approving our proposal for modifying our voting policy in the United Nations," said that "he felt we were not making as much impression as we should in Peking. He was inclined to think that we needed a man of more experience and weight than Hutchison. He realised that it would be inappropriate to send Mr. Dening, who is known as Ambassador Designate . . . [but] he thought about someone like Lord Lawson, formerly Mr. Jack Lawson, M.P. . . . [He] felt Lord Lawson, without attempting anything in the nature of negotiations, might well succeed in convincing the People's Government of the sincerity of our intention."[24] The Foreign Office opposed the idea of a special mission, claiming that Hutchison had done a good job in Peking.[25] However, the heated debate had not proceeded very far when the Korean War broke out.

From the start, the Korean War meant different things to London and Washington. From the American point of view, the conflict proved the NSC–68 thesis and provided a golden opportunity to implement policy options prescribed in the document. In other words, a general rearmament against the Soviet Union all around the world was quickly put into action. As far as China was concerned, the geographical closeness between Korea and China presented an equally good chance for the administration to package the three problems together by implementing the "Dulles Formula." As soon as the Korean War broke out, Acheson proposed at a cabinet meeting that the Seventh Fleet be used to neutralize the Taiwan Strait. There was no opposing opinion at the meeting. In fact, the president went so far as to say that he wanted "consideration given to taking Formosa back as part of Japan and putting it under MacArthur's command." Acheson replied that he "had considered this move but had felt that it should be reserved for later and should not be announced at this time."[26]

The Korean War came as a great shock to London. The Labour government was even more shocked by the Acheson decision to use the Seventh Fleet to neutralize the Taiwan Strait. Such a quick announcement on Washington's part indicated a preemptive move that could throw all Bevin's efforts to establish diplomatic relations with Peking down the drain.

Bevin quickly realized that this decision would push Peking to an extreme position, thus forfeiting all the British attempts to achieve certain stability in the Far East. In New York, the U.K. delegation, which had already been instructed to vote for Peking's seat, was in great confusion. Kenneth Younger reported to Prime Minister Attlee two days after Truman's 27 June declaration on Korea and Taiwan that, "As you know the reaction of [the] American Government to our proposed action was so unfavourable that it was finally decided to make no change in our line at the meeting of the 19th June. . . . Recent events in Korea and President Truman's statement of the 27th June have introduced unexpected and completely new elements into the Far Eastern situation. . . . [They] signify the emergence of a positive U.S. policy, the effects of which it is too early to assess with any certainty but which may well have important implications on our position particularly in our relations with the Central People's Government."[27]

London was extremely irritated by the fact that the preemptive nature of the Truman declaration indicated a deliberate effort to trick the other Atlantic allies into defending the U.S. China policy by forging an automatic connection between events in Korea and China. Because the allied relationship was defined by the NATO treaty, Bevin found it hard not to support the American position on Korea, but he could not accept Washington's policy to package Korea and China together. On 7 July, Bevin sent a long message to Ambassador Douglas in London stating that although the Americans had the wholehearted backing of world opinion in the initiative they took to deal with the aggression in Korea, he did not believe they could rely on the same support for their declared policy in connection with Formosa. Bevin went on further:

> Not only would many powers, particularly Asian powers, dislike the prospect of an extension of the dispute which might follow if the Central People's Government were to attempt an attack on Formosa, but some undoubtedly feel that now that the Central People's Government are in control of all Chinese territory, it would not be justifiable, in view of the pledge under the Cairo declaration, to take steps which might prejudice the ultimate handing over of the territory to China. . . . In general I think that the United States Government would be wise in their public statements to concentrate on the Korean issue and play

down the other parts of the President's statement of 27th June, otherwise there may be a risk of a breach in the international solidarity happily achieved over Korea.[28]

Bevin's message upset Acheson terribly because of its cogency and articulation in pointing out the major faults in his policy. In an equally frank reply, Acheson said that the United States government had no intention of retreating from the position taken by Truman in his statement. Acheson also said that the Americans would "do what we can to prevent an extension of the Korean conflict, but as the fiction of no So[viet] and Chi[nese] involvement wears thin, questions will be raised of the gravest importance to us all." Acheson defended the Taiwan Strait decision on the ground of military necessity and added that it "did not purport to deal with the many complicated political questions involved." He angrily pointed out that, "In all frankness, I do not see any likelihood of harmonizing our policies toward Chi[na] by any significant change in the basic attitudes on which US policy is founded." After listing eight indictments of the Chinese Communist regime, Acheson reminded Bevin of the British appeasement in the 1930s and said he hoped he would not see it again.[29]

To Bevin, Acheson's message was a severe charge. When Ambassador Douglas handed the message to Bevin, who was at a hospital, Douglas reported to Acheson later, the ailing foreign secretary was "a little taken aback at the vigor of your response." But Bevin insisted on adding a caveat that "the UK's position with respect to Korea is not to be construed as a commitment that the same position is taken with regard to Formosa as that of the US."[30]

A few days later, Douglas met with Strang, Younger, and Dening, who indicated that Bevin was hurt, if not outright offended, by Acheson's message.[31] But the British refused to back off from the position that Truman's 27 June statement directly contradicted what the U.S. president and Acheson had said in January regarding Taiwan. On 15 July, Bevin sent another message to Acheson, where he clarified: "I recognise that you attach great strategic importance to Formosa. What I am anxious to avoid is that we should give the Russians a chance to divide Asia from the West on an Asian problem. . . ." Bevin continued to stress that,

What I am afraid of is that the present situation will, if we are not careful, push China further in the direction of the Soviet Union. On our information in China, though reacting violently to your declaration on Formosa, has committed herself no more than Russia over Korea. . . . Therefore I say that we must be very careful not to add China to our enemies by any actions or attitudes of ours.

He believed that the UN objectives should be: (1) North Koreans must be repelled back to the Thirty-eighth Parallel, (2) there can be no submitting to Soviet blackmail, and (3) the question of Chinese representation in the UN should be considered in the UN and not in relation to any possible Soviet blackmail connected with Korea.[32]

Bevin's suggestion of using the UN-seat issue as a breaking point in dealing with Peking inevitably fell on deaf ears in Washington. Yet his calculation of Peking's initial intentions regarding Korea seemed to have been accurate. During the months before General MacArthur crossed the Thirty-eighth Parallel, various sources reported that the Chinese Communists did not want to mix their claim on Taiwan with any ambitions in Korea. The Indian ambassador in Peking, M. M. Panikkar, more than once had conversations with Chinese leaders. In July, the ambassador reported a tête-à-tête with Chou En-lai, during which the Chinese premier intimated that, "the Chinese had every intention of avoiding implication in present hostilities unless forced upon them."[33]

Washington, however, was not receptive to any signals coming from different channels that the Chinese were prepared to fight, if forced to. Certainly no effort was made to accommodate the Chinese in order to keep them out of the Korean conflict. On the contrary, not only did the administration refuse to budge on the issues of Taiwan and China's UN seat, but it seemed quite complacent before General MacArthur's military plans, which, from the Chinese perspective, seemed so provocative as to be designed not only to unify all Korea but also to carry the war over the Chinese border. It is not surprising that, from very early on, Mao had decided to draw the line at the Thirty-eighth Parallel.[34] MacArthur himself never hesitated to make his ambitions known. More importantly, the flamboyant general had many supporters within the administration. John Foster Dulles sent a memo to Paul Nitze on 1 August, stating that the UN forces must go beyond the Thirty-eighth Parallel.[35] In a memo dated 18 August, the Central Intelligence Agency (CIA) also urged the need to "conquer all Korea."[36] The State Department, for its part, was somewhat ambivalent about MacArthur's plans. A memo for NSC circulation dated 23 August pointed out that, "It is U.S. policy to help bring about the complete independence and unity of Korea." But the memo also suggested that the Korean problem must be dealt with in the wider framework of the conflict between Communist and non-Communist countries; hence, it recommended deferring the decision on crossing the parallel.[37]

Within the State Department, some voices were even heard in favor of the British position. These weak opposing views were often voiced by those who disagreed with the basic assumptions of the NSC–68. Charles Bohlen, for example, concurred with London that "the greatest danger of this arises from the possible entry of Communist China into the conflict."[38] In his memoirs, Bohlen recalled bitterly that "NSC–68's misconception of Soviet aims misled, I believe, Dean Acheson and others in interpreting the Korean War."[39] A disgruntled George Kennan wrote a long memo a few days before his unhappy departure from the State Department in late August, warning that the American policy in the Far East was heading for serious trouble. Kennan articulated that

> (a) we have not achieved a clear, realistic, and generally accepted view of our objectives in Korea; sectors of our public opinion and official establishment are indulging themselves in emotional moralistic attitudes toward Korea which, unless corrected, can easily carry us toward real conflict with the Russians and inhibit us from making a realistic agreement about that area; (b) by permitting General MacArthur to retain the wide and relatively uncontrolled latitude he has enjoyed in determining our policy in the North Asian and Western Pacific areas, we are tolerating a state of affairs in which we do not really have full control over the statements that are being made—and actions taken in our name; and (c) our policy toward the rival Chinese regimes is one almost sure to run us into serious conflict with England, the Commonwealth, and other Asian countries, and to strengthen the Peiping-Moscow solidarity rather than weaken it.[40]

Kennan's memo was, by far, the most devastating criticism of the U.S. policy in the Far East from the within the administration.

The Foreign Office was thinking along the same line. On 19 July, Kenneth Younger reported to Attlee that, "Although it now seems unlikely that U.S.A. will take any provocative action, it would be unwise to assure that no clash leading to hostilities between China and

U.S.A. can occur. . . . [If] this does happen we may be faced with a decision whether to dissociate ourselves firmly and publicly from this quarrel, or whether to risk becoming involved with China ourselves." Younger predicted strong reaction from Washington if London decided to get out of the conflict: "In their present mood, the Americans would react most strongly to a refusal by us to join them in what they would regard as part of the same struggle as Korea." On the other hand, "hostilities between ourselves and China would have the gravest effect upon our position in the Far East, especially in Hongkong . . . [and] would endanger our relations with India. They would probably also endanger the unity of the Parliamentary Labour Party over Far Eastern policy."[41]

On 1 September, Bevin told Australian Foreign Minister Percy C. Spender that so far Mao Tse-tung had kept clear of Korea and that the British were anxious not to force him into it. Bevin emphasized that, although opinion in Britain was intense and almost unanimous against the Russians, there was no strong feeling against Mao Tse-tung. Likewise, there was no support of Chiang Kai-shek.[42]

Since August, London had become acutely aware of the danger that might result from the provocative policy and style adopted by General MacArthur, who as both American and UN commander had begun to act, even more than usual, like an independent government. Sir Oliver Franks told Acheson on 13 August that MacArthur's official visit to Formosa earlier that month had greatly upset London.[43] The general became even more reckless after the trip. On 28 August, he delivered an unauthorized message to the Veterans of Foreign Wars Convention in Chicago, announcing that, "Nothing could be more fallacious than the threadbare argument by those who advocate appeasement and defeatism in the Pacific that if we defend Formosa we alienate continental Asia. Those who speak thus do not understand the Orient."[44] The message was so vexatious that President Truman had to order its withdrawal.[45] In the meantime, Ambassador Franks, under instruction, told H. Freeman Mathews, deputy undersecretary for political affairs at the State Department, that the British government had grave anxiety over the Formosa problem and the U.S. policy regarding it. Philip Jessup candidly told Franks that it might be desirable to have a plebiscite that could lead to an independent Formosa. Franks replied in shock, "the attraction of such a course is intellectual but that its practical application is horrid."[46]

As London began to realize the impossibility of altering Washington's two-China policy, the Foreign Office had to concentrate on preventing armed conflict between the PRC and the United States. Shortly before an Anglo-French-American tripartite conference of foreign ministers scheduled to be held in New York in September, Bevin thought a summit meeting between Truman and Attlee was opportune before the conference. Confiding the idea to Franks in Washington, Bevin said:

> Prime Minister and I, after mature consideration believe that time is coming when a meeting between the President and Prime Minister would be useful. . . . The position as I see it is as follows: The international situation has become increasingly dangerous and the chance of further outbreaks on the Korean model must be taken into account . . . .The best way to prevent it is for the Western Powers and their associates to be effectively and organically prepared. If we can put ourselves in this posture, the Russians, who are realists, will then think twice before themselves breaking the peace.[47]

Franks was, however, against the trip because it would come during a fall congressional election season and could embarrass the administration.[48] Bevin accepted Franks's argument, but told the ambassador that he would not drop the idea.[49] Attlee did not make his trip until December, after the Chinese had already entered the war. It is commonly believed that Attlee's trip was made in reaction to the Chinese intervention and talks in Washington about using atomic bombs in retaliation. In reality, the summit idea came up well before the Sino-U.S. military confrontation and was designed to settle a whole range of Anglo-American differences in the Far East.

At the end of August, Bevin prepared a long cabinet memo entitled "Review of the International Situation in Asia in the Light of the Korean Conflict." In it he argued that the policy pursued by His Majesty's government had been the right one, and that British support of nationalism in Southeast Asia provided the best possible counter to communist subversion and penetration. He added that since the British position in the Far East had been severely weakened as a result of the war, on the one hand, they were unable to exercise much influence upon the course of events, but on the other hand, they were less immediately involved in the debacle in China and Korea and were, to some extent, thus, freer than the United States to determine their future policy in the Far East. In very sharp language, Bevin reminded his colleagues in the cabinet that,

In the Far East ... the United States have tended to be a law unto themselves since the end of the war, with results which have been far from happy. ... In China, the late President Roosevelt's policy of cultivating the friendship of that country failed dismally for the reason that American support was given to the regime which, through its failure to introduce promised reforms, eventually lost the confidence of the overwhelming majority of the Chinese people.

Paradoxically, Bevin pointed out further:

The United States Government, having denounced this regime in a White Paper, on the same occasion proclaimed its hostility to the Communist regime even before it had been set up. Yet at the same time they continued and still continue to give support to Chiang Kai-shek. Thus it is true to say that the United States lack all direction in their policy towards China. That this state of affairs is dangerous is demonstrated by the Formosa situation.

As far as Anglo-American relations were concerned, Bevin recalled cynically that for the first time since the war, the U.S. administration had shown a desire to consult with and consider the views of the British on Far Eastern affairs. The Americans also showed signs of appreciating the importance of Asian (particularly Indian) opinion in dealing with these matters. Thus, Bevin concluded, "The U.S. Administration, as I have indicated, will not change its policies in response to purely British suggestion, [although] it may be willing to modify those policies in response to a majority view in the UN Assembly."[50]

Shortly before his departure for New York to attend the tripartite conference, Bevin further elaborated his objective at a cabinet meeting: "to induce the U.S. Government to look at Asia as a whole and to pay due regard to the desire of Asiatic countries to avoid any appearance of domination by the West." He believed that the U.K. government had recognized the emergence of new forces in Asia by granting self-government to India, Pakistan, Ceylon, and Burma, but that the United States had been much slower to perceive the new spirit of independence in the continent. Thus, Bevin was convinced, a steady influence must be brought to bear on American public opinion in order to reduce the risk of conflict between the United States and China over Taiwan.[51]

Three days before Bevin reached New York, General MacArthur

scored a surprising victory at Inchon. Upon Bevin's arrival, the British foreign secretary sensed that the Inchon victory had mellowed the U.S. attitude toward China's UN seat, which was one of his objectives at the tripartite conference.[52] But he was wrong. Bevin soon found out that Washington did not regard MacArthur's military advantage as a good opportunity to seek political settlements with Peking. On the contrary, the spirit of "hot pursuit" was gaining momentum in Washington.

Bevin was increasingly worried that MacArthur's saber-rattling was making Peking nervous. Since September, various intelligence sources from Hongkong, Peking, and New Delhi had reported that the Chinese Communists would not sit back and watch MacArthur march through the Thirty-eighth Parallel. The American consulate general in Hongkong had also on many occasions reported that Peking was prepared to fight. Chou En-lai even conveyed a message via India that Peking was not interested in Korea per se.[53] John Paton Davies pointed out that Peking had so far "declined to snatch the Moscow chestnut from the fire."[54]

Despite all the signals, General MacArthur ordered the air bombing of the Manchurian border area in September. After the operation, Bevin received an urgent message from New Delhi that Chou had stated that China might have to intervene in Korea for her security.[55] Pressured by Bevin, Acheson agreed to let India tell Peking that the bombing was an "accident." In fact, the Truman administration was quite ambiguous about MacArthur's action. On the one hand, the Inchon success promised to fulfill the objective of unifying the whole Korean peninsula. On the other, Washington hoped that the Chinese would not enter the war. But the administration also found it difficult to manage the situation since the general showed increasing signs of insubordination due to his utter contempt for Washington's political judgment—a situation painfully similar to that endured in 1945 with Patrick Hurley.

This ambiguity, which stood in the way of a firm policy to control MacArthur, was reflected in NSC–81/1, dated 9 September and originally drafted by the State Department. The document pointed out that, while the UN forces "have a legal basis for conducting operations north of the 38th Parallel," they "should undertake no ground operations north of the 38th Parallel in the event of the occupation of North Korea by the Soviet Union or Chinese Communist force." However, since no such occupation had yet occurred, General MacArthur was effectively left with the decision as to the occupation's likelihood. Moreover, MacArthur, who dismissed Peking's warnings as mere "bluffing," appeared to have support from the Pentagon, including the usually cautious General George C. Marshall, the new secretary of defense, who seemed to agree on the necessity of "hot pursuit when the enemy was on the run." Thus, only extremely serious factors could bar such a tactic. Under the circumstances, General MacArthur's judgment on China's intentions became decisive.

The British were remarkably alarmed by this phenomenon. While still on board the *Queen Mary* on the way back to London, Bevin received an emergency message about Chou's statement. He quickly instructed the Washington Embassy to confer with the State Department.[56]

In London, Sir Roger Makins, deputy undersecretary of state at the Foreign Office, reported urgently to Prime Minister Attlee that,

> General MacArthur . . . is discounting the Chinese reactions as bluff. . . . It is clear that if there is a clash between American and Chinese forces a number of countries will withhold support from the Americans. If Mac-Arthur carries out his plans and if the Chinese carry out theirs, the result may be a clash between the Americans and Chinese in North Korea which in our view will rapidly spread. This would immediately create most serious difficulties for us in regard to our China policy and especially in regard to Hongkong.

Sir Roger concluded: "From a general point of view, a clash between China and the United States would absorb a high proportion of American war effort for an indefinite period, weakening our defenses elsewhere. . . . We shall make recommendations . . . to settle the Korean affair by political rather than by military means."[57]

Meanwhile, in Tokyo, General MacArthur continued to discount the significance of the Chinese intention. To London, MacArthur had always been an abomination. Britain's problems with him dated back to the war against Japan, but Korea greatly sharpened that dislike. Early in 1950, Dening complained in a Foreign Office minute that MacArthur, while sitting in Tokyo, was exerting a malign influence on American China policy. Dening explained that poor General Alvary Gascoigne, British representative in Tokyo, had never been given an adequate picture.[58]

The Korean War drastically changed the Anglo-Chinese relations as well. London, for example, had to control strategic exports to China in

July.[59] But the Chinese were cautious in reaction to British support of the American policy and its own subsequent military involvement in Korea. John Hutchison, chargé at Peking, noted that the Chinese did not utilize the British action in Korea to further stir up troubles in Malaya or Hongkong. Hutchison believed that Peking would not wish to destroy an already tenuous yet potentially valuable relationship with London at this stage.[60]

Yet the fact that the two governments were taking opposite sides in the Korean War brought a halt to Anglo-Chinese talks over establishing diplomatic relations. The channels of communication became increasingly more difficult. London realized that, since the U.S. administration was unable to restrain MacArthur's behavior, the Chinese side must be informed of this fact so that Peking would not react too irrationally. Shortly before the Chinese intervention was known in October, the Foreign Office sent Dening, ambassador-designate to Peking, on a top-secret mission to China, although ostensibly his assignment was to visit other Asian and Pacific countries. The mission was so guarded that even Dening's own private secretary was not aware of it.[61] The idea of sending a high-caliber special envoy to Peking had always been on Bevin's mind, for he was concerned with Hutchison's weak representation in China. However, Dening's trip came a little too late to be effective. Before his departure, Dening told Sir William Strang that he would "encourage the Chinese to vent their grievances, whether real or imaginary, and try to convince them that their suspicions are unfounded and that a measure of good will on their part is likely to find a response in the rest of the non-communist world."[62] But the Foreign Office may have made a mistake by sending an ambassador-designate to visit Peking. The new regime did not like the idea of a "forced entry" without prior progress in negotiations over establishing formal diplomatic ties. And as the Chinese were hesitating to issue an entry visa to Dening, events in Korea had become irreversible.

MacArthur carried out his plans, as Sir Roger Makins had feared, and so did the Chinese. Before the General moved northward toward the Chinese border, President Truman arranged a meeting with MacArthur on Wake Island in the midst of the Inchon euphoria, not least in order to boost the Democratic Party's prospects in the forthcoming congressional elections. Although the president told MacArthur to avoid unduly provoking the Chinese, he was reassured by the general that Korea could be unified without a Chinese intervention. Two days later Truman capitalized on the Wake Island meeting by delivering a highly rhetorical political speech. The British embassy in Washington immediately surmised that the speech had been the real motive behind the Wake Island trip, noting that there were some new developments in the administration's propaganda techniques.[63]

London was by no means reassured by the meeting. Bevin informed Acheson that he intended to convey a message to Chou En-lai via Pandit Nehru, telling Chou to "hold his hands for the present." When the message was actually delivered, Chou emphasized again that the Chinese government had no intention of taking any action if American forces did not cross the Thirty-eighth Parallel.[64]

Washington continued to ignore warnings from London. As late as 12 October, a CIA report predicted that, "barring a Soviet decision for global war, such action [i.e., Chinese intervention] is not probable in 1950."[65] On 24 October, before Dening's arrival in Hongkong, MacArthur issued an order to remove any restrictions on operations north of the Thirty-eighth Parallel.[66] A week later, Walter Bedell Smith, director of the CIA, reported to Truman that "Fresh, newly-equipped North Korean troops have appeared in the Korean fighting, and it has been clearly established that Chinese Communist troops are also opposing UN forces."[67]

Washington's first reaction was to condemn the Chinese at the United Nations. London was vehemently against such a move. Bevin believed that, "This might make it more rather than less difficult for the Chinese to climb down and avoid open commitment."[68]

In Korea, the massive offensive launched by the Chinese was quickly changing military maps. In late November, MacArthur conceded that "we face an entirely new war." The general issued a communiqué conveying that, "all hope of localizing the Korean conflict . . . can now be completely abandoned."[69] Reacting strongly, Bevin asked Washington: "Is MacArthur getting us into a full-scale war with China?"[70]

Unable to enter China, Dening instead went to Tokyo in November. In his report to London, Dening expressed deep doubts about the UN commander: "I am not satisfied as a result of my visit to Japan and Korea that the U.S. Government will necessarily succeed in preventing General MacArthur from creating situations which may lead us all into difficulties" Dening was convinced that "the sabre-rattling which has gone on in Tokyo for some months has given encouragement to the

Chinese to believe that they are the next objective of attack." He emphasized further that:

> In these circumstances and in their ignorance of what goes on in the outside world the Chinese may quite genuinely refuse to believe any assurances which we or the U.S. may give. The fact is that the impression one gains in Tokyo is quite different from that which appears to prevail in Washington and New York.

He concluded that: "The Chinese have now gone so far that they may feel unable to retreat. I wish I could feel more confident that General MacArthur's action and utterances will give them no excuse for believing that they are in the right. . . . Our chances of doing this are going to be seriously jeopardized if General MacArthur is able to do and say what he likes."[71]

In London, Bevin had not yet given up hope for a political solution to the Korean conflict. In late November, the foreign secretary planned to instruct Sir Gladwyn Jebb, U.K. representative to the United Nations, to discuss with the Chinese an offer of a "demilitarized zone" in Korea. Acheson was consulted, but his reaction was furious. He told Bevin that Anglo-American divergences had better be concealed at this stage of military operations when General MacArthur was about to launch an offensive. Bevin reluctantly agreed.[72]

Instead of encouraging Bevin to seek a political solution, Washington asked London if it would be acceptable to carry on the war across the Yalu River into Manchuria. A shocked Bevin replied: "I cannot endorse the United States suggestion that violation of the Manchuria border may be necessary."[73] What worried London more was the loose talk in Washington about the possibility of using the atomic bomb against the Chinese. Although using the bomb ran the risk of a nuclear clash with the Soviet Union, American officials saw little harm in discussing it in order to chasten Peking.

Meanwhile, Washington made a further attempt in November to commit the United Nations to the American policy toward Taiwan. Washington proposed a resolution in support of the neutralization of the Taiwan Strait. Sir Pierson Dixon, deputy undersecretary at the Foreign Office, commented bitterly that,

> The Americans have behaved very badly over this question. By modifying their earlier view and stalling on discussion of the question of

Formosa in the Assembly, they have now landed the UNO in a difficult position. . . . The Americans are endeavoring to make the UN endorse that [i.e., Truman] declaration and say that any attempt by the Chinese to disturb the state of affairs created by it, will be the affair of the UN.[74]

Immediately after the mid-November congressional elections, the Labour cabinet decided to proceed with the long-planned summit meeting between Truman and Attlee. Although Washington found no compelling reason to reject the idea, there were strong suspicions and speculations about the British objective. Most of the press reports believed that Attlee's trip was prompted by the deep British concern about the possible use of atomic bombs in Korea. Julius Holmes, the American minister in London, offered another speculation: "Certain aspects [of the] U.K. economic situation . . . will be most prominently involved in [the] President's talks with Attlee."[75] But, as it turned out, he was wrong; Attlee was preoccupied with the subject of the U.S. China policy.

One nightmarish scenario for the administration was that Attlee would come to Washington for an extensive peace effort, putting the U.S. government in an awkward position. At an inner conference held at the Pentagon, Acheson told Defense Secretary Marshall and others that, "We must anticipate that someone will propose a cease-fire, for example, Attlee. We can get support for not abandoning Japan and support for not abandoning Korea. There would be no support on Formosa or on the question of seating the Chinese Communists." General Omar Bradley pointed out that the political price for cease-fire would be too great. Paul Nitze put it more bluntly: "If the Soviets put forces into Korea in support of the Chinese, there would be a slight chance of holding our European allies. It is not possible to hold the UK in line for early hostilities with the Soviet Union."[76]

London, too, went to the meeting with a deep distrust of Washington. Shortly before the summit, Attlee and Bevin invited French Prime Minister René Pleven and Foreign Minister Robert Schuman to London. During the conversations, Attlee told his guests that he was strongly against the American resolution at the UN naming the Chinese as an aggressor. He explained that,

The British and French are more alive to Asiatic sentiment than are the Americans. For example, the suggestion that the atomic bomb might be used in Korea showed a lack of understanding for Asiatic mentality, in that it suggested that Europeans and Americans have a low regard for the value of Asiatic lives.[77]

On the same day Attlee departed for Washington, Bevin, who did not accompany the prime minister on the trip, expressed his view on the ongoing war in a telegram to the British embassy in Washington, stating that, "There is a lack of sound military and political judgment in Tokyo. . . . If we cannot hold the redoubt [in Korea], then we must be prepared to withdraw under pressure, which we imagine is what is meant by a 'Dunkirk.' "[78]

Prime Minister Attlee arrived at Washington on the morning of 4 December. Ignoring the fatigue, he agreed to start talks immediately in the afternoon. What followed were six intense conferences over five days between Attlee and Truman. During the talks, both sides showed considerable intransigence. Moreover, Attlee seemed to want to settle all Anglo-American divergences over Asian policies since the end of the war against Japan. The confrontation between the two leaders, thus, became both specific and broadly philosophical. The atmosphere was so tense that, after the first meeting, Acheson felt compelled to suggest a "more relaxed" environment.[79]

The first meeting brought up most of the salient points of departure. Attlee lost no time in stating that the British government was very eager to avoid the extension of the Sino-U.S. conflict. He emphasized that he had "tried to look at the matter from the way in which the Chinese felt. . . . The Chinese Communists are not members of the United Nations and, therefore, are not obliged by any of those considerations." Attlee added that "[the Chinese Communist] attitude seems to include an element of fear, a genuine fear of the United States and of European nations generally. . . . They want to have the fullest position of any Chinese government in recent times. They feel strongly about Formosa and a little less strongly about Hongkong." Attlee went on to propose a package deal to settle the Sino-American problem.

The Americans reacted most unfavorably to Attlee's exposition. At the request of the president, Acheson countered Attlee's argument by saying that, "The Chinese Communists were not looking at the matter as Chinese but as Communists who are subservient to Moscow. All they do is based on the Moscow pattern, and they are better pupils even than the Eastern European satellites." And, "if we yield to the Chinese Communists," Acheson wondered "whether we would be able to keep the Japanese and the Filipinos in hand." The secretary of state then asked rhetorically, "If no settlement is made with the Chinese Communists, are we worse off than if we do make such a settlement?" According to him, "This depends on what we do next. This moment for negotiations with the Communist movement is the worst since 1917. . . . We must refuse to recognize their gains."

In reply, Attlee told Truman that opinions differed on the extent to which Chinese Communists were satellites. He asked: "When is it that you scratch a communist and find a nationalist?" He was probably referring to Lord Curzon's famous quib that "scratching a Mullah's beard and you find the Union Jack." Truman retorted, "They are satellites of Russia and will be satellites so long as the present Peiping regime is in power. . . . The only way to meet communism is to eliminate it." Acheson added that, "It is a saying in the State Department that with communistic regimes you can't bank goodwill, they balance their books every night." After General Marshall also made a comment to reinforce Acheson's argument, Attlee replied dryly that, "Tito is also a full Communist." He then shifted to the question of Asian opinions, stating that, "Asiatics think that [the Korean conflict] is their show." He recalled the attitude he had found in India almost twenty years ago regarding the Japanese.* Attlee concluded that, "how we could avoid being bled in the East so that we could save the West. It would be wise today to consider the most immediate problem," namely, European defense and recovery.[80]

The Anglo-American differences were so sharp that Acheson had to hold a follow-up conference with Attlee's entourage in the evening. During the meeting, Acheson insisted that "a surrender to the Chinese would probably result in the loss of the island chain." Sir Roger Makins, on the other hand, summed up the first summit meeting by saying, "Our two countries differ in our estimate of Chinese attitude and intentions."[81]

The next morning, Acheson held an inner conference with his subordinates, during which the secretary of state recounted that Prime Minister Attlee had taken the position that at this time the U.S. govern-

---

*Attlee, as a Labour leader, had been sent to India on a fact-finding mission twenty years before.

ment had no choice but to negotiate with the Chinese, although President Truman asserted that the Americans were not prepared to do this. Referring to Attlee's argument that Europe was really more important than the Far East, Acheson emphasized that,

> We could not separate our foreign policy into two compartments—the Far East and the European. . . . Americans would not accept a surrender in the Far East in accord with the desire of some of our Allies who have urged us to be conciliatory in the Far East. Americans demand that we must be vigorous everywhere.[82]

This mentality was perfectly compatible with the NSC–68 spirit.

At the second meeting, President Truman indicated that he would rather fight to a finish. Prime Minister Attlee, however, focused on the record of American China policy since the end of the war. He could not help but remind his hosts that, after all, "China had been made a great power by Franklin Roosevelt . . . at the time they [Britain and the United States] had not agreed in thinking China was still in an inchoate mass." Attlee added that, "The Indian nationalists had waged a violent campaign against the British. The British gave them what they wanted and a very considerable change had occurred." He stressed that the United States needed a historical perspective: "Chinese civilization is very old and is accustomed to absorbing new things. They may wear the red flag with a difference. The question is what we could do to prevent the Chinese looking to the USSR as their only friend." According to Attlee, "If we say that China is just a part of the USSR, we link them together and play the game of Russian imperialism." He concluded:

> The United States thinks that the Chinese are completely subservient to the USSR and they are not only Communists but Stalinists. There was a great difference here. They can be Marxists and yet not bow to Stalin. . . . It is easy to say that China is entirely in the hands of the Russians. This is [a] fatalistic attitude. At least you hope that if you back nationalism you can get Chinese imperialism opposed to Russian imperialism.[83]

An emotional Acheson countered that, "The Chinese have undone fifty years of American friendship with them. No matter what happens now, it will take at least a decade for the American people to get over what the Chinese have done to them."[84] Attlee was appalled that the United States was apparently prepared to let the Sino-American relationship drift into a frozen and bitter end. Despite Attlee's powerful arguments, the Americans were not impressed by Britain's experience in managing her imperial decline. On the same day, Attlee sent Bevin a telegram, indicating little progress had been made in Washington. He stated that the United States would not allow the Communists to occupy Formosa or to become members of the Security Council. In addition, he related Acheson's branding the Chinese Communists as aggressors and calling for economic sanctions against them. Attlee also said President Truman thought there was no hope of any successful negotiation with China. However, the prime minister added, "I think Marshall has a more realistic attitude than Acheson."[85]

Attlee was even less successful on the issue of Taiwan. The verbatim transcript on this subject at the Truman Library in Independence, Missouri, is interesting in that it shows far more drama than the bland version in the State Department record. The president apparently reacted strongly to the prime minister on the Taiwan issue, saying: "We can't open our whole left flank now by giving up Formosa to that country.... I am not in any mood for unconditional surrender to that vicious government. I think in the long run, though, the Chinese will realize that their real friends are not in Siberia, they are in London and Washington." The prime minister replied: "You won't bring them to that realization by continuing hostilities." The president then retorted: "No, but I won't back out of Korea.... And I won't give up anything else, I'm never licked until I'm licked. I don't think you do either. You didn't at Dunkirk. Neither do we. We are like you. After all, we inherited that from Great Britain."[86]

Nevertheless, the British delegation felt relieved over at least two issues: the use of the atomic bomb and the need to control MacArthur. At the fifth meeting, President Truman made a comment that was stricken out of the record. According to a top-secret memo, Truman promised to consult with London before the actual use of the atomic bomb in Korea. Attlee at once pressed for a written promise, which Truman declined to give, declaring that, "If a man's word wasn't any good it was not made any better by writing it down."[87]

Attlee was delighted to notice that his American hosts were, in private, equally worried about General MacArthur's behavior. The flamboyant general, who had little respect for Washington's direction, was increasingly an awkward liability for the Allied troops. Shortly before Attlee's visit, Acheson stated at an NSC meeting chaired by the president personally that, "We should be sure he [MacArthur] understands his directive." Acheson further indicated that the U.S. objective at this stage was not to carry the war over the Chinese border, but "to find a line that we can hold and [to] hold it."[88]

During an after-dinner, off-the-record conversation on 7 December, Attlee's deep concern about MacArthur was echoed by his American hosts. It is, however, puzzling to note that Acheson immediately thereafter attempted to deny any role in denigrating the general. He deliberately told his subordinates the next morning that he had "stayed out [of] this portion of the conversation." But, according to the British record, Acheson was especially virulent about MacArthur. The British records have him saying: "There are two questions. First, whether any government has any control over General MacArthur. . . . Secondly, the question of what arrangements should be made for consultation in the future." General Marshall gave a more subtle opinion by stating that he would not like to see a future Allied commander in Europe of the same type as MacArthur.[89]

Although Attlee could claim some satisfaction from his trip, the summit, like so many previous dialogues between London and Washington over the subject of the Far East, was unable to smooth over the deeply rooted differences between the two. By year's end, their differences were further sharpened when Washington named China as an aggressor at the United Nations. In a message to Congress dated 8 January, 1951, President Truman pointedly invoked the familiar specter of appeasement of the 1930s:

> If the democracies had stood up against the invasion of Manchuria in 1931, or the attack on Ethiopia in 1935 or the seizure of Austria in 1938, if they had stood together against aggression on those occasions as the UN has done, the whole history of our time would have been different.[90]

Attlee wrote to Truman: "I am greatly disturbed by present developments in the Far East. It now appears from the information we are receiving . . . that the U.S. Government may wish to substitute for a policy of localising the conflict in Korea a policy aimed at developing limited action against China." He added, "The kind of action against China for which the U.S. Government appear to be pressing at the UN will, in our view, almost certainly provoke China to extend hostilities."[91] Truman replied emphatically that, "If the truth be that aggression has occurred let us not shrink from stating that truth because of the fact that the power which launches it is formidable."[92]

Before the New Year arrived, Washington also announced a freezing of all Chinese government assets in the United States. The war between the two countries, thus, entered a new stage. Ill and fragile, Bevin watched disapprovingly as Washington headed for more trouble in Asia. As the Korean War escalated at the end of the year, Bevin thought that, "The next six months would be most vital in the world's history."[93] Death soon intervened before he could reconsider any other options.

Finally, the British realized that Anglo-American differences over China could not be resolved. Robert H. Scott, Dening's successor as assistant undersecretary for Far Eastern affairs, was a key figure on Attlee's entourage in Washington. In a lengthy minute written shortly after the summit, Scott summed up the British mood thus: "The Russian toreador has been enticing the American bull into the China shop by waving a bit of red bunting and the bull has been suitably goaded by cutting himself on bits of China until he is fighting mad." Describing the British aim in China, Scott clarified: "We never expected dividends from the China policy, unless you can have negative dividends. . . . Our China policy was definitely a long term lock-up investment which may yet justify itself. . . . If we had gone the American way, we would not only have had some extremely difficult passages with India, but we would have had a crisis over Hongkong and possibly would have lost it." As far as China's future was concerned, Scott made this farsighted prediction:

> I do not believe that we or anyone else can drive a wedge between Russia and China, but I do believe that a rift will appear in course of time spontaneously . . . What we could have done—and what Americans have done—is to rivet Russia and China together, so that a rift will take longer to appear and the alliance is more solid than it need have been.

Scott concluded that, "Anglo-American solidarity is and must remain our first objective in foreign affairs." But "let us stand shoulder to shoulder and not hang on to Uncle Sam's apron (and money) strings when he is in one of his moods," and "when he is facing the wrong way, let us gently nudge him around so that we are still standing shoulder to shoulder but looking in a different direction."[94]

Notes

1. U.K. PRO, Franks to Bevin, January 1950, FO371 83243/FC1022/26.
2. *FRUS*, 1950, 6:258.
3. For the full text of Acheson's speech, see U.S. State Department *Bulletin*, 23 January 1950, pp.111–18.
4. U.K. PRO, Strang to Tokyo, 7 January 1950, FO371 83279/FC1022/30.
5. U.K. PRO, Millard Publishing Company, *Monthly Report,* FO371 83243/FC1019/21.
6. U.K. PRO, Minute by Coates, 21 January 1950, FO371 83243/FC1019/17.
7. Acheson to Bruce, *FRUS*, 1950, 6:294.
8. U.K. PRO, FO Memo, 2 March 1950, FO800/FE50/9.
9. Mao Tse-tung, *Selected Works*, v. 5, p. 65.
10. U.K. PRO, Bevin to Strang, 25 January 1950, FO800/517.
11. *FRUS*, 1950, 3:1609.
12. U.K. PRO, Cripps-Hoffman correspondence, March 1950, FO800/US/50/10.
13. U.K. PRO, Franks to Bevin, 8 March 1950, FO800/US/50/8.
14. *FRUS*, 1950, 1:303.
15. *FRUS*, 1950, 3:858.
16. *FRUS*, 1950, 6:71.
17. U.K. PRO, Memo by Bevin, CAB 134/290, FE (O) 50 /16.
18. U.K. PRO, Memo of Conversation, 10 May 1950, FO800/US/50/19.
19. *FRUS*, 1950, 3:1630.
20. *FRUS*, 1950, 6:76.
21. *FRUS*, 1950, 6:347–48.
22. *FRUS*, 1950, 1:315.
23. *FRUS*, 1950, 6:349–51.
24. U.K. PRO, FO Memo, 12 June 1950, FO371 83327/FC1051/4.
25. U.K. PRO, ibid., Memo by Shattock, 15 June 1950.
26. *FRUS*, 1950, 7:178–80.
27. U.K. PRO, Younger to Attlee, 29 June 1950, FO800/FE/50/4.
28. *FRUS*, 1950, 7:330.
29. Ibid., p. 349.
30. Ibid., p. 361.
31. Ibid., p. 380.
32. Ibid., pp. 396–99.
33. Ibid., p. 488.
34. See Memoirs of Marshal Nie Rongzhen, vol. 3, pp. 733–39 and *Peng Dehuai Zishu* (Autobiography of Peng Dehuai), pp. 257–58.
35. *FRUS*, 1950, 7:514.
36. Ibid., p. 600.
37. Ibid., p. 653.
38. Ibid., p. 521.
39. Charles Bohlen, *Witness to History, 1929–1969*, p. 291.
40. *FRUS*, 1950, 7:623–28.
41. U.K. PRO, Younger to Attlee, 19 July 1950, FO800/US/50/25.
42. U.K. PRO, Memo of Conversation, 1 September 1950, FO800/FE50/32.

43. *FRUS*, 1950, 6:431.
44. Ibid., p. 453.
45. Ibid., p. 454.
46. Ibid., pp. 464–65.
47. U.K. PRO, Bevin to Franks, 14 August 1950, FO800/US/50/31.
48. U.K. PRO, FO800/US/50/33.
49. U.K. PRO, FO800/FE/50/34.
50. U.K. PRO, Memo by Bevin, "Review of the International Situation in Asia in the Light of the Korean Conflict," 30 August 1950, PREM8/117.
51. U.K. PRO, Ibid., Cabinet Records, 4 September 1950.
52. U.K. PRO, Ibid., Bevin to Attlee, 6 October 1950.
53. *FRUS*, 1950, 7:742.
54. Ibid., p. 753.
55. Ibid., p. 795.
56. U.K. PRO, 2 October 1950, FO800/FE/30/37.
57. U.K. PRO, Makins to Attlee, 3 October 1950, FO800/FE/50/12.
58. U.K. PRO, FO Minute, 4 January 1950, FO371 83279/FC1022/30.
59. CAB 129/41 CP(50)157.
60. U.K. PRO, Hutchison to FO, FO371 83293/FC1022/439.
61. For a detailed discussion of Dening's trip, see James Tuck-Hong Tang, *Britain's Encounter with Revolutionary China, 1949–54*, pp. 92–95.
62. Ibid., p. 93.
63. U.K. PRO, FO Minute, 20 October 1950, FO371 81630/AN1025/7.
64. *FRUS*, 1950, 7:896–97.
65. Ibid., p. 934.
66. Ibid., p. 995.
67. Ibid., p. 1025.
68. Ibid., p. 1033.
69. Ibid., pp. 1237, 1239 (footnote 1).
70. Ibid., p. 1241.
71. U.K. PRO, Dening to Bevin, December 1950, FO800/FE/50/46.
72. *FRUS*, 1950, 7:1210.
73. Ibid., p. 1172.
74. U.K. PRO, FO Minute by Dixon, FO371 83301/FC1024/116.
75. *FRUS*, 1950, 3:1703.
76. *FRUS*, 1950, 7:1323–34.
77. U.K. PRO, FO800/FE/50/47.
78. U.K. PRO, Bevin to Washington, 4 December 1950, FO800/FE/50/48.
79. *FRUS*, 1950, 7:1832.
80. Ibid., pp. 1361–74.
81. Ibid., p. 1375.
82. Ibid., pp. 1383–86.
83. Ibid., pp. 1392–1408.
84. Verbatim Transcript, Truman-Attlee Talks, 5 December 1950, Truman Papers, President's Secretary's Files, box 164, Truman Library.
85. U.K. PRO, Attlee to Bevin, FO800/FE/50/49.
86. Verbatim Transcipt, Truman-Attlee Talks, Truman Papers, President's Secretary's Files, box 164, Truman Library.

87. *FRUS*, 1950, 7:1462.
88. Ibid., p. 1246.
89. U.K. PRO, Memo of Conversation, 7 December 1950, FO800/FE/50/53.
90. U.K. PRO, FO800/FE/51/6.
91. Ibid., FE/51/3.
92. Ibid., FE/51/6.
93. Ibid., FE/50/54.
94. U.K. PRO, FO Minute by Scott, FO371 92235/FC1207/3.

Concluding Remarks

Several salient points may be made about Anglo-American relations in China from 1945 to 1950. First, throughout the period, the two allies did not collaborate in any significant way in China. This suggests that their differences were over long-term interests rather than over sentimentality between the successor and the succeeded in the predominant position in Far Eastern politics.

Second, the Anglo-American dispute over China must be put into a broad context of global strategy and general outlook. A Cold War framework alone cannot explain why the two countries failed to see eye to eye in the Far East. Dimensions of imperial rivalry in both Southeast Asia and Europe affected considerations in the Far East. This is particularly evident in the case of Great Britain.

Third, from an Anglo-American perspective, there seemed to have been no "lost chance" in China in 1949 and 1950. The United States did not have a consistent policy of creating a "Chinese Tito" in Mao. On the contrary, Washington seemed bent on antagonizing the Communist regime through a policy of nonrecognition. Even if this policy were meant to coerce Mao into becoming like Tito, its utter ineffectiveness was expected in London.

Finally, the Korean War itself did not radically change the American position vis-à-vis Communist China. By June 1950, the cards were all on the table in Washington. Supported by NSC–68, the only U.S.

policy option was continued hostility toward Peking. The year 1950 marked the peak of American global power; the United States had an opportunity to flex its muscle. But the year may have also started a process of decline that led to the Vietnam trauma. In this situation, Great Britain, the quintessential Western imperial power in the Far East, felt that the Americans were mismanaging their newly acquired Asian hegemony. Worse yet, the U.S. failure in Asia had spoiled Britain's own efforts to salvage the rich remnants of its own imperial past. In the end, however, London, felt it had no choice but to tie Britain's fate to a misbehaved United States. Meanwhile, Britain's jaded wisdom might find useful employment in counseling its headstrong American successor, while guarding its profits on the side.

Bibliography

Acheson, Dean G. Papers. Harry S. Truman Library, Independence, Missouri.

————. *Present at the Creation: My Years in the State Department.* New York: W. W. Norton, 1969.

Allen, Louis. *The End of the War in Asia.* London: Hart-Davis, MacGibbon, 1976.

Attlee, Clement Richard. *As It Happened.* London: Heinemann, 1954.

Ballard, Jack S. *The Shock of Peace: Military and Economic Demobilization After World War II.* Washington, D.C.: University Press of America, 1983.

Barnett, A. Doak. *China on the Eve of Communist Takeover.* New York: Praeger, 1963.

Beal, John Robinson. *Marshall in China.* Garden City, N.Y.: Doubleday and Co., 1970.

Berlin, Isaiah. *Washington Despatches.* Chicago: University of Chicago Press, 1981.

Bianco, Lucien. *Origins of the Chinese Revolution, 1915–1949.* Translated by Muriel Bell. Stanford: Stanford University Press, 1971.

Blum, Robert M. *Drawing the Line: The Origin of the American Containment Policy in East Asia.* New York: W. W. Norton, 1982.

Boardman, Robert. *Britain and the People's Republic of China 1949–74.* London: Macmillan, 1976.

Bohlen, Charles Eustis. *Witness to History, 1929–1969.* New York: W. W. Norton, 1973.

Borg, Dorothy, and Heinrichs, Waldo, eds. *Uncertain Years, Chinese-American Relations, 1947–1950.* New York: Columbia University Press, 1980.

Buhite, Russell D. *Patrick Hurley and American Foreign Policy.* Ithaca, N.Y.: Cornell University Press, 1973.

————. *Soviet-American Relations in Asia, 1945–1954.* Norman: University of Oklahoma Press, 1981.

Bullock, Alan. *The Life and Times of Ernest Bevin.* Vol. 3. London: Heinemann, 1983.

Byrnes, James Francis. *Speaking Frankly.* New York: Harper, 1947.

————. *All in One Lifetime.* New York: Harper, 1958.

Cairncross, Alec. *Years of Recovery: British Economic Policy, 1945–51.* London: Methuen, 1985.

Campbell, Thomas, and Herring, George C., eds. *The Diaries of Edward R. Stettinius, Jr., 1943–1946.* New York: New Viewpoints,1975.

Carton de Wiart, Adrian. *Happy Odyssey: The Memoirs of Lieutenant-General Sir Adrian Carton de Wiart.* London: Jonathan Cape, 1950.

Chakravarti, Prithwis Chandra. *India's China Policy*. Bloomington, Ind.: Indiana University Press, 1962.

Chen, Jerome. *China and the West: Society and Culture, 1815–1937*. Bloomington, Ind.: Indiana University Press, 1979.

Chern, Kenneth S. *Dilemma in China: America's Policy Debate, 1945*. Hamden, Conn.: Archon, 1980.

Churchill, Winston S. *Winston S. Churchill: His Complete Speeches, 1897–1963*. New York: Chelsea House, 1974.

Clemens, Diana Shaver. *Yalta*. New York: Oxford University Press, 1970.

Cohen, Warren I. *America's Response to China: An Interpretative History of Sino-American Relations*. New York: John Wiley and Sons, 1971.

Cohen, Warren I., ed. *New Frontiers in American-East Asian Relations: Essays Presented to Dorothy Borg*. New York: Columbia University Press, 1983.

Colville, John. *The Fringes of Power: Downing Street Diaries, 1939–1955*. London: Hodder and Stoughton, 1985.

Cumings, Bruce. *The Origins of the Korean War*. 2 vols. Princeton: Princeton University Press, 1981, 1990.

Darby, Phillip. *British Defence Policy East of Suez, 1947–1968*. London: Oxford University Press for the Royal Institute of International Affairs, 1973.

Davies, John Paton. *Dragon by the Tail: American, British, Japanese, and Russian Encounters with China and One Another*. New York: W. W. Norton, 1972.

Dennett, Tyler. *Americans in Eastern Asia in the Nineteenth Century*. New York: Macmillan, 1922.

Dilks, David, ed. *The Diaries of Sir Alexander Cadogan, O.M., 1938–1945*. London: Cassell, 1971.

Donovan, Robert J. *Conflict and Crisis: The Presidency of Harry S. Truman, 1945–1948*. New York: W. W. Norton, 1977.

Dulles, Foster Rhea. *China and America: The Story of Their Relations Since 1784*, 3d ed. Princeton: Princeton University Press, 1972.

Eden, Anthony. *The Memoirs of Sir Anthony Eden, Full Circle*. London: Cassell, 1960.

Elsey, George M. Papers. Harry S. Truman Library, Independence, Missouri.

―――. *Roosevelt and China: The White House Story*. With commentary by Riley Sunderland. Wilmington, Del.: Michael Glazier, 1979.

Fairbank, John K. *The United States and China*, 4th ed. Cambridge: Harvard University Press, 1983.

Feis, Herbert. *The China Tangle: The American Effort in China from Pearl Harbor to the Marshall Mission*. Princeton: Princeton University Press, 1953.

Foot, Rosemary. *The Wrong War: American Policy and the Dimensions of the Korean Conflict 1950–1953*. Ithaca, N.Y.: Cornell University Press, 1985.

Fraser, T. G. "Roosevelt and the Making of America's East Asian Policy, 1941–1945." In *Conflict and Amity in East Asia, Essays in Honour of Ian Nish*, ed. T. G. Fraser and Peter Lowe, 92–105. Hampshire, U.K.: Macmillan, 1992.

Gaddis, John Lewis. *The United States and the Origins of the Cold War, 1941–1947*. New York: Columbia University Press, 1972.

Gallicchio, Marc S. *The Cold War Begins in Asia: American East Asian Policy and the Fall of the Japanese Empire*. New York: Columbia University Press, 1988.

Gardner, Richard. *Sterling Dollar Diplomacy.* New York: McGraw Hill, 1969.

Gittings, John. *The World and China, 1922–1972.* London: Eyre Methuen, 1974.

Grasso, June M. *Truman's Two-China Policy, 1948–1950.* Armonk, N.Y.: M. E. Sharpe, 1987.

Grew, Joseph Clark. *Turbulent Era: A Diplomatic Record of Forty Years, 1904–1945.* Edited by Walter Johson with Nancy Harvison Hooker. Boston: Houghton Mifflin, 1952.

Griswold, A. Whitney. *The Far Eastern Policy of the United States.* New York: Harcourt, Brace and Co., 1938.

Harriman, William Averell, and Abel, Elie. *Special Envoy to Churchill and Stalin, 1941–1946.* New York: Random House, 1975.

Head, William P. *America's China Sojourn: America's Foreign Policy and Its Effects on Sino-American Relations, 1942–1948.* Lanham, Md.: University Press of America, 1983.

Howard, Michael E. *The Lessons of History.* New Haven: Yale University Press, 1992.

Hu Sheng. *Imperialism and Chinese Politics.* Reprint ed. Beijing: Foreign Languages Press, 1981.

Hull, Cordell. *The Memoirs of Cordell Hull.* Vol. 2. New York: Macmillan, 1948.

Hunt, Michael H. *The Making of a Special Relationship: The United States and China to 1914.* New York: Columbia University Press, 1983.

Iriye, Akira. *The Cold War in Asia: A Historical Introduction.* Englewood Cliffs, N.J.: Prentice-Hall, 1974.

James, D. Clayton. *The Years of MacArthur.* Vols. 1–3. Boston: Houghton Mifflin, 1975.

Kahn, E. J., Jr. *The China Hands: America's Foreign Service Officers and What Befell Them.* New York: Viking, 1975.

Kennan, George Frost. *American Diplomacy, 1900–1950.* Chicago: University of Chicago Press, 1951.

———. *Memoirs, 1925–1950.* Boston: Little, Brown, 1967.

Kennedy, Paul M. *The Realities Behind Diplomacy: Background Influences on British External Policy, 1865–1980.* London: George Allen and Unwin in association with Fontana, 1981.

King, F. H. H. *A Concise Economic History of Modern China.* Bombay: Bombay House Publishing, 1968.

Koen, Ross Y. *The China Lobby in American Politics.* Edited with introduction by Richard C. Kagan. New York: Harper and Row, 1974.

Kolko, Gabriel. *The Politics of War: The World and the United States Foreign Policy, 1943–1945.* New York: Random House, 1968.

Kolko, Joyce, and Kolko, Gabriel. *The Limits of Power: The World and the United States Foreign Policy, 1945–1954.* New York: Harper and Row, 1972.

LaFeber, Walter. *America, Russia, and the Cold War, 1945–1975,* 4th ed. New York: John Wiley and Sons, 1976.

Leahy, William D. *I Was There: The Personal Story of the Chief of Staff to Presidents Roosevelt and Truman Based on His Notes and Diaries Made at the Time.* New York: Whittlesey House, 1950.

Liu Xiao. *Shijie zhishi* (World Knowledge), no. 3.

Locke, Edwin. Papers. Harry S. Truman Library, Independence, Missouri.

Louis, William Roger. *Imperialism at Bay: The United States and the Decolonization of the British Empire, 1941–1945*. New York: Oxford University Press, 1978.

Luard, Evan. *Britain and China*. London: Chatto and Windus, 1962.

Mao Tsetung. *Selected Works of Mao Tsetung*. Vol. 5. Beijing: Foreign Languages Press, 1978.

Martin, Edwin W. *Divided Counsel. The Anglo-American Response to Communist Victory in China*. Lexington, Ky.: University of Kentucky Press, 1986.

May, Ernest R. *The Truman Administration and China, 1945–1949*. The America's Alternative Series, ed. Harold M. Hyman. Philadelphia: J. B. Lippincott, 1975.

May, Gary. *The China Scapegoat: The Diplomatic Ordeal of John Carter Vincent*. Washington, D.C.: New Republic Books, 1979.

Morgan, Kenneth O. *Labour in Power, 1945–1951*. Oxford: Oxford University Press, 1984.

Morrison, Herbert. *Herbert Morrison: An Autobiography*. London: Odhams, 1960.

Mosley, Leonard. *Marshall—Hero of Our Time*. New York: Hearst Books, 1982.

Murfett, Malcolm H. *Hostage on the Yangtze: Britain, China, and the Amethyst Crisis of 1949*. Annapolis, Md.: Naval Institute Press, 1991.

National Archives of the United States (NAUS), Washington, D.C. General Records of the State Department. RG 59.

———. Decimal Files. RG 59. Microfilm.

———. Lot Files 110.

———. Records of the Office of the Executive Secretariat. RG 59.

———. Records of the Office of European Affairs.

———. Records of the Policy Planning Staff.

———. Stettinius Records.

Nicholas, Herbert George. *The United States and Britain*. Chicago: University of Chicago Press, 1975.

Nie Rongzhen. *Nie Rongzhen huiyilu* (Memoirs of Marshal Nie Rongzhen). Beijing: PLA Press, 1986.

Office of Strategic Services. R & A Report. 13 June 1945, microfilm no. 3316.

Osgood, Robert Endicott. *Ideals and Self-Interest in America's Foreign Relations: The Great Transformation of the Twentieth Century*. Chicago: University of Chicago Press, 1953.

Ovendale, Ritchie. *The English-Speaking Alliance: Britain, the U.S., the Dominions, and the Cold War, 1945–1951*. London: Allen and Unwin, 1985.

Pelcovits, Nathan A. *Old China Hands and the Foreign Office*. New York: King's Crown Press under the auspices of the American Institute of Pacific Relations, 1948.

Pelling, Henry. *The Labour Governments, 1945–51*. London: Macmillan, 1984.

Peng Dehuai. *Peng Dehuai zishu* (Autobiography of Peng Dehuai). Beijing: People's Publishing House, 1981.

Pepper, Suzanne. *Civil War in China: The Political Struggle, 1945–1949*. Berkeley: University of California Press, 1978.

Pogue, Forrest C. *George C. Marshall*. Vols. 1 through 4. New York: Viking, 1973, 1987.

Porter, Brian E. *Britain and the Rise of Communist China: A Study of British Attitudes, 1945–1954.* London: Oxford University Press, 1967.

Purcell, Victor. *The Chinese in Southeast Asia.* London: Oxford University Press under the auspices of the Royal Institute of International Affairs, 1965.

Purifoy, Lewis Carroll. *Harry Truman's China Policy: McCarthyism and the Diplomacy of Hysteria, 1947–1951.* New York: New Viewpoints, 1976.

Reardon-Anderson, James. *Yenan and the Great Powers: The Origins of Chinese Communist Foreign Policy, 1944–1946.* New York: Columbia University Press, 1980.

Rothwell, Victor H. *Britain and the Cold War, 1941–1947.* London: Jonathan Cape, 1982.

Royal Institute of International Affairs. *The British Empire.* Oxford: Oxford University Press, 1938.

———. *Political and Strategical Interests of HongKong.* Oxford: Oxford University Press, 1939.

Sbrega, John Joseph. *Anglo-American Relations and Colonialism in East Asia, 1941–1945.* New York: Garland, 1983.

Schaller, Michael. *The U.S. Crusade in China, 1938–1945.* New York: Oxford University Press, 1978.

Schwartz, Benjamin Isadore. *Chinese Communism and the Rise of Mao.* Cambridge: Harvard University Press, 1979.

Shai, Aron. *Britain and China, 1941–1947: Imperial Momentum.* London: Macmillan in association with St. Antony's College, Oxford, 1984.

Smith, Gaddis. *Dean Acheson.* New York: Cooper Square, 1972.

Strang, Lord. *Home and Abroad.* London: Andre Deutsch, 1956.

Stueck, William Whitney, Jr. *The Road to Confrontation: American Policy Toward China and Korea, 1947–1950.* Chapel Hill, N.C.: University of North Carolina Press, 1981.

———. *The Wedemeyer Mission: American Politics and Foreign Policy During the Cold War.* Athens, Ga.: University of Georgia Press, 1984.

Tang, James Tuck-Hong. *Britain's Encounter with Revolutionary China, 1949–54.* New York: St. Martin's Press, 1992.

Thorne, Christopher G. *The Limits of Foreign Policy: The West, the League, and the Far Eastern Crisis of 1931–1933.* London: Hamilton, 1972.

———. *Allies of a Kind: The United States, Britain, and the War Against Japan, 1941–1945.* London: Oxford University Press, 1978.

———. *The Issue of War: States, Societies, and the Far Eastern Conflict of 1941–1945.* New York: Oxford University Press, 1985.

———. *Border Crossings: Studies in International History.* New York: Basil Blackwell with the East Asian Institute, Columbia University, 1988.

Truman, Harry S. *Memoirs.* Vol. 1, *Year of Decisions.* Garden City, N.Y.: Doubleday, 1955.

———. Papers. President's Secretary's Files (PSF). Truman Library, Independence, Missouri.

———. President's Personal Files (PPF). Truman Library, Independence, Missouri.

———. Confidential Files. Truman Library, Independence, Missouri.

Truman Library, Independence, Missouri. Name Files.

————. The White House Central Files.

————. Sumner Files: China.

Tsou, Tang. *America's Failure in China, 1941–50.* Chicago: University of Chicago Press, 1963.

Tucker, Nancy Bernkopf. *Patterns in the Dust: Chinese-American Relations and the Recognition Controversy, 1949–1950.* New York: Columbia University Press, 1983.

U.K. *Hansard Parliamentary Debates,* Commons (1944 to 1945).

U.K. Parliament. *The Korean War: Summary of Events.* Cmd. 8078. 1950.

————. *The Prime Minister's Visit to the United States.* Cmd. 8110. 1950.

U.K. Public Record Office (PRO). "Attlee Papers." PREM8.

————. "Churchill Papers." PREM11.

————. "The Far Eastern Committee." CAB 134.

————. "Cabinet Minutes." CAB 128.

————. "Private Papers, Clark Kerr, Carton de Wiart, etc." CAB 127.

————. "Foreign Office Political Correspondence." FO371.

————. "Ernest Bevin Papers." FO800.

————. "Treasury Files Concerning China, 1948–1949." T3236.

————. "Colonial Office Files." CO371.

————. "Board of Trade Files Concerning China, 1946." BT60.

U.S. Department of State. *Foreign Relations of the United States (FRUS), 1944–1951.* Washington, D.C.: Government Printing Office, 1966–77.

————. *Bulletin.*

————. *United States Relations with China, with Special Reference to the Period 1944–1949.* Washington, D.C.: Office of Public Affairs, 1949.

Watt, D. Cameron. *Succeeding John Bull: America in Britain's Place, 1900–1975.* New York: Cambridge University Press, 1984.

Wedemeyer, Albert C. *Wedemeyer Reports!* New York: Holt, 1958.

Whiting, Allen Suess. *China Crosses the Yalu: The Decision to Enter the Korean War.* New York: Macmillan, 1960.

Wu Xiuquan. *Zai waijiaobu bunian de jingli* (Eight Years at the Ministry of Foreign Affairs). Beijing: Shijie Zhishi, 1983.

Xianggang yu Zhongguo (Hong Kong and China: A Collection of Historical Material). Hong Kong: Wide Angle, 1981.

Ye Fei. *Ye Fei huiyilu* (Memoirs of General Ye Fei). Beijing: PLA Press, 1988.

Zhongguo Gongchandang lici zhongyao huiyi (Major Meetings of the Chinese Communist Party), Vol. 1. Shanghai: Central Party School, Shanghai People's Publishing House, 1982.

Zhonghua remin gongheguo duiwaiguanxi wenjianji (Collected Documents on the Foreign Relations of the People's Republic of China), 4 vols. Beijing: Shijie Zhishi, 1957.

Index

Lanxin Xiang, born and educated in China, is a graduate of Fudan University in Shanghai. He completed graduate work at the Johns Hopkins University and also lived in Europe for four years. From 1992 to 1993, Professor Xiang was an Olin Fellow of Military and Strategic History at Yale University. He has published in the *Journal of Contemporary History*, *Orbis*, and others. He is working on two new manuscripts: one on the Boxer War based on multinational sources, and the other on "Mao's generals." Professor Xiang teaches at Clemson University.